MARLBOROUGH'S SHADOW

by the same author:

Biography
Captain-General and Rebel Chief; The Life of James Duke of Monmouth (1979)
Lionel Edwards, Master of the Sporting Scene (1986)
Millais: Three Generations in Nature, Art and Sport (1990)
Blue and Scarlet: an Autobiography (1990)

Regimental Studies
Sefton: The Story of a Cavalry Horse (1983)
The Story of the Blues and Royals: Royal Horse Guards and 1st Dragoons (1993)
Through Fifteen Reigns: A Complete History of the Household Cavalry (1997)
Guardsmen of the Sky: An Account of the Involvement of Household Troops in the Airborne Forces (1997)

Polo
The World of Polo: Past and Present (1986)
A Concise Guide to Polo (1989)
Hanut: Prince of Polo Players (1995)

Equestrian and Field Sports
The Book of Foxhunting (1997)
Victorian and Edwardian Field Sports from Old Photographs (1978)
British and Irish Hunts and Huntsmen, Vol I (1982)
British and Irish Hunts and Huntsmen, Vol II (1983)
British and Irish Hunts and Huntsmen, Vol III (1987)
Collecting Sporting Art (1988)
A Concise Guide to Hunting (1988)
Horse and Carriage: The Pageant of Hyde Park (1990)
The Green Guide to Field Sports (1991)

Fiction
Gannet: The Story of a Terrier (1990)
Puffin at the Cabin (1994)

House History
Dorneywood (1993)

Anthology
The World's Greatest Horse Stories (1979)
The World's Greatest Dog Stories (1985)

MARLBOROUGH'S SHADOW

THE LIFE OF THE FIRST EARL CADOGAN

by

J. N. P. WATSON

LEO COOPER

First published in Great Britain 2003 by
LEO COOPER
an imprint of Pen & Sword Books Ltd
47 Church Street,
Barnsley,
South Yorkshire, S70 2AS

Copyright © 2003 by J. N. P. Watson

ISBN 1 84415 008 9

Typeset in Original Garamond by
Phoenix Typesetting, Burley-in-Wharfedale,
Ilkley, West Yorkshire

Printed in England by
CPI UK.

THIS BIOGRAPHY IS
DEDICATED TO
VALENTINE WOYKA,
CAVALRY OFFICER *PAR
EXCELLENCE*

I do believe the greatest part of Lord Marlborough's victories are owing to him [Cadogan] and even the Pensionary [Antoine Heinsius, First Minister of the Dutch Republic] said to me, "*Si vous voulez avoir un duc de Marlborough un Cadogan est Necessaire.*"

The soldier-diplomat Earl of Strafford to the Lord Treasurer, Robert Harley, Earl of Oxford.

Contents

Maps and Diagrams

Introduction

Military historians and other biographers of the great Duke of Marlborough have portrayed William Cadogan as simply the 'big bluff Irishman' who handled his chief's commissariat during the War of the Spanish Succession. But Cadogan's bluffness hid a restless energy, a subtle intelligence, a quicksilver mind and great practical ability. Nor was he really an Irishman, despite the fact that he came from Dublin, for both his parents were of Welsh extraction.

It is true that Marlborough – having first recognized the young officer's outstanding courage, administrative ability and flair for leadership since seeing him in action at the siege of Cork, aged 18, in 1690 – had him promoted, nine years later, to the brevet rank of colonel, to be Quartermaster General of the army of the Grand Alliance. But as Cadogan's other talents emerged with experience, the young man became the Captain General's alter ego. For Marlborough, already in his fifties and suffering from migraines and what he called 'the spleen', had lost much of the physical energy of his youth. And here was an officer not only of exceptionally high intelligence (and of a rather higher standard of education than Marlborough himself had received), who was not only his equal, in many respects, in terms of capability if not of genius, but who was also of sufficient youthful vigour to lead all those special missions that were imperative to the success of the campaigns. At the same time Cadogan, emulating his chief in every way, served, par excellence, his senior-officer apprenticeship. There were many similarities in their respective personalities.

Given Cadogan's physical courage, quick thinking and capacity for leadership, he frequently found himself – at sieges, or in manoeuvre or in open battle – allotted vital tasks as a front-line general. His penetrating mind, tenacity of purpose and lively imagination led to his employment as chief of intelligence and master spy, while his tact and charm were well practised in several diplomatic missions. Studying his career during those melodramatic campaigns of 1701–1711, one can scarcely help being astonished at this young officer's facility for fulfilling his myriad duties, often with the minimum of sleep. Queen Anne's Captain General would trust none other than Cadogan with those tasks.

Marlborough was well known for his avarice (Winston Churchill, in his splendid four-volume biography, was at pains to cover up for his illustrious ancestor). Notwithstanding the Captain General's genius he was blatantly and frequently naive in the manner in which he asked for *douceurs* or, indeed, took money that was not his to take. Marlborough felt keenly that his (honestly earned) capital was not equal to his grand status. He needed extra funds, too, to complete the building of Blenheim Palace, for he was determined to have a country property that would outmatch any other private house in Britain. There was no doubt that his protégé Cadogan, took a leaf out of his chief's book; and, as the Dutch authorities claimed, he was at least as dishonest. He, too, was a family man. He, too, required an income commensurate with his rapidly escalating rank. He, too, needed capital to become a man of estates.

We see this darker side of the so-called 'bluff and burly Irishman's' complex nature, particularly during his period as a member of the four-man government (two Dutchmen, Marlborough and himself) of the southern Netherlands, during the period 1707–1708, when he was condemned by the Dutch for his arrogant and bullying manner as well for his extortion and corruption. Nor have these aspects of his character been revealed, previously, in any profound study of his life. Marlborough is on record as giving away feelings of guilt by a shifty or diffident demeanour, whereas Cadogan, in the same situation, became more authoritarian and domineering.

There have been countless biographies of Marlborough; but none in depth, of this remarkable man who was the Captain General's right-hand officer during that last war against Louis XIV. Robert Pearman, a chartered surveyor at one time employed by the Cadogan estate, wrote an excellent outline of the general's life, which was commissioned by the 7th Earl Cadogan and published by the Haggerston Press in 1988. My thanks are due to Mr Pearman for his account of Cadogan's family background which I did not personally research. Also for some details of the last decade of Cadogan's life.

I have been fascinated by the Spanish Succession War ever since being required to study the famous 1704 march of the Grand Alliance from the Netherlands to the Danube, for the military history paper of an army promotion exam many years ago. I was amazed then, as I have been since, at the 32-year-old Cadogan's foresight, ingenuity and stamina in organizing the logistics of that marathon.

Following Marlborough's deprivation and self-imposed exile at the end of 1711 Cadogan joined him to be his eyes and ears and man-of-action on the Continent where the great Captain General was planning an invasion of England to forestall (as he imagined) the Tories' attempt to make way for the enthrone-ment of the Jacobite Pretender. And the younger officer's facility for intrigue and espionage were again used to the full – until 1714 when George I ascended the throne. Reinstated then, in the rank of lieutenant general, Cadogan commanded the force that finally quelled the 1715 rebellion, and was thus the man who effectively brought the Highlands into the United Kingdom. Being a skilful negotiator and accomplished linguist, and having accumulated considerable diplomatic experience during the war, he was deemed fit to hold senior ambassadorial rank, which he did, between 1715 and 1720, with great aplomb. And, on Marlborough's death, in 1722, the King appointed him

Captain General of the army. Cadogan died four years later, at the age of 54. But what a life!

The following also deserve my sincere thanks for their help in the preparation of this biography: Rosemary Baird, the archivist at Goodwood House, and her asistant, Ellen Westbrook; Melanie Blake, of the Courtauld Institute; Earl Cadogan; his son, Viscount Chelsea, who discovered (in a trunk, in a Perthshire loft), during the summer of 2000, a packet of more than twenty letters appertaining to Cadogan, along with a warrant, signed by George I, sending him on a mission to Berlin and Vienna in 1719. The family believe that these documents cannot have seen the light of day since the 18th century. And I feel enormously privileged to be the first author enabled to quote from them. I am also grateful to their principal secretary, Susan Wizard; to the military historian David Chandler, particularly for his permission to reproduce certain sketches from his excellent *Art of Warfare in the Age of Marlborough*; to Ellis Ni Dhuibhne and Joanna Finegan, of the National Library of Ireland; to Godfrey Davies (author of *The Seamy Side of Marlborough's War*; Patricia Dickson (author of *Lieutenant General William Cadogan's Intelligence Service*; to Tom Gilseman of the Irish National Archives; to Edward Gregg (author of *Marlborough in Exile*); to Doctor Ian Hart and Doctor R.C.E. Hayes, of the Royal Commission on Historical Manuscripts; to the Earl of Lytton, who lent me books; to Elizabeth Kirwan, of the National Library of Ireland; to Joshua Lunn, the issue desk manager and his staff at the Manuscripts Reading Room of the British Library; to Alastair Massie and his staff at the Reading Room of the National Army Museum; to M. O'Connor of the Registry of Deeds, Dublin; to Mary L. Robertson of the Huntington Library, in California, USA; to David Notley, who composed the maps; to Eddie Smith, of Westminster School; to Stuart ÓSeanÓir, of Trinity College Library, Dublin; to Marcella Senior, the Secretary's office, Trinity College; to the West Sussex Record Office, at

Chichester, especially Mr Timothy McCann; to Helen Walch, of the Blenheim Palace administrative office; to Sheila Watson, my literary agent; and to the staff of the London Library for, as ever, their faithful cooperation. And, above all, to my wife Lavinia, for her staunch support throughout the work involved, quite apart from typing the entire text, etc, along with the copious correspondence connected with it.

I have, on several occasions quoted 'Coxe'. Archdeacon William Coxe, having quarried the archives at Blenheim Palace, wrote his life of the great Duke of Marlborough during the 1820s. Sometime after that many letters and other documents went missing from the muniments room, either lost, stolen or destroyed. Thus Churchill, Trevelyan and other biographers of Marlborough and his Duchess have had recourse, in their research, to Coxe.

JNPW
Pannett's Shipley Sussex

ABBREVIATIONS

GMT	=	George Macaulay Trevelyan
WSC	=	Winston Spencer Churchill
BL	=	British Library
DNB	=	Dictionary of National Biography
HMC	=	Report on the Historical Manuscripts Commission
PRO	=	Public Record Office
SP	=	State Papers
SAHR	=	Society for Army Historical Research

Prologue

The state funeral of the great Duke of Marlborough took place on 9 August 1722. Leading the procession of generals who followed the coffin was the officer who had succeeded him as commander-in-chief of the British army and as Master-General of the Ordnance, William, Earl of Cadogan. According to the Dictionary of National Biography Cadogan behaved in a most unseemly manner on this occasion, appearing 'indecorously dressed and betraying his want of sympathy by his looks and gestures'. (The originator of that entry must have been a Jacobite and for some reason have been very biased.) But, notwithstanding that the new C-in-C had always adored and adulated Marlborough, he would have attended that funeral with very mixed feelings. For Cadogan, who was still a bare 50 years old, had, for over half his life, prospered under the great Duke's shadow.

As stated in the introduction, Marlborough, a born talent spotter, having recognized Cadogan's outstanding flair as a young regimental officer, appointed him Quartermaster General to the Grand Alliance army of the Netherlands, an army composed of half-a-dozen different nationalities, an enormous responsibility for a youth not yet 30 years old. Then, as the young officer's gifts became increasingly apparent as the Spanish succession war progressed, the Captain General employed him in a variety of other senior roles – as chief of staff, chief of intelligence, formation commander, leader of *coup de main* parties, diplomat and civil administrator. Marlborough admitted, on several occasions, that he entirely depended upon him. And, indeed, whenever there was a mission of vital importance to be carried out Cadogan was invariably nominated to lead it.

The soldier-diplomat Earl of Strafford wrote, in a letter to Marlborough's avowed enemy, Lord Treasurer Harley, that 'I do believe the greatest part of Lord Marlborough's victories are owing to him [Cadogan]; and even the Pensionary [Heinsius, first minister of Holland] said to me, *'Si vous voulez avoir un duc de Marlborough un Cadogan est Necessaire.'*

In 1715 Cadogan commanded the army that ultimately defeated the Jacobite uprising in Scotland, and he was subsequently employed as ambassador to Holland with particular missions to the courts of Austria and Prussia. However, Marlborough being still nominally at the army's helm (although a sick man) the shadow remained. But since, on 9 August 1722 that shadow vanished, Cadogan might be forgiven for expressing his sense of relief by displaying a little abandon and insouciance. He was at last his own man, perhaps for a while the greatest figure in the Kingdom. Shadow or no shadow, before turning to Cadogan's background and boyhood it must first be admitted that this life study has partially failed if it does not portray the subject as being at least as subtle and complex a character as Marlborough himself, and unless it reveals Cadogan as possessing and exploiting at least as many skills and aptitudes as his more famous chief. Since there was no such place as Cadogan sufficiently substantial to carry the word "of", his title was subsequently reduced to 'Earl Cadogan'.

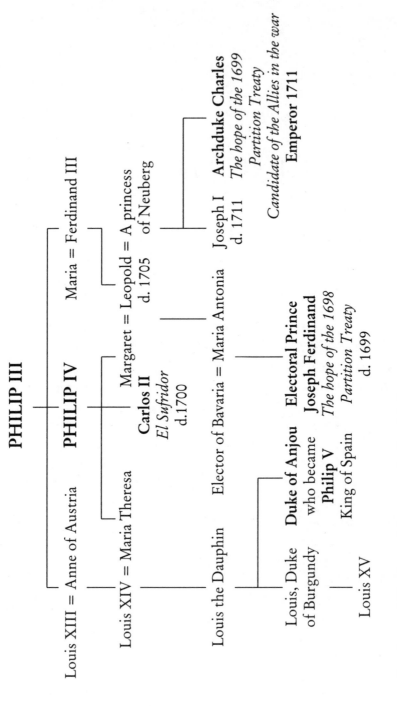

PHILIP III

Louis XIII = Anne of Austria

Maria = Ferdinand III

Louis XIV = Maria Theresa

PHILIP IV

Margaret = Leopold = A princess
            d.1705   of Neuberg

Carlos II
El Sufridor
d.1700

Joseph I   **Archduke Charles**
d. 1711   *The hope of the 1699*
           Partition Treaty
     Candidate of the Allies in the war
           Emperor 1711

Louis the Dauphin

Elector of Bavaria = Maria Antonia

**Electoral Prince
Joseph Ferdinand**
*The hope of the 1698
Partition Treaty*
d. 1699

Louis, Duke
of Burgundy

Duke of Anjou
who became
Philip V
King of Spain

Louis XV

Bourbon and Hapsburg claimants to the Spanish throne

1

YOUNG WILLIAM

(1672–1690)

Cadogan was originally a Welsh name, Cadwgn; the clan was of fighting stock; indeed the very name Cadogan is translated from the Celtic as 'battle-keenness'[1]*. The grandfather of the subject of this biography, another William, emigrated to Ireland in the 1630s . Born in Cardiff, in 1600, 'Old William', a clever lad with a legal education behind him, was appointed private secretary to the ill-fated Thomas Wentworth, Earl of Strafford, Charles I's Irish Lord Deputy (who was not to be saved by his weak King, in 1641, from the scaffold). 'Old William' not only stayed on in Dublin with Strafford's successor (from 1639), but also became a member of the Irish House of Commons. He was astute enough in the turbulent 1640s to be against the King. He rose to the rank of major in Cromwell's army and was appointed Governor of Trim castle[2], a stronghold on the Boyne in Co. Meath.

'Old William's' first wife having died young, he remarried one, like himself, of Welsh extraction, Elizabeth Roberts, of Caernarvon. Their one son, Henry, was the father of 'Young

---

* See Notes at end of each chapter.

William'. 'Old William' died in 1660, a few weeks before the Restoration. Henry Cadwgn, who was to change his name to the more locally pronounceable Cadogan, was a law student at Trinity College, Dublin, at the time of his father's death. It was not long before he became a man of considerable property with a substantial estate at Liscartin, Co. Meath.

Henry also married a Welsh woman, Bridget, daughter of Sir Hardress Waller, another leading Cromwellian (he was one of the committee of five delegated to decide on the time and place for the King's execution). 'Young William', the second of the five children of Henry and Bridget, was born in 1672. The eldest son, Ambrose, while serving in the Irish army, died in 1639. There was a third son, Charles, who also features in this account, and two girls, Frances and Penelope. Their father, who put in a stint as High Sheriff of Co. Meath, was ambitious to extend the Cadogan domains. He acquired another estate in Co. Limerick, which included a 13th century castle, near Adare.

Henry, determined that his intelligent and lively son, William, should follow him in the legal profession, envisaged him as a Trinity Dublin student as he himself had been. To prepare and qualify him for a place there he sent him, at the age of ten, to London, to Westminster school, whose pupils were largely composed of boys destined for the clergy. Westminster was then ruled, dictatorially, by Doctor Richard Busby, who had occupied the headmastership since 1638. Busby insisted on his pupils conversing only in either Latin or Greek. And woe betide them if they failed to do so, for he believed – more than most in that age, when corporal punishment was the standard correction – in the adage 'spare the rod and spoil the child'. His answer to any misdemeanour was the cane. The architect Christopher Wren, the poet John Dryden, the philosopher John Locke, the poet and diplomat Matthew Prior, the founder of the Bank of England, Charles Montagu, Earl of Halifax, and James Brydges, Paymaster General to the Forces (and subsequently 1st Duke of Chandos), who was to be a close colleague of 'young William's', were among those whose boyhoods had thrived, or were to prosper, during Busby's regime. Although bullying was rife at Westminster 'Young William', a lad of singular courage, and exceptionally tall, broad and strong for his age, would have known exactly how to cope with bullies.

The 1680s were turbulent times in London, with the country divided for the first time between the Whig and Tory factions and Titus Oates inciting the Protestant mob to resist the (virtually nonexistent) Popish Plot. To what extent, one wonders, did 'young William' and his fellow-pupils join the mourning at the death of Charles II? Busby, a faithful Royalist (until Catholic James displayed his zealotry and began his series of excesses) would have encouraged that. Did 'Young William' hear the cannons rolling down the streets from the Tower to join King James's army marching to resist the Western rebellion? Perhaps he even witnessed the beheading of Monmouth on Tower Hill, a fortnight later, as many thousands of others did. 1685 being, too, the year of the *Dragonnade*, the revocation of the Edict of Nantes, Louis XIV's ethnic cleansing of Protestants, William Cadogan may also have encountered some of the French Huguenot refugees, who found their way to London, many of them in due course enriching England's talents and trades.

In 1687 William, now aged 15 and with a well-grounded education behind him, was back in Dublin and was accepted during March of that year as a law student at Trinity. Youths grew up fast in those days and William Cadogan was no young saint. In the Dublin of the late 1680s he befriended another young tearaway, his contemporary Lord Raby (later 3rd Earl of Strafford), who was to be a lifelong companion, and who, in particular, was to be of much help to him during the War of the Spanish Succession. Now, as their correspondence indicates – it may be read in the Strafford Papers (BL22,196) in the British Library – they frolicked and drank and wenched together to their hearts' delight. Yet 'Young William' was also

3

a conscientious law student. Likewise Raby, who was studying to become a diplomat.

Meanwhile the London he had left behind was in tumult. James II, encouraged by his Italian Queen and priests, was hell-bent on the misguided policy of attempting to Catholicize his three kingdoms. The Cadogan family, being staunch Protestants, must have viewed the removal of officers of their denomination from the Irish army, and their replacement by Catholics – under the direction of the Irish lieutenant general, Robert Talbot, Earl of Tyrconnel – with deep concern. King James, in proposing to gratify his Catholic subjects at the expense of the Protestants, clearly found Ireland, a fundamentally Catholic country, a most convenient place to start.

Protestants everywhere received the news of the birth of a Prince of Wales in 1688 with further consternation. Were England, Scotland and Ireland to be subject to a Catholic dynasty, they were wondering. Would there be another Gunpowder Plot or a repetition of 'Bloody Mary's' rule? Would there be a return to despotic government such as that of the French King? Nor was James to be deflected from his aims. Such was the troubled and angry mood in England that summer of 1688, that a delegation of seven Protestant grandees crossed secretly to Holland to invite another William – Prince William of Orange, James's nephew and husband of James's elder daughter, Mary – to come to England at the head of an army to displace his bigoted father-in-law.

News travelled from London to Dublin within three or four days, given an easterly breeze over the Irish sea. The Cadogan family as well as the Protestant hierarchy and undergraduates at Trinity would have been overjoyed to hear of Dutch William's landing at Torbay on 5 November and of King James's failure either to challenge him with his substantial army or to prevent his other son-in-law, Princess Anne's consort, Prince George of Denmark, or the Earl of Clarendon's son, Lord Cornbury, or Brigadier General John Churchill, among others, leading defecting units of the Royalist army over to the invader.

William Cadogan, who was always to have a strong feeling of his own destiny, must have taken a closer interest than most young thinking men in the unfolding of these events and those that followed – the flight of James and his Queen and their Prince to France, and the crowning of Dutch William and Princess Mary in April, 1689. It is likely that young William would be aware, too, that Louis XIV might plan retribution, perhaps an invasion of England, with Ireland as the springboard and James as the figurehead and claimant of his throne. For William of Orange, William III, was an unattractive figure and never a popular one. And that is precisely what in March, 1689, Louis did – he sent James to lead a French army, 100,000 strong, to conquer Ireland as a first step towards recovering his throne.

There was panic on the streets of Dublin as James's army (which rapidly became a Franco-Irish army) marched north from Cork and Kinsale, rapidly occupying the country in the name of the ex-King. Trinity was in desperate straits for money; no rents had been coming in, while plate which the Fellows had sold for building more chambers for residents fetched less than half its true value; fellows, dons and scholars were on a starvation diet; in September they were all turned out of the campus, which was occupied by the Jacobite army.[3] What were the students to do, their family homes having been requisitioned? There was one hope. When Tyrconnel called on Derry and Enniskillen to surrender he was rebuffed. Seventeen-year-old William Cadogan (his higher education no more than halfway through) was among the Trinity students who, deftly avoiding the enemy, made their way north. The two Ulster garrisons needed young men of his calibre as officers. And it was with the Enniskillen Brigade that his military career began. He was now a cornet of dragoons.

The outposts still resisting the invaders went under command of the Huguenot Duke of Schomberg – when his

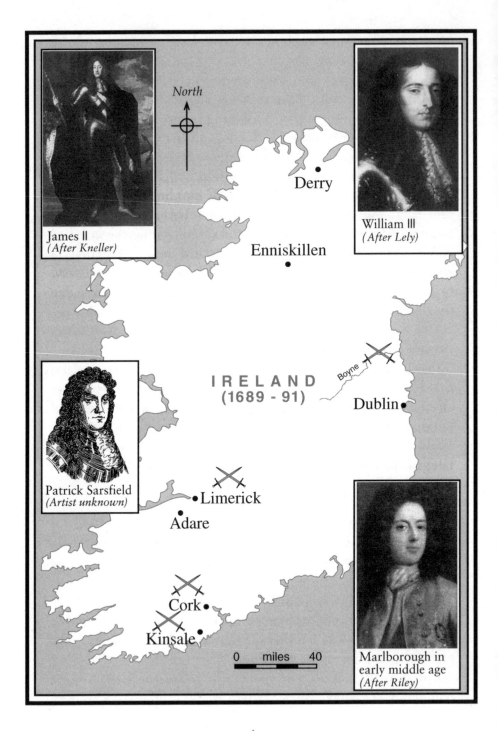

North

Derry

Enniskillen

James II
(After Kneller)

William III
(After Lely)

I R E L A N D
(1689 - 91)

Boyne

Dublin

Patrick Sarsfield
(Artist unknown)

Limerick

Adare

Cork

Kinsale

Marlborough in
early middle age
(After Riley)

0   miles   40

contingent arrived in Ulster from England. Schomberg suffered an appalling volume of casualties from sickness and disease, and it was not until after June, 1690, when King William arrived with reinforcements and took command, that the tide began to turn against ex-King James. Dutch William's 36,000, including William Cadogan in the Enniskillen Brigade, pushed southwards, driving the Franco-Irish army back towards Dublin. Ex-King James stood his troops behind the Boyne to receive them. King William attacked on 1 July and sent them helter-skelter, the Irish infantry – many of whom young Cadogan would meet again as the Wild Geese in Louis XIV's army – being among the first to flee. The Franco-Irish were by no means inspired by ex-King James, who had been careful not to expose himself near the fighting, and who fled back to France as fast as his horse, and a ship waiting at Kinsale, could carry him. But Cornet Cadogan, of the Enniskillen Brigade, had shown himself to be a warrior.

It was in the vicinity of ex-King James's flight from Ireland that Cadogan saw tough action for the second time in 1690, the enemy forces now being under the competent command of James's son (by Marlborough's sister, Arabella Churchill), the Duke of Berwick, with Patrick Sarsfield (Earl of Lucan) at the head of the Irish element. Sarsfield sent the Enniskillen Brigade to besiege Cork. While William III was conducting the siege of Limerick, Marlborough (who had gained an earldom in the Coronation honours), commanding the forces in England and being one of Queen Mary's Regency council, proposed a daring project that stood a good chance of hastening the end of the war in Ireland.

This was to launch an amphibious attack against Cork, followed by Kinsale, the two principal ports through which reinforcements, arms and other supplies were still reaching the enemy from France. Although Marlborough's plan was rejected by the majority of the Regency Council Queen Mary had the suggestion sent to her husband at Limerick. Dutch

William's jealous generals attempted to veto Marlborough's proposal, but the King, notwithstanding his personal prejudice against Marlborough, saw the plan's merit and gave it his blessing.

The expeditionary force embarked at Spithead on 30 August; but, owing to turbulent weather, the fleet was kept in port for nearly three weeks, not sailing until 17 September. Three days later Marlborough's ships were anchored in Cork harbour, by which time a mixed force of Dutch, Huguenot, Danish and Ulster units were converging on the city from Tipperary. Cork fell on the 27th, Kinsale on 15 October, Marlborough's victories being widely acclaimed as the most cleverly executed operations of the Irish Campaign. It was during the strenuous fighting for these crucial coastal fortresses that Marlborough took particular note of the gallantry, efficiency and flair for leadership of a certain young subaltern, tall, heavily-built Cadogan. 'Young William', having been fulsomely praised by a soldier who was clearly due for promotion must have felt himself to be due for promotion, too. Anyhow all thought of continuing his law studies had now evaporated.

Notes

1 Pearman, *The Cadogan Estate*, 28.
2 The certificate for his governorship, in 1655, is in BL Add MS 46936A, f23.
3 McDowell, R.B. and Webb, D.A., *Trinity College, Dublin* 28–29.

2

Marlborough's Right-Hand Man

(1691 – 1701)

Lieutenant William Cadogan continued to serve in Ireland, in a keeping-the-peace role, for another three years after the fall of Limerick in 1691. Regimental promotion in the English, Scottish and Irish armies was essentially by purchase, as it would continue to be for about the next two centuries. Cadogan was a young man of modest private means, his family having recovered their properties and other assets. England was at war with France again and a young officer with military aspirations needed to be where the action was. In 1694 the 22-year-old subaltern of dragoons bought a captaincy with a unit on active service in Flanders, Brigadier General Thomas Erle's Regiment of Foot.[1]

In May 1691 Dutch William, accompanied by Marlborough, had crossed to The Hague to coordinate the operations of the combined armies of the League of Augsburg, a force amounting to about 70,000. The French, although numerically inferior were a much more closely-knit force. Commanded by the redoubtable Duke of Luxembourg, they had the best of those early years of this war. In particular the Allies suffered crippling defeats at the Battles of Steinkirk (1692) and Neerwinden (1693).

Soldiering during the next four years (1694–98) in the southern Netherlands added considerably to Cadogan's military education, especially regarding the infantryman's arts, the administrative aspects of the profession and the finer points of siege warfare, a tactical branch of which the French were the acknowledged masters.

The world's greatest military engineer, Maréchal Sebastien de Prestre de Vauban had served his apprenticeship in siege warfare under Condé and Turenne. In 1698, after Louis XIV appointed Vauban *Commissaire Général des Fortifications*, this expert proceeded to strengthen the frontier fortresses of the

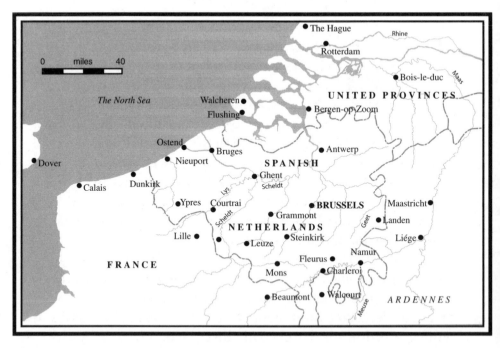

The Main Fortresses in the Spanish Netherlands

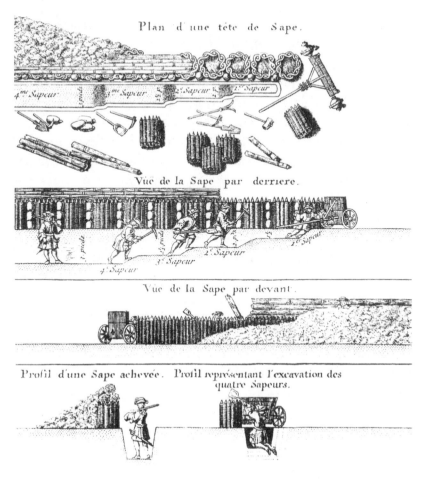

Plan d'une tête de Sape.

4.me Sapeur   3.me Sapeur   2.e Sapeur   1.er Sapeur

Vue de la Sape par derrière.

4.e Sapeur   3.e Sapeur   2.e Sapeur   1.er Sapeur

Vue de la Sape par devant.

Profil d'une Sape achevée.   Profil représentant l'excavation des quatre Sapeurs.

Contemporary drawings relating to aspects of Siege Warfare

southern Netherlands and to oversee the reduction of nearly forty others which had been in Dutch hands.

Entering a captured fortress for the first time Captain Cadogan would have found that defensive designs à la Vauban were at once alarmingly formidable and extremely complex. First, he would take careful note of the glacis, the stronghold's sloping exterior which afforded the defenders clear fields of view and fire; then the outer bank, the palisade, with its parapet

11

protecting the covered way where those defenders not in action sheltered. Closer to the centre was the counterscarp, the outer wall of the great ditch, behind which rose a ring of demilunes, or ravelins, mutually supporting triangular works with close all-round defence. Next in depth, and a little higher, he would have taken note of the hornworks with their twin salients in musket range of their neighbours, thus also mutually supporting, and tactically linked with the demilunes and the bastions housing the artillery pieces. On each bastion there was a cannon emplacement. In between those lay a stone-faced ditch, which often bristled with a palisade of sharpened spikes. Finally there was the toughest nut of all to crack, the citadel. Vauban's defences were thus designed in considerable depth.

Cadogan would have learned that successful investment and capture of a fortress involved carefully constructed circumvallations. As for the force carrying out the attack they would have dug contravallations as the siege earthworks were known. Those were the radius of parallel trenches, connected by saps, communication trenches, by which the contravallations with their infantry and heavy guns, breaching batteries, were brought ever closer to the fortress – until the enemy, cowed and crippled by artillery bombardments, faced the final assaults by musketeers and grenadiers.

In 1695 Cadogan, among other siege operations, led his company at the siege of the mighty fortress of Namur which had been taken by the French under Vauban and Luxembourg in 1692 and was now held by another highly experienced French soldier, the veteran Maréchal Boufflers. The Allied corps forming the lines of circumvallation held off several attempts by Maréchal Villeroi to relieve Boufflers. The Allies overran the defences and took the town on 3 August, but almost another month passed before the citadel fell. Boufflers thus became the first *maréchal* to surrender a fortress. This counted as one of the greatest triumphs of William III's military career.

1695 was, in general, a good year for the Allies, their most notable achievement being that of the English navy, whose ships, holding sway in the Mediterranean, kept the French fleet largely anchored at Toulon. Although both sides were ready for peace in 1695 and negotiations began, the Congress did not sit at Rijswik (Ryswick) until April of the following year and the treaty was not signed until September 1697. By that peace France was obliged to relinquish all the towns and districts she had seized since the Treaty of Nijmegen (1679), retaining only Strasbourg. Louis also undertook to recognize William III as King of England and to give no further aid to James II. But being Louis, he would fail to keep that promise. For Cadogan there was further promotion.

In 1698 he learned that the post of major in the Enniskillen Dragoons had just become vacant and he applied for it. That autumn, having bought the appointment, he returned to Ireland and took up his duties. The office of regimental major, or second-in-command, also carried the responsibilities of quartermaster.

When dragoons were first established in the English army during the 1660s they were employed as mounted infantry. They rode with the cavalry (the Horse), but dismounted for battle, three men out of every four advancing on foot, while the fourth held the horses. Like cavalrymen, recruits to the dragoons were required to bring a horse with them on enlistment. (But horses of a lower quality were acceptable for dragoons. In Ireland their mounts were mostly *garrons* – hardy local ponies.) By the turn of the century, however, the dragoon regiments were increasingly allotted the roles of true cavalry, that is taking on the enemy cavalry by shock action, or interspersing their troops with the companies of Foot in a mutually supporting role, or as reconnaissance troops, or in rearguard action or guarding convoys. Not surprisingly Cadogan proved to be a most hardworking, imaginative and able second-in-command and quartermaster of dragoons. The Enniskillens could not have found a more efficient and industrious major.[2]

He must have already sensed that his military future greatly depended upon the General who, in 1690, had been sufficiently impressed by his leadership, courage and administrative foresight to have enquired his name. Accordingly, Major Cadogan would have been dismayed, to say the least, to hear of Marlborough's setbacks during King William's reign. For, as a start, King William and Queen Mary had become increasingly irritated by the influence exerted by Marlborough and his Countess over the heiress to the throne, the Queen's sister, Princess Anne, and her Danish consort, Prince George, both of whom the King despised and was at pains to put down. Early in 1692 Dutch William deprived Marlborough (his gentleman of the bedchamber, as well as his foremost English general) of all his posts.

When Anne continued to defy her sister by having her best friend and lady-in-waiting, Sarah Marlborough, in attendance at court functions the Queen lost her temper. Marlborough was sent to the Tower, the pretext – on forged evidence – being that he was in treasonable correspondence with the Jacobite Court at St Germains (which he was, notwithstanding that the fact that the testament on which he was charged should have been inadmissible).

When the falsity of the evidence was revealed in June, 1692, he was released. Meanwhile Louis being still intent upon an invasion of England with a view to replacing William and Mary with ex-King James, the hectic troop movement between the French channel ports continued unabated. In the summer of 1694 William planned an amphibious attack between Camaret Bay and Brest. In the event the assault force was almost entirely annihilated. So it was clear that the enemy had foreknowledge of the project. Marlborough, whose links with St Germains were as close as anyone's, was among those accused of giving the game away. But, although he was a devious individual he was not one who would deliberately put English lives at risk.

Besides which, the English government had known since April the measure of opposition the expeditionary force was likely to face. The 'Camaret Bay' operation had been ill-fated from the start, as Cadogan must have realized.

Following popular Queen Mary's death at the end of 1694, Louis reckoned that the English people would certainly now prefer Stuart ex-King James to Dutch William. A Jacobite plot to ambush and assassinate William as he returned from a hunting trip in February, 1696, was foiled, and heads rolled. Louis proved wrong. Although William was by no means loved by the English people, as a wise and shrewd statesman and brave soldier he was highly respected; certainly the bulk of the Protestant population did not wish to see him exchanged for James.

As Cadogan would have heard, with rather more than passing interest, King William not only restored Marlborough to all his former places in 1698, but also appointed him governor of the heir presumptive, Princess Anne's frail little son, the Duke of Gloucester (who was to die, aged 11, two years later – another occasion for Jacobite rejoicing).

1698 was also marked by the burning down of most of Whitehall Palace and the election of an artful and extremely ambitious young man to be Speaker of the House of Commons, Robert Harley, who would have some detrimental influence on Cadogan's career in the years ahead.

In December, 1700, an event occurred which must have convinced the Enniskillen Dragoons major that his campaigning days were soon to return. In that month the decrepit and childless Carlos II of Spain, *Carlos el Sufridor*, died, his vast dominions – Spain, Milan, Naples, Sardinia, the Balearics and those in the Netherlands, South America and the Indies – being left to Louis XIV's grandson, the 16-year-old Philip, Duke of Anjou, whose claim was through Louis' Queen, the Infanta Maria Theresa, the senior of the Spanish Princesses. Naturally, neither the Protestant powers nor the

Austro-Hungarian empire considered the prospect of a Franco- Spanish hegemony to be in any way acceptable.

There had been two other claimants to the Spanish throne, both Austrian. The first was the Archduke Charles, the son of Emperor Leopold, whose Empress was the Infanta's sister; and the other was Leopold's grandson, the baby Joseph Ferdinand, Electoral Prince of Bavaria. By the Partition Treaty of 1698, signed by France and the Grand Alliance powers, it was agreed that the Electoral Prince should be chief heir to Carlos and that the Dauphin (Anjou's father) would have the bulk of the Italian states, except Milan, which would go to the Archduke Charles. To the great consternation of the Grand Alliance powers the infant Electoral Prince died in January, 1700. Further negotiation resulted, in February, in the signing of the Second Partition Treaty, whereby the Austrian Archduke was designated as King of Spain, while the Milanese was added to the Dauphin's share.

That autumn, however, the powers in Madrid, objecting to a division of the Spanish empire, had persuaded Carlos to leave his entire empire to Prince Philip, Duke of Anjou. Louis, given his habitual treachery, accepted the will without question. And, scarcely had Carlos breathed his last than the French monarch's grandson was posted to Madrid as Philip V of Spain. In the words of the Spanish ambassador to Versailles, *"Maintenant il n'y a plus de Pyrenees"*. Cadogan would have known, this was a *casus belli* if ever there was one.

Also of great significance for England and Cadogan's future was the death in September, 1701, of James II, and Louis' recognition of the ex-King's son, James (the 'Old Pretender') as the lawful King of England, in revocation of the French monarch's former promise – a clear breach of the Treaty of Ryswick. In the same month the Grand Alliance – England, Holland and the Austro-Hungarian Empire – was renewed and war declared. Other powers were soon joined to the Alliance – Denmark and most of the German princes. But the Elector of Bavaria, who was also nominal governor of the southern Netherlands, sided with France, although Bavaria was a province of the Empire.

William III, at 51, was a sick man. Another commander must lead the Grand Alliance. The King was a shrewd judge of character. While fully aware of the unscrupulous and financially acquisitive side of Marlborough's personality, the King had accurately sized up the English general's genius both as a military commander and as a diplomat. In May 1701 he appointed him to lead the English[3] forces in Holland, with a view to taking over the supreme command and to be Ambassador Extraordinary and Plenipotentiary with the right 'to conceive treaties, without reference, if needs be, to King or Parliament'.

Marlborough, sensing that times of great challenge lay ahead, wanted the most gifted administrative officer in the army to be his quartermaster general. The great commander having seen for himself Cadogan's outstanding conduct during the Cork campaign of 1690 (it was perhaps of benefit to the young officer that he also stood head and shoulders above his fellow men in physical stature!) had heard nothing but the highest praise for the young officer since then – both during the War of the League of Augsburg and as second-in-command and quartermaster of the Enniskillen Dragoons. So, notwithstanding the major's youth he had him advanced, in June, 1701, to the brevet rank (exceptional promotion) of colonel, and ordered him to come over from Ireland, along with twelve battalions. On 1 July Cadogan accompanied the King and Marlborough to Holland, promptly taking up his duties (and causing considerable jealousy among those who were thus passed over).

Was there a wistful sigh from Marlborough, one wonders, as he pondered on this young officer upon whom he had conferred such rapid promotion. For perhaps the veteran surmised that his own army career might have turned out somewhat differently had he not devoted so many years in the service of the Royal Duke who became the King he despised and deserted. As it was Marlborough was now over fifty, while his protege was not yet thirty. Perhaps he saw in Cadogan the military high achiever he wished he himself had been as a young man. Perhaps he saw him as a replacement for the only son he and his Sarah had lost. Certainly he recognized in Cadogan a restless energy and strength which in himself was already starting to wane.

Marlborough and Cadogan enjoyed a profound and happy mutual respect and had a great deal in common, one of their principal shared virtues being generosity (uncannily coupled with avarice, as we shall see). William Seward makes this comment in his *Anecdotes*:

> Though no epicure himself the Duke had, in common with Louis XIV, a pleasure in seeing others eat, and, when he was particularly pleased, exercised this pleasure, though it cost him something. Lord Cadogan used to say that he remembered seeing the Duke completely out of humour one day, a thing very unusual with him, and much agitated; in the evening, however, a messenger arrived who brought him some news which he liked. He immediately ordered the messenger to be placed in a situation where no one could speak to him and ordered his coach to be opened, and some cantines to be taken out, containing hams and other good things, and spread before some of the principal officers, he looking on and tasting nothing.[4]

Cadogan was similarly open-handed, although, in his case the messenger would not have been hidden! He said later, when Marlborough was disgraced, that he would never desert 'the great man to whom I am under such infinite obligations, I would be a monster if I did otherwise'.[5]

Notes

1   E. S. Jackson, *The Inniskilling Dragoons*, 241
2   Jackson, *op cit*, 240–41; W. Y. Carman, article in Journal of SAHR, Vol 46, *The Dress of Erle's Regiment in 1704 and 1709*, 1968. The DNB asserts that Cadogan held a previous commission with the Inniskilling

Dragoons. However, E. S. Jackson's carefully researched history of the regiment, along with the lists of officers accompanying the book, shows no Cadogan until 1698, when it has Cadogan registered as the major with effect from 1 August.

3   The term 'English' then also included the Scots and Protestant Irish
4   WSC I, 413, Quoting William Seward, *Anecdotes*, 257
5   *Ibid*, 466 2

3

Marriage

(1702–1704)

During his leisure time in Amsterdam, in the spring of 1702, Colonel Cadogan met and fell in love with a beautiful Dutch girl called Margaretta Munter, the member of a noble, landowning Amsterdam family. She was heiress to the substantial castle and estate of Raaphorst, some 10 miles from the Hague. Her father was a councillor in the court of Justice at the Hague, her mother (born Margaretta Trip) was the scion of a family of aristocratic architects. It was not long before Cadogan, already bilingual in French, added Dutch to his language accomplishment. His gift for languages was to prove invaluable in the many dealings he was to have with Austrian and German officers and diplomats, among others.

His romance with Margaretta began about the time that William III died. Sorrel, the King's charger, stumbled on a molehill when King William rode the horse out from Hampton Court one morning early in February, 1702, causing him to be thrown and to break his collar-bone. A sick man anyway, further complications set in and he died on 8 March (prompting cynical Englishmen everywhere to raise their glasses 'to the little gentleman in black velvet' – the mole which had initiated the unpopular monarch's final illness).

Thirty-eight-year-old Anne – the victim of sixteen miscarriages and the death, in childhood, of her only surviving offspring – was now Queen. She was at least as sanguine as her predecessor and her politicians to fight the grandiloquent, self-important, deceitful, expansionist Louis XIV. Few sovereigns were to have reigns of such success and popularity as Queen Anne was to enjoy. In 1692 she had prophesied to Sarah Marlborough that the day of her succession would be '. . . a Sun Shine day . . . England will flourish again'. And when she first addressed her Parliament she told the members, 'I know my heart to be entirely English', a barbed reference to the late King. However, Anne would be the last truly English monarch for many generations. For, by the Act of Settlement of 1701 she was to be followed by James I's granddaughter, Sophia, Electress of Hanover and the heirs of that German princess. But a considerable element of the British (as it would be from 1707) population, the pro-Jacobite faction, strongly disagreed with the Act of Settlement, a reality which would be of great significance later on in William Cadogan's career.

The signatories of the Grand Alliance made their formal declaration against France on 15 May 1702. Thus began the War of the Spanish Succession which was to humble France, reduce Holland, render England the most powerful nation in the world and bring Cadogan to the pinnacle of his profession. Settling into his post of Chief of Staff and Quartermaster General, he soon formed close liaisons with Marlborough's brother, Charles Churchill, the senior General of Foot; Henry Lumley, the senior cavalry general; the Huguenot Adam de Cardonnel, Marlborough's military and political secretary; the Revd Doctor Francis Hare, the Captain-General's chaplain and diarist; and Colonel Holcroft Blood, the chief Gunner, not to mention such officers at general headquarters as the commissary-general, the provost-marshal, the surgeon-general, the waggon-master-general; Colonel John Holcroft, the chief engineer; and the various major generals of Horse and Foot. By this time Cadogan also had dealings with Holland's Grand Pensionary, Antoine Heinsius, and with Austria's envoy at the Hague, Count Wratislaw.

The French had in Louis XIV a king and commander-in-chief whose word was absolute, who held sway over some 400,000 soldiers, and who, from Versailles, coordinated his strategy with a highly experienced eye and hand. For he had been in supreme command since early youth. When hostilities were renewed that May the situation looked bleak for the Allies. The French had the upper hand in the Mediterranean, in Italy, Germany and Spain. They had reoccupied almost the whole of the Spanish Netherlands (with the exception of the mighty Meuse fortress of Maastricht) threatening Holland herself. Marlborough, commanding the Allied forces in Flanders and operating along the valleys of the Meuse and the Rhine, was up against the five Dutch field deputies – who were no better than political commissars. For the Dutch parliament, the States General, refused to have their troops committed to any fighting without the approval of those Deputies attached to the Allies' headquarters. And, since it was Dutch policy not to engage in open battle (or any bold initiative for that matter) the Captain General's plans were repeatedly frustrated. Nevertheless the Allied forces in Flanders frequently outwitted Maréchal Boufflers, took several fortresses and were generally in the ascendant by the close of the 1702 campaign.

Consequently the Queen made Marlborough a Duke, while Colonel Cadogan who, at the tender age of thirty, had distinguished himself as the senior staff officer and administrative chief, was granted a financial bonus ('. . . which same her Majesty is graciously pleased to allow him in consideration of his extraordinary charge, care and pains in the execution of his said office of Quartermaster-General during the last campaign'.) And on 2 March 1703 the Queen further honoured him with the Colonelcy of the 6th Horse. Known during the war as Cadogan's Horse, the regiment was to become the 5th Dragoon Guards.[1] Cadogan's Horse being then stationed in Ireland, their Colonel wanted them with him in Flanders and he aimed to have a truly heavy regiment to suit his own figure and frame of mind. 'I must beg leave to recommend to your protection the three troops I have in Ireland,' he wrote to Robert Southwell, the war secretary, on 5 June 1703, 'the Duke of Marlborough has promised they shall be here the next campagne, in order to fit them for it I have desired Coll [George] Kellum to turn out the little men and the unserviceable Horses to enable the captains to recruit it will be necessary for some reasonable time to allow the vacancys att the musters, that being the only way to make the Squadrons better'.[2]

The English parliament, with the Whigs in power, as they would be for the next nine years – voted an additional 20,000 troops for the 1703 campaign, which was fought once again by the armies of Flanders on the Meuse and the Rhine. Despite further obstruction by the Field Deputies and lack of co-operation, too, by the Dutch generals, the Allies fought another successful Flanders campaign, which resulted in the reduction of a further ten fortresses and which continued until 15 December with the capture of Guelder in the province of Cleves. So far as the Field Deputies were concerned Cadogan had this to say: 'The resolution and vigour the Deputies show were enough to put their Generals out of countenance if they were not equally incapable of shame and reason'.[3] In August Marlborough intended to attack Villeroi's Lines opposite Ramillies, but the Dutch refused him. They opted for a siege of Limburg.

Cadogan had struck up a close and useful friendship with England's envoy to Prussia, Lord Raby (their copious original correspondence being contained in the Strafford Papers, now held in the British Library). In a letter to Raby of 20 September 1703, Cadogan refers to an administrative problem: 'I have been till now on the road of all posts, being employed to find horses in the country for drawing the cannon from Liège to Limburg; those whose business it properly was having so wholly neglected it that there wanted above 1,000 which with much ado I have got at last and sent away to Liège'. Then he adds a gossipy enquiry: 'Your Lordship in your letter speaks of your old mistress in Ireland, but I had much rather have news of the new ones you make at Berlin . . .'[4] (He must have smiled to himself as he wrote that, recalling the days when the two wild undergraduates drank at the taverns and chased after girls in their 'teenage Dublin days'.)

A week later, regarding the siege of Limburg, Cadogan had a similar message for Robert Southwell:

> The preparations for our siege of Limburgh goe on but lamely and I am sent back to this place [the Allied camp at St Fron] in order to get Horses out of the country for the carrying to Limburgh the Artillery and Mortars yet behind. I suppose the Batterys will be ready against Fryday att Farthest, and that probably in three or four days we shall be Masters of the Place.[5]

The best news for the Allies in 1703 was that of the defection from France of Portugal, whose economy had been crippled by the Anglo-Dutch naval blockade; and the Italian state of Savoy, whose leaders were aggrieved at Louis' failure to grant them promised additional financial aid. The worst news was that of the almost unprecedented storm that struck northern Europe on 26 November, and, among other victims, destroyed much of the English battle fleet.

On the Danube front and in southern Germany things had not gone well. Maréchal Claude- Louis-Hector, Duc de Villars and the Elector of Bavaria inflicted a crushing defeat on Count Styrum's Austrian army at Hochstadt. That coup allowed Maréchal Tallard to take the key German fortress of Landau without interference, and enabled another French corps to outflank the Imperial Lines of Stollhofen (thirty miles south of Landau on the upper Rhine). [see map p 33] Meanwhile, on 14 October Villars had won a victory against Prince Louis, Margrave of Baden (the architect of the Stollhofen Lines at Friedlingen, also on the Upper Rhine). Given those successes, France posed a very real threat to Austria herself, even Vienna, particularly as the Hungarians were in revolt against their Austrian overlords. In Italy Vendôme was supreme. At home the Tories continually complained about the War. These were the principal reasons for Marlborough's decision to carry the main thrust of the war to the Danube and Bavaria in 1704. It was to be an adventure that would test Cadogan's capability to the full.

Raby, an officer with a gallant and efficient regimental record behind him, held the Colonelcy of England's second senior cavalry regiment[6], the Royal Dragoons, who, to his dismay, were posted to Portugal. Not only that, but when they arrived they were allotted the most indifferent horses available. Raby wrote compaining of this treatment to Cadogan who sympathized and told him that 'the Duke of Marlborough would not if he could have avoided it parted with any of the Horse and Dragoons'.[7]

Warfare was a seasonal occupation, campaigns being largely dictated by the conditions of roads and waterways and the availability of grazing. The winter was not a time for active soldiering, but for replenishing and training. The 1703 campaign over, indefategable Cadogan supervised the return of the Allies to their garrisons, where he faced the problems not only of apportioning quarters and billets, but of finding the sources of rations for the soldiers for four or five months, supplying new coats and shoes, and overwintering many thousands of horses on very limited pasture, corn and hay. But he also found a good deal of time to visit Margaretta.

There was a drama in store for him when, early in March 1704,

25

he crossed to England on business. His packet boat was attacked by a French privateer. When it looked as though the Frenchmen were about to board his boat he threw his confidential papers overboard. But that proved unnecessary; for, just then, a strong east wind blew up, carrying him safely to Harwich, where he anchored on 7 March.[8]

In London, during the next fortnight, Marlborough secured an interview for Cadogan with the Queen. Anne – corpulent and riddled with arthritis, bearing the signs, too, of a heavy drinker, wearied by her many miscarriages, still devastated by the loss of the only child that had survived birth – was a sad woman who cannot have been an attractive sight. Yet she showed a great sweetness, which was reflected in her lilting voice and childlike manner. And there was a stubborness and a steel, too, with which Cadogan would soon become acquainted.

He also had the pleasure of meeting the staunch Lord Treasurer, Lord Godolphin, a financial wizard yet one whose heart was closer to Newmarket and the breeding of horses than it was to London and the Treasury. Sidney Godolphin was the Marlboroughs' closest friend; his only son, Francis, had married their eldest daughter, Lady Henrietta. While Godolphin remained Lord Treasurer the English army would never lack the wherewithal to wage war, evidence of which was already clear to Cadogan.

In December 1703, Leopold, the new Austro-Hungarian Emperor, aware of the imminent threat to his country posed by the French armies, was prompted to 'look abroad and solicit the assistance of the most powerful Allies and particularly the Queen of England and the States General were importuned for speed and Effectual succours'.[9]

Marlborough, in his turn, knew that, if the French reached Vienna, they would have virtually won the war. He was determined to frustrate their plans. He was now in possession of Anne's 'Order in Council' for his proposed expedition to the

Danube. At home only she and Godolphin were fully informed of the Grand Design.

Cadogan was soon to cross to Holland again and, during the fourth week of April, to marry his beloved Margaretta.

Notes

1 Cannon, *The 5th, or Princess Charlotte of Wales Regt of Dragoon Guards*, pp17–18
2 BL Add MS 21, 494, f64
3 HMC, Chequers Court, 119–21; BL Add MS 29547, f41; GMT, I, 316
4 Strafford Papers, Sloane 3392
5 BL Add MS 21, 494, f68
6 The Royal Regiment of Horse Guards (The Blues), which did not acquire Household Cavalry status until the 19th century, was then the senior cavalry regiment. As a Guards regiment the Blues were never of the Line. Raby's regiment was the Royal Dragoons. The two regiments were amalgamated, as the Blues and Royals, in the Household Cavalry, in 1969.
7 *Op cit*, ff 5, 13, 15
8 Pearman, 35
9 Hare's Journal, 6

4

Long Trek Commissary

(1704)

On 19 April 1704, when the thirty-two-year-old Colonel Cadogan boarded the yacht *Peregrine* at Harwich bound for Holland, he found himself in excellent company. Besides the Captain General and his brother, General Charles Churchill, there were Lieutenants General the Earl of Orkney and Henry Lumley, along with the Captain General's brilliant Secretary, Adam de Cardonnel. Of those the Captain General had confided only in Cadogan and de Cardonnel that he intended to march the army of the Grand Alliance to the Danube 'to save the [Austro-Hungarian] Empire'. Apart from those only the Queen, the Lord Treasurer Godolphin and Antoine Heinsius, knew of it. If William Cadogan was seriously daunted by the fact that, as Quartermaster General, he would be responsible for all aspects of the administration of that gigantic army on their long trek he did not, apparently, reveal it. They sailed at noon. A large convoy of transports, bearing four complete regiments of Foot, a squadron of Cadogan's regiment of dragoons, other reinforcements, and a protective squadron of men o'war, accompanied the flagship. 'We were infested in our passage with a whole fleet of little thieving 'Privateers', wrote Cardonnel; 'I fear they stole one or two of our small traders.'[1] That, however, was among the least of the anxieties of the High Command as regards the forthcoming endeavour.

Louis XIV, masterminding the French strategy from Versailles, still fielded massive land forces, who were deployed in no fewer than nine armies. One of those, commanded by Marlborough's nephew, the Duke of Berwick, operated in Spain; three more looked after French interests in Italy – in Lombardy, Piedmont and Savoy. A corps, commanded by the Comte de Coigny, was held in Alsace. Maréchal Villars, at the head of another army, attempted to quell the Huguenot peasants, known as Camisards, who had risen in rebellion in the Cevennes. The combined forces of the Elector of Bavaria and Maréchal Marsin, referred to at the end of the last chapter, were awaiting sufficient reinforcements to strike at Nuremburg, then Vienna. Louis would soon order Tallard (lately ambassador to England), who was keeping a watch on the Rhine, to march over the mountains of the Black Forest with his army and to provide those reinforcements.

Villeroi, the enemy *maréchal* who held the military responsibility for the Spanish Netherlands, believing the Allies to be heading for the Moselle valley, shadowed them, and continued shadowing them, beyond the Moselle. He left behind a small force, under the Marquis de Bedmar, to face Overkirk. Thus the Dutch, being now in considerable superiority in the Netherlands, could afford to reinforce the English and their attached mercenaries, which Overkirk would do to the tune of 15,000 troops. This was, of course, on the unwritten understanding that the expedition would venture no farther south than the Moselle valley. A Dutch division under Lieutenant General van Goor was already in southern Germany.

The Dutch (with the exception of Antoine Heinsius) knew nothing of the Danube plan. Marlborough, who had been determined to dispense with interference by the States-General and their dreaded Field Deputies, left most of the Dutch force behind, under command of Veldtmarshal Overkirk, to hold the Spanish Netherlands. Marlborough would lead only the English troops (about 19,000 men) and such Dutch, German and Danish mercenaries who were to join them on the marathon march. He gave the States General the impression that his objectives were the fortresses in the valley of the Moselle.

The Allied army began their march to the Rhine from Maastricht on 6 May, crossing the Meuse on the 14th. They reached the Rhine, close to Bonn, on 23 May where the ominous news reached them that Maréchal Marsin's army had linked up with that of the Elector of Bavaria at Villingen on the Danube, making a total force of nearly 50,000. Now that Franco-Bavarian host was to march eastwards along the Danube valley, pointing at the heart of Austria. We now turn to the start of that march which was to prove the first great test of Cadogan's career as Quartermaster General.

It proved to be a disastrous summer. So far it had been flat country, a landscape, said Captain Andrew Bonnell, of the Artillery, in a letter to his father, 'of Great Heaths and adorned with pleasant villages, Castles and Cloysters'. Then the countryside altered. 'It is now different from our Vale for we are coming to prodigious mountins almost impossible for our Artillery to Pass . . . in which Hills abound with Vines and ye lower Ground with plenty of Corne'[2]. The army was approaching the Rhine.

Apart from atrocious weather, everything – thanks largely to Cadogan – was beautifully organized. The men's rations, forage for the horses and other local commodities were all paid for en route. Henry Davenant, the army's financial agent, based at Frankfurt, having received the credits from Godolphin, forwarded all that was needed, to Cadogan, to pay the commissars and German sutlers. 'Notwithstanding the continual marching,' wrote Marlborough to Godolphin, 'the men are extremely pleased with this expedition, so that I am sure you

30

will take all the care possible they may not want.'[3] Cadogan and his assistant commissaries never lacked for money to pay for local produce. 'I must needs say he perform'd that March with very good Conduct,' wrote Sergeant Millner, of the Royal Irish, 'by beginning every Day's March by Break of Day or Sunrising; so that every Day, before it was extream hot or Noon, we were fully encamp'd in our new Camp. So that the remaining Part of the Day's Rest was nigh as good as a Day's Halt.'[4] But the roads, no more than stony blistering tracks, when they were not deep in mud, were not kind to the feet of heavily burdened troops.

At Coblenz, where the Moselle flows into the Rhine, almost everyone in Marlborough's army, from generals downwards, along with French spies in the town, anticipated that the 'scarlet caterpillar' (as the late Winston Churchill called it) would turn south-west along the Moselle. 'Now, when we expected to march up the Moselle,' Captain Robert Parker, also of the Royal Irish, wrote in his journal, 'to our surprise we passed that river over a stone bridge and the Rhine over two bridges of boats.'[5] Louis and his marshals were foxed, wondering how on earth they should react to this extraordinary turn of events. Clearly the Allies were now intent upon a campaign on the Rhine: but how to respond? Marlborough was determined that the secrecy of his mission must be guarded. The whole distance – some 260 miles – was to be covered as quickly as possible, but the Captain General, by agreement with Cadogan, would weary neither his men nor his horses unduly. They would rarely march more than 12 miles a day starting at first light, reaching their next camp before midday. And they would be adequately catered for at every halt.

Cadogan had overall responsibility for march discipline; for ensuring that intervals were kept; confirming the establishment of field hospitals en route; for seeing that stragglers were either tended for their sickness or injuries, or were urged to catch up; and he checked that the cavalry escorting the columns were alert. This was a contented army, happy to venture into the green hills of Germany, to have a change from the Low Countries; an army having great confidence in their incomparable commander-in-chief and his adminstrative staff. The troops were greeted enthusiastically wherever they went by the local population. Captain Richard Pope, a cavalry troop leader, commented in a letter home, that 'the troops are in fine condition. At least 200 Ladies come to see us on the march, some of them very much handsomer than we expected to find,'[6]

The soldiers sang as they marched, songs such as this:

> We shall lead more happy lives
> By getting rid of brats and wives
> That scold on both night and day,
> When over the Hills and far away!
> Over the hills and over the main
> To Flanders, Portugal and Spain.
> Queen Anne commands and we'll obey,
> Over the Hills and far away
> Courage boys 'tis one to ten,
> But we return all gentlemen,
> While conquering colours we display
> Over the Hills and far away.

It was mid-May. The sun was bright, the air fresh, the meadow flowers shone in profusion, the bird song was delightful. The weather told them little of the cold, wet summer they were soon to endure.

South of Coblenz the Allied columns were obliged to leave the Rhine valley, for want of an adequate road, and to strike into the Taunus mountains, 'a very steep and tedious road', said Sergeant Millner; 'where, the same day, there fell a great Shower of Hail, each thereof as large as a Musket-Ball'[7] Bonnell's estimate of the hail was much larger. 'I remember and shall as long as I live a Storme of Haill which happ'd ysday [yesterday]. It

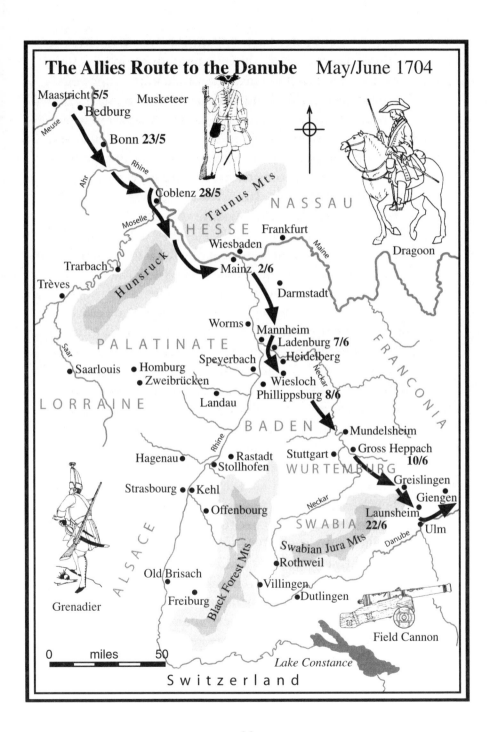

The Allies Route to the Danube May/June 1704

Maastricht **5/5** Musketeer

Bedburg

Bonn **23/5**

Meuse

Ahr

Rhine

Coblenz **28/5**

Taunus Mts

NASSAU

Moselle

HESSE Frankfurt

Wiesbaden

Maine

Dragoon

Trarbach

Trèves

Hunsruck

Mainz **2/6**

Darmstadt

Saar

PALATINATE

Worms

Mannheim

Ladenburg **7/6**

Speyerbach

Heidelberg

FRANCONIA

Saarlouis Homburg

Zweibrücken

Wiesloch

Neckar

LORRAINE

Landau

Phillippsburg **8/6**

BADEN

Mundelsheim

Rhine

Rastadt

Stollhofen

Stuttgart

Gross Heppach

10/6

Hagenau

Strasbourg Kehl

WURTEMBURG

Greislingen

Neckar

Giengen

Offenbourg

SWABIA

Launsheim

22/6

Danube

Ulm

Swabian Jura Mts

Rothweil

ALSACE

Black Forest Mts

Old Brisach

Villingen

Dutlingen

Grenadier

Freiburg

Field Cannon

0 miles 50

Lake Constance

Switzerland

33

was as big as a large Walnut and fell with yt [that] violence yt it laid down all ye corne where it came beate down all ye young frute of ye Trees and frightened all our horses into ye Woods'[8]

Having seen to the marching columns (and having handed over responsibility to a subordinate) Cadogan would ride ahead each morning with his camp reconnaissance party to select and establish a suitable site for the next night's encampment. It must have adequate space, ready access and egress and proximity to water; and it must afford ready security, so as to be easily defended if need be. After making that decision he would indicate where the tent-lines and horse-lines were to go. He would see the bread ovens put together and that sufficient bread, the soldiers' staple diet, was baked daily. He would ensure that replacement clothing and equipment was available. 'As we marched through the countrys of our Allies Commissaries were appointed to furnish us with all manner of necessaries for Man and Horse: these were brought to the ground before we arrived and the soldiers had nothing to do,' as Captain Parker observed, 'but to pitch their tents, boil their kettles and lie down to rest. Surely never was such a march carried on with more order and regularity and with less fatigue.'[9] Due credit to Cadogan.

Cadogan may be readily envisaged, tall, thickset, energetic, efficient, having organized a camping-ground, seated at his table by his Quartermaster-General's tent and office, receiving the regimental and battalion seconds-in-command and quartermasters, indicating their allotted areas and issuing particular orders. Then he would watch the soldiers disperse. The infantrymen, who comprised some 70 per cent of the army, wore a heavy knee-length, full-skirted coat with deep pockets, a waistcoat, shoes, stockings and a three-cornered hat (a less ornate one than that worn by Chelsea Pensioners today), with, in some cases, on the back and sides, leather flaps, which could be lowered against rain or intense heat. Crimson and scarlet were the English colours; the coats distinguished their wearers from the enemy. Colour was about esprit de corps and instilling fear in the enemy. Those red colours meant English troops, the best-trained soldiery in Europe.

Each infantryman was armed with a flintlock musket and wore a sword as well as a bayonet. His bayonet was the new 16-inch ring pattern which fitted over the musket's muzzle. He wore white crossbelts for his cartridge boxes and a bandolier from which hung a dozen powder charges. He was also burdened with a knapsack, a rolled cloak, a blanket, a spade, a cooking pot and 24 rounds of shot, all of which, with musket and ramrod, cannot have weighed much less than 60 lbs – quite a load to carry on a twelve-mile march. The officers, more ornately dressed and much less heavily burdened, sported full-bottomed wigs under their tricornes, and gorgets – metal half-moon-shaped appendages – around their necks.

Each battalion deployed 13 companies, at least one of which would be a pike company, whose primary role was to form a 'hedge square' of metal points to deter enemy cavalry while their musketeer comrades re-loaded. (There were 26 drill movements involved in the handling of the flintlock.) There were also the battalion's grenadier companies, each of which was composed of tall, strong, hand-picked men, who, in addition to the same equipment issued to the musketeers, carried a pouchful of grenades, and wore, strapped to a wrist, a slow-burning fuse with which to prime them. They wore mitred caps to render their grenade-swinging arms free movement.

The heavy rains persisted. On the night of 30 May the army 'encampt by the Rhine side', wrote Sergeant Wilson, of Howe's Regiment,

> but there faling such Floods of Rain by which there came such a torrent of Water from ye Mountains that ye Roades were render'd soe bad that there was no Possibilite of moving ye Train [of Artillery]. and ye Campe being on a level Ground by

ye Violence of ye Water was in Danger of being washed away into ye Rhine. But ye Roades soe bad and ye Grounde so boggy with ye excessive Raine that no one piece of Canon could be moved. Upon which there was Orders for ye Country [local farmers, etc] to bring in fresh Straw for ye Men and another day's Forage for ye Horses.[10]

Notwithstanding such abysmal conditions the Elector of Mainz reviewing the Foot Guards on 2 June, observed 'not only their order, but their cleanliness, and their arms, accoutrements, clothes, shoes'. He said to General Churchill commanding the infantry, 'Certainly all these gentlemen are dressed for the Ball. Sergeant Wilson added that 'the Army appeared that Day fully as Clean and Compleat as if they had marched out of their Quarters into the Field. Of which his Electoral Highness took notice.'[11]

It is doubtful whether most battalions of the line displayed quite such an impressive appearance. For the army contained more conscripts than volunteers. Cadogan was as familiar with the background of the average recruit as well as any officer in the army. As he had seen for himself recruiting was largely from the dregs of society. Vagrants were press-ganged; men dying of starvation took the 'Queen's shilling' in order to eat the Queen's bread, murderers awaiting the death sentence were released from prison to fill the depleted ranks. Such types were hounded to the Savoy, London's dreaded recruiting depot, often with buttons removed from their breeches, lest having taken the 'Queen's shilling', they absconded. Desertion was rife. Here is Sergeant Kite in Farquhar's *The Recruiting Officer*:

Hunger and ambition, the Fears of Starving, and the Hopes of a Truncheon led me along to a Gentleman with a fair Tongue, and fair periwig who loaded me with promises; but 'gad it was the highest load that ever I felt in my whole life. He promised to advance me, and indeed he did so – to a Garret in the Savoy. I asked him why he put me in prison: he called me Lying Dog, and said I was in Garrison; and indeed 'tis a Garrison that may hold out till Domesday before I should desire to take it again.

And Farquhar knew what he was talking about. He had been a recruiting officer. As that deeply religious Cameronian officer, Major John Blackadder, recorded:

> This is a sad corps I am engaged in; vice raging openly and impudently. They speak just such language as devils would do. I find this ill in our trade, that there is now so much tyranny and knavery in the army, that it is a wonder how a man of straight, generous honest soul can live in it . . . Armies which used to be full of men of great and noble souls, are now turned to a parcel of mercenary, fawning, lewd dissipated creatures, the dregs and scum of mankind.[12]

Nor could this army afford to be on bad terms with the German populace, to be guilty of crimes involving villagers or private property. So discipline was very tight. Offenders were fined, flogged or, in extreme cases, hanged. The army's consequent good order and discipline paid off very well. The German townsfolk, villagers and farmsteaders, who had dreaded the advent of the 'scarlet caterpillar', were amazed at their good behaviour.

The infantry officers were often not much better than the men. They were mainly ill-educated and ill-trained, while some were unkempt drunkards, or fellows who gambled away what little money they possessed, or who joined the army to avoid debtors' prisons.

The cavalrymen, being largely genuine volunteers were, on the whole, of a higher calibre than the Foot. For the most part they supplied their own mounts on enlistment, although a limited number of horses were available for cavalry recruits, but they were required to pay for them, usually through stoppages of pay. The cavalry were dressed much as the Foot were, except that their breeches were more protective and they wore thigh-length boots instead of shoes. Some of the dragoon regiments wore leather leggings. Regiments of Horse and dragoons were mostly composed of eight or nine troops subdivided into three or four squadrons, which, for tactical purposes, were semi-independent. At each encampment Cadogan would have given a special welcome to the officers and men of his own regiment, of which he was immensely proud.

The artillery and sappers would be the last to reach camp. Cadogan would have shown the Gunners' representative the gun park, Colonel Holcroft the engineers' place and the waggon-master-general where to put the echelon horses and carts. It was a wet summer and the guns caused the worst problems on those appalling roads. The uneven tracks were often transformed into quagmires. The artillery train, composed of 34 guns, fired stone or cast-iron cannon balls from their 16- and 12-pounder culverins, with an effective range of about 1,000 yards; or grapeshot, for closer-range work, from the smaller sakers and minions. Cadogan would have acquainted himself with those statistics and a host of other tactical detail.

Since Marlborough raced on with the squadrons of Horse during most of that celebrated southwards march, leaving his brother, Charles, to plod on with the Foot, the guns and other horse-drawn paraphernalia, Cadogan must have been usually galloping ahead with his reconnaissance party to make arrangements for the cavalry, leaving a subordinate to see in the remainder of the army. His workload was such that he surely felt exhausted each evening. 'This march has hardly left me time to eat or sleep' he wrote to Raby, now serving with the English Embassy in Berlin, on 30 May, by which time the army's destination was no longer a secret:

We continued it with all imaginable diligence towards the lines of Stolhoffen where the Luneburgers Hessians and Dutch already are who must compose the army . . . which will consist of forty-five Battalions and about seventy or eighty Squadrons . . . 'tis absolutely necessary to hasten putting in execution the project of reducing the Elector of Bavaria . . . it will be an army left in the lines of Stolhoffen sufficient to prevent the French forcing them or passing the Rhine below Philipsburgh . . . [we] design forming two armies each of above forty thousand and to enter by two wayes into Bavaria, one by Donauwert and other between Ulm and the Lake of Constance which will oblige the Elector either to divide his Force to oppose both armies . . . or els to keep his Force entire and act against one and so leave the other a free passage to Munich and Ingoldstad this must necessarily bring him to reason unless he will hasard inevitable ruine by being shut up between two armies each stronger than his own that must certainly happen after the taking the two forementioned places. The whole success of the Expedition depends on preventing the French either to force the Lines of Stolhoffen or to pass the Rhine below Philipsburgh which they will probably attempt when their Great Detachment from the Maese has joined their army in the Rhine as the only way left to succour the Elector, we having got so far before them as to make their sending any further succour by the Black Forest so late. Monsr Villeroy commands the Detachment coming from the Maese, it consists of thirty-five Battalions and about forty or fifty Squadrons, amongst whom is the Maison du Roy.[13]

That was the plan at the end of May. But early in June the strategic vision changed. The Captain General tricked Louis and his marshals into believing he would operate in Alsace, with Landau as his principal objective, by requesting the Governor of Philippsburg to have a pontoon bridge constructed across the Rhine there. However, having crossed the Neckar at

Ladenburg the 'scarlet caterpillar' – now a myriad of other colours, being joined by more Hessians, Danes and Dutch – veered away from the Rhine and continued southwards, going over the Neckar again at Lauffen.[14]

As early as 23 May, when the expeditionary force was at Bonn, the Captain General heard that Tallard had linked up with the Elector of Bavaria on the Danube at Villingen. On 8 June Tallard and Villeroi met at Zweibrucken to discuss their future. They wrote to Louis proposing alternative measures. A fortnight later the King ordered Villeroi to Offenburg, to keep watch on the Rhine, with special reference to the Lines of Stollhofen.

Marlborough and Cadogan met 41-year-old Prince Eugène of Savoy – who was then Europe's leading military commander – for the first time just beyond the Neckar, at Mundelsheim. Eugène had a chequered career behind him. He was the son of the Count of Soissons and a grandson of the Duke of Savoy. His mother, a niece of Cardinal Mazarin, had been one of Louis XIV's mistresses. When she was accused of poisoning her husband, Louis exiled her and took custody of Eugène. From early childhood the boy showed a passionate interest in soldiering; but Louis, with his predilection for organizing the lives of others, considered that Eugène would make a good priest and duly found him a place in the Church. Jibbing at that Eugène soon escaped from France and, having offered his services to the Austro-Hungarian Emperor made a considerable name for himself in the Austro-Turkish War. He became a field marshal before his thirtieth birthday. Following a brilliant career fighting the French in Italy, he was recalled to Vienna to be the Imperial Commander-in-Chief. However, during this summer of 1704 he contrived to desert his war office desk for command of a field army. Not everyone found him an attractive person. 'His nose spoils his face,' thought the Duchess of Orleans; 'he is always dirty and has lanky hair which he never curls.' During their discussions Eugène and

Marlborough, accompanied by Cadogan, rode to Gros Heppach to review the English cavalry and

> His Highness [Eugène] was very much surprised to find them in so good a condition after so long a march, and told his Grace he had heard much of the English Cavalry, and found it to be the finest he had ever seen. But, says he, money which you don't want in England, will buy cloths and fine forses, but it cannot buy that lively air I see in every one of these troopers' faces. To which his Grace replied that that must be attributed to their heartiness for the public cause, and the particular pleasure they had in seeing his Highness.[15]

The Captain General worked Cadogan to the extremes of physical endurance not only as Quartermaster General and Chief of Staff but also as his diplomatic representative. Next day 'as Count Wratislaw informed his Grace that Prince Lewis himself [the Margrave of Baden] was coming Post to meet him, his Grace sent Colonel Cadogan to compliment and conduct that Prince to the Camp,' said Hare. 'The Colonel met him, with Prince Lobkowitz his nephew at Elsinghen.'[16]

Eugène told Marlborough of his grave misgivings regarding the integrity of Prince Lewis, who commanded another Imperial army and who joined their councils at Gros Heppach. The Dutch element of Marlborough's army was under command of the competent Lieutenant General van Goor, who, during the previous campaigning season, had such an altercation with Baden (who was, patently, in the wrong) that the States-General instructed their general to return his troops to Holland. But now Goor stayed while Baden agreed to a request by Marlborough, in that context, that he would let bygones be bygones.

Anyhow, Baden, Eugène and Marlborough concurred that, for the moment, Eugène should proceed to Stollhofen and confront Villeroi's forces on the Rhine, while Marlborough and the Margrave invaded Bavaria. Meanwhile, in late June, the weather had turned even nastier, rendering the roads worse than ever and prompting Marlborough to tell his Duchess that 'as I am writing I am forced to have a fire in the stove in my chamber. But the poor men, that have not such conveniences, I am afraid will suffer from these continual rains.' Sergeant Millner was one of them. 'The Way was very heavy, deep and tedious,' he recorded in his journal, 'which then and several other Times detain'd us from expeditious Marching. There [at the village of Erlickheim] we saw the first cut Corn of the Year.'[17]

Notwithstanding that the roads were reduced to deep mud and the ascents were as steep as ever Marlborough's cavalry joined forces with the Margrave of Baden's 50,000 strong army on 22 June at Launsheim, which was only about fifteen kilometres from the camp occupied by Marsin and the Elector of Bavaria, close to Ulm on the Danube. Tramp, tramp, tramp. Each footstep, each hoof, was sucked from the glutinous mud. Five days later Charles Churchill caught up with the Foot and the guns. The long trek was over. Private John Marshall Deane, of the Foot Guards, gives another fair idea of the conditions suffered by the army:

> It had rayned 32 days together more or less and misserable marches we have had for deep and dirty roads and through tedious woods and wildernesses and over vast high rocks and mountains, that it may be easily judged what our little army endured and what unusuall hardship they went through.[18]

Back at home William Penn the Quaker expressed his concern regarding 'this mighty march to the Danube with so prodigious an artillery requiring 200 horse to draw it . . . to give a turn to the French affairs; and may England, poor England ever prevail.'[19]

'Marlborough has joined Lewis of Baden,' wrote Lediard.

'Success will either gain him a great Reputation and very much shelter him from his enemies (which are not a few) or be his Ruin.'[20] For Cadogan, having already hitched his wagon to Marlborough's star, it was much the same. The future was packed with hazard. 'If he [Marlborough] fails,' promised Sir Edward Seymour, a member of the Council, 'we will break him up as hounds upon a hare.'[21]

In those fifty-two days and nights Cadogan, under the tutelage of England's great Captain General, completed the most important administrative apprenticeship of his life. But the stiffest challenges of the whole enterprise were still to be faced. At home the Tories – who, notwithstanding the Whig government,boasted a majority in the House of Commons – vented their fury on Marlborough for leading the Queen's army so far from home. The Hungarian rebels, closely assisted by the French, were not far from the gates of Vienna. Marsin and the Elector withdrew their forces further west along the valley, to Lauingen, while Tallard had successfully raced along the last miles of the Black Forest to increase the strength of the Franco-Bavarian army of the Danube to over 60,000. A mighty fortress barred the Allies' way into Bavaria. Called the Schellenberg it dominated the Danube town and bridge of Donauwörth. Marlborough's immediate aim was to capture the Schellenberg, and, with it, Donauwörth, with a view to entering Bavaria and persuading that State's Elector to desert the French and return to the Imperial fold.[22]

Notes

1 BL Add MS 28, 918; Cardonnel Letters, 22.4.1704
2 Letters of Andrew Bonnell, 25.6.1704
3 Coxe, I, B331
4 *Journal*,83
5 *Two Soldiers of Marlborough's Wars*, 30
6 HMC, Cowper, III, 36
7 *Journal*, 85
8 Letters, 25.6.1704

9   Chandler, *op cit.*

10 Diary of Sgt Wilson, 82

11 *Ibid.*

12 Blackadder, *Diary* (1700–1728) (Ed.A Crichton, 1824), 129–30

13 BL Add MS 22196 (Cadogan-Raby corres), ff 16–18

14 BL Add MS 9114, (Hare) f 35 Millner, *Journal*, 88; Coxe 1, 163; WSC II, 775

15 Hare *op cit*, f 35

16 *Ibid*, f 36

17 *Journal*, 89

18 *Journal*, SAHR, special publication No 12, f 5

19 GMT, I, 354

20 Lediard, I, 319

21 WSC II, 780

22 Fuller accounts of the march to the Danube are to be found in GMT I, 347–55; WSC II, 740–843

5

Unhorsed at the Schellenberg

(1704)

Marsin and the Elector had been preparing to besiege Nuremberg, but the advent of the army of the Grand Alliance frustrated that plan, and they withdrew to Dillingen. The main Allied force being now on the Danube and interposed between the Franco-Bavarian army and Austria, the immediate threat to Vienna was also over (from French invasion if not from the Hungarian insurgents). The Allies had secured the strategic initiative. That situation warranted, too, a fresh administrative perspective for Cadogan. Marlborough's expeditionary force could no longer rely on the Rhine and its magazines. By arrangement between Cadogan and Raby the Allies' line of communication and supply was switched from the vulnerable north-north-west to north-east, through Franconia to Nuremberg and Frankfurt, magazines being set up at Heidenheim and Nördlingen, where the hospital was to be established. Cadogan's agents, contractors and commissaries were already purchasing supplies and hiring transport in Franconia. The security of the new route rendered the capture of the Danube town of Donauwörth and its adjacent fortress, the Schellenberg, still more important. Maréchal Villars had warned the Elector of Bavaria in 1703: 'Fortify your towns, and, above all, the Schellenberg, that fort above Donauwörth, the importance of which the great Gustavus taught us'.[11] (Sweden's King Gustavus Adolphus was, in 1632, the only commander who had ever stormed and captured the Schellenberg.)

As for the Allies' Imperial confederate, the Margrave of Baden, he calmly announced, at this juncture, that he would move independently eastwards to attempt a river crossing at Neuberg. The Captain General remonstrated, pointing out that to divide the armies would be madness – especially before the Danish cavalry squadrons (who were due in a few days to boost the English, Dutch and German contingents) arrived, and before a Swabian detachment, also due, reinforced the Margrave's own army. The Imperial contingent on the Danube, Marlborough argued, should stay united with their Allies. Baden was persuaded to fall into line. Meanwhile the wet

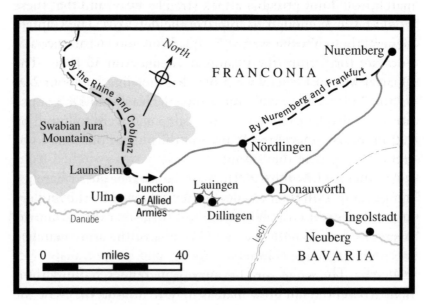

Cadogan's new administrative communications via Nuremberg

weather continued without interruption and the nights bitterly cold. But the soldiers were impatient.

The fortress of Schellenberg was situated on top of a steep hill, but its walls and ramparts were in need of repair. To reach it the Allies must cross a rivulet called the Wernitz. On 30 June a friendly local man reported that the enemy occupied the fortress with a garrison of 13,000 and that they were now improving the ramparts and entrenching themselves. 'Hereupon his Grace sent the Quarter Master General,' the Captain General's chaplain tells us, 'with a party of 400 Horse to gain more particular intelligence. These went within sight of the Schellenberg upon which they perceived several of the enemies Batterys lying encamp'd.' In accordance with the High Command custom of those days, Marlborough and the Margrave alternated in supreme command day by day. On 1 July 'it being his Grace's turn to command the next day he resolv'd to attack'.[2]

The enemy imagined that the Allies, following their gruelling march, could not possibly attack straight away, and that there would be time enough to improve the defences. The Captain General thought otherwise. 177 squadrons and 76 battalions of Foot set forth from their camp at Giengen on 30 June. 'The Quarter Master General went out that morning [at about 2am on the 2nd] with several Squadrons of Horse and Dragoons,' says the Chaplain, 'to mark out a camp and were followed by 400 Pioneers to level the Ways and thirty-six Pontoons to be laid in Bridge over the Wernitz.'[3]

At 2am on 2 July the 6,000 men of the advance guard marched out of camp with their cavalry escort, followed by the artillery under the expert Colonel Blood, and at the rear the 'Countrey Waggons' loaded with fascines. The rest of the army marched at 5am in two huge columns.

As the day wore on the enemy watchers behind their ramparts on the hill grew increasingly anxious as they saw the splashes of colour below grow more frequent and deploy. At around 10am they detected much movement near the Wernitz as Cadogan's pioneers worked to establish pontoons. Meanwhile at about 9am Cadogan with the Quartermasters and their escort had reached the heights above the Wernitz and had started making out a camp and assembly area. By 5pm the spearhead force, under the command of General van Goor, was in position half way up the ascent on which the fortress lay. At 6.15 they advanced under the protection of a barrage from Colonel Blood's guns, and also under withering Bavarian artillery fire from the walls.

When the Allied cavalry prepared to charge up the hill, Colonel Cadogan, having carried out his various administrative functions, rode to the head of Cadogan's Horse to lead them in the wake of the Foot. It was a hard, steep climb, a great effort for Cadogan's charger, carrying as the horse did, an exceptional weight.

Fifty yards or so from the parapet ran a road bordered by steep banks. This was totally unexpected; and, believing it to be the ditch of which they had been informed in their intelligence briefing, the leading ranks of dragoons and infantrymen threw

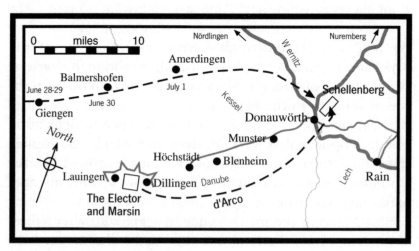

The Advances to the Schellenberg

into it the fascines which they were carrying. That was a grave error, for the breastwork ditch, of which they had been notified, was 20 yards further up the hill. Thus, coming towards the parapet and obstructed by that ditch, they were unable to storm across it, but could only, for the moment, stand and suffer the enemy's dreadful cannonade and fusilade.

What followed was one of the fiercest fights in history. This is how Colonel Jean Martin de la Colonie, commanding an enemy regiment, portrays the tussle at the ramparts:

> It would be impossible to describe in words strong enough the details of the carnage that took place during the attack, which lasted a good hour or more. We were all fighting hand-to-hand, hurling them back as they clutched the parapet; men were slaying, or tearing at the muzzles of guns and the bayonets which pierced their entrails; crushing under their feet their own wounded comrades, and even gouging out their opponents' eyes with their nails, when the grip was so close that neither could make use of their weapons. I verily believe that it would have been quite impossible to find a more terrible representation of Hell itself than was shown in the savagery of both sides on this occasion.[4]

By 8.30 pm Marlborough's army were masters of the Schellenberg. And, while they consolidated within the fortress, the Margrave of Baden's cavalry slipped through between the fortress and the town of Donauwörth and captured a great haul of weapons and stores of which wounded Cadogan took charge. The defenders were utterly routed. Many who escaped the Allies' firearms, swords and bayonets, drowned in the Danube in their hectic flight. But the Allies lost heavily, too, suffering several thousand casualties, General van Goor being counted among the many senior officers who were killed. Cadogan, whose charger was shot and killed under him, escaped with a wounded thigh, a blackened face and a mighty

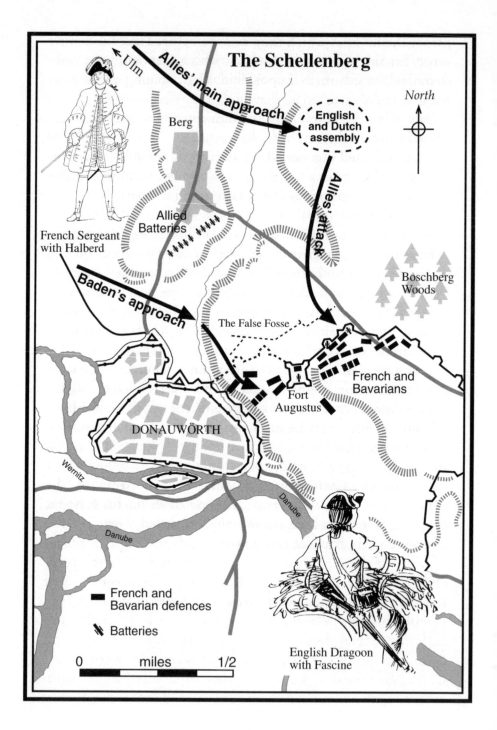

The Schellenberg

Ulm

Allies' main approach

Berg

English and Dutch assembly

North

Allies' attack

Allied Batteries

French Sergeant with Halberd

Baden's approach

The False Fosse

Boschberg Woods

French and Bavarians

Fort Augustus

DONAUWÖRTH

Wernitz

Danube

Danube

■ French and Bavarian defences

☳ Batteries

0   miles   1/2

English Dragoon with Fascine

perspiration. (History does not relate whether a second charger was provided for him.) The cavalry officer, Captain Pope, aptly described the victory as 'a considerable advantage, purchased at a dear rate'.[5]

However, this was not too high a price to pay for that splendid open gateway into Bavaria. The Allies went on to capture Rain and Neuberg, and with those fortified towns, as well as Donauwörth, in their possession, Cadogan's new Franconian supply line was greatly strengthened. Next, the Captain General – with a view to persuading the Elector to return to his Imperial fidelity – set about having the Bavarian villages burned.The Elector set great store by his governorship of the Spanish Netherlands and was much tempted by King Louis' promise of the Austro-Hungarian throne once Emperor Leopold was toppled. Set in the balance beside those enticements, however, was the smoke arising from his beloved Bavarian parishes and his wife's entreaty to change sides. He was in fact about to sign the document whereby he would desert the French when he received a letter from Tallard informing him that the reinforcements for which he had been waiting, would soon be at Augsburg. The Franco-Bavarian army on the Danube would thus number over 60,000 troops and 90 guns, (a surely invincible strength, they imagined). That news prompted the Elector, in his eagerness to be on 'the winning side', to lay down his quill and shake his head. So far as he was concerned the Allies' fate was sealed. There was no question of his changing sides now.

Notes

1   WSC II, 787, Quoting L. P. Anquetil, *Vie du Maréchal Villars* (1784)
2   Hare, *op cit*, f42; WSC II, 792
3   Hare, *op cit* f 43
4   Horsley (ed), *Chronicles of an Old Campaigner*, 135
5   Journal *op cit*, 114

6

Chief-of-Staff at Blenheim

(1704)

The French and Bavarians were now in a position to cross to the north bank of the Danube and threaten the communications of the Grand Alliance with Franconia, from whence Cadogan drew their supplies. On 10 August the enemy crossed the Danube to Dillingen. And the three *maréchals*, Tallard, Marsin and the Elector, were congratulating themselves that the successful passage of their combined armies over the great river would be sufficient in itself to force the Allies to withdraw entirely from Bavaria. Already, they reckoned, the cause of the Two Crowns had achieved a considerable victory, and without a shot being fired. Four days before that, Eugène, having marched his army with great speed from the Rhine, had linked up with Marlborough's cosmopolitan force at Schrobenhausen, making an Allied total of about 56,000 men and 55 guns, which was somewhat fewer than the enemy.

The Franco-Bavarian army was next advanced eastwards to a new position on a four-mile front, with their right flank anchored on the Danube village of Blenheim, their left on hilly woodland, and with the security of a broad marshy stream, the

Nebel, in front of them. But it was clear, from the character of their encampment, that they were not expecting battle.

Although the Captain General and his Imperial ally were determined to force their way over the Nebel and attack the Franco-Bavarian host, despite being somewhat numerically inferior, neither Marlborough nor Eugène wished to cooperate with the unreliable Baden. So they suggested to him that he lead his troops to besiege Ingoldstadt, to which the Margrave readily conceded.

Morale was not high in the Franco-Bavarian ranks, which had been weakened by desertion, sickness and fatigue (following their own marathon marches), while the virulent disease of glanders (or farcy) – the symptoms of which are abcesses in the lower jaw, ulcers on the mucous membranes and discharges from the nostrils – had run through their horse lines like wildfire. However, although the three Franco-Bavarian commanders were by no means of a single mind there was one issue on which they all agreed. It was that the army of the Grand Alliance, being outnumbered and 'outgeneralled', had but one choice: to withdraw from Bavaria and make clear the road to Vienna for the forces of King Louis.

Yet Marlborough decided to attack without delay. Sergeant Millner tells us that, on 12 August, 'about Six the Duke and Prince Eugène called to them on a Rising Ground all the Generals, and gave them the necessary Directions to attack the Enemy; and then our Army advanced into the Plain, and were drawn up in Order of Battle about seven'.[1]

Cadogan's campaigns in the Low Countries at the turn of the century had been more or less comprised of a series of sieges while the recent storming of the Schellenberg heights was a steep frontal attack to seize an objective. Blenheim was to be his first set-piece battle and he would be Chief of Staff. The commanders of old, leading massive armies, did not make as much use of the terrain as modern tacticians do. They thought in terms of feint, of drawing the enemy's strength to one point,

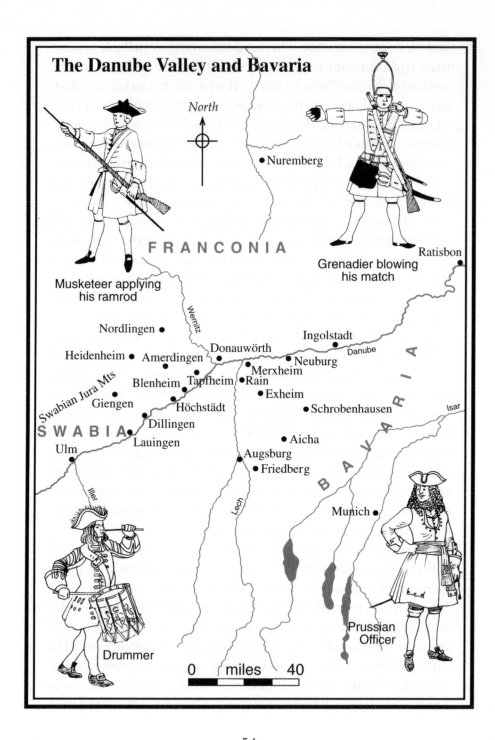

The Danube Valley and Bavaria

North

Musketeer applying
his ramrod

Grenadier blowing
his match

FRANCONIA

- Nuremberg

Ratisbon

Nordlingen •

Wernitz

Heidenheim •

Amerdingen •

Donauwörth •

Ingolstadt •

Danube

Neuburg •

Merxheim

Swabian Jura Mts

Blenheim Tapfheim • Rain

Exheim •

Giengen •

Höchstädt •

Schrobenhausen •

Isar

SWABIA •

Dillingen

Lauingen

Aicha •

Ulm •

Augsburg •

Friedberg •

BAVARIA

Iller

Lech

Munich •

Drummer

Prussian
Officer

0   miles   40

then striking at another. They endeavoured to outflank him, to make frontal assaults successful with the use of overwhelming superiority in numbers; to terrify the enemy with their artillery and their musketry and the awesomely dazzling colours of their regiments. Infantry divisions took up 500 square yards of ground and so did cavalry brigades. Armies deployed en masse. Blenheim was to be fought on a three-and-a-half mile front.

The Allies' general plan of attack was for Lieutenant General Lord Cutts, 'the Salamander'[2], commanding the left wing, to keep the enemy's stronghold at Blenheim village occupied, while Eugène conducted a holding operation on the right, with Lutzingen as his main objective, following which Marlborough would assault on the decisive centre, which was pivoted on the village of Oberglau. This was to be the first test of William Cadogan's capacity as Chief of Staff in a set-piece open battle. His principal tasks were to coordinate the team of hand-picked aides-de-camp through whom the Captain General transmitted his orders; to ensure that the sappers and pioneers – who would advance with bridging equipment and fascines, to facilitate the crossing of the Nebel – knew exactly what to do; to see that Colonel Blood, the artillery commander, interpreted Marlborough's instructions faithfully; to make certain that replenishments of ammunition were brought forward without delay; and to point out to the surgeons where they should site their field aid posts and hospitals. His administrative roles were, for the moment, delegated.

The Comte de Mérode-Westerloo, a Flemish officer commanding an enemy cavalry brigade, wrote a graphic account of the battle. At six o'clock on the morning of 13 August a servant woke him in Blenheim with the news that the army of the Grand Alliance was approaching. 'Where?' asked the Count incredulously. 'There!' replied the servant opening the barn door, 'and drawing my bed curtains, the door opened straight on to the fine, sunlit plain beyond – and the whole area appeared to be covered by enemy squadrons. I rubbed my eyes in disbelief, and then coolly remarked that the foe must at least give me time to take my morning cup of chocolate.' The Count then dressed, mounted his charger, sent for his ADC and galloped off to rouse his regiments:

> All was quiet, not a single soul stirred as I clattered out of the village. The same sight met my gaze when I reached the camp – everyone still snug in their tents – although the enemy was so close that their standards and colours could easily be counted. They were already pushing back our piquets, but nobody seemed at all worried about it . . . I still had received no instructions, but I ordered my regiments to mount by way of precaution; I went in person to the standards of each squadron to give them this order, making sure that the trumpeters did not sound 'boot and saddle' or 'mount'. Soon everyone was on his horse, and I kept them all drawn up at the head of their tents, and then . . . and only then . . . did I notice the first signs of movement in Blenheim village.[3]

The Captain General's left wing and central force had started out on their approach march towards the eastern bank of the Nebel in nine columns at three o'clock that morning while Eugène's contingent made difficult progress through the scrubland of the foothills to the north, in his endeavours eventually to come abreast with Marlborough's right flank. Blood's guns played on the enemy camp, while the French artillery responded with similar ferocity, one cannon ball falling near the feet of Marlborough's and Cadogan's chargers as the two men conversed. On the left wing Rowe's brigade, leading the assault, was to lose at least a third of its strength to the defenders of Blenheim village. However, 'Salamander' Cutts then passed five squadrons over the Nebel. Those, being charged by the Gendarmerie from the front and attacked from the flank by musket and cannon fire from the village, began to recoil. Then the Allies' Lieutenant General Count Bülow, commanding the Lunenburg troops, brought across fresh squadrons of dragoons to sustain the reeling first line. With Bothmar's Hanoverian regiments, five more squadrons under Ross, together with his own dragoons, Bülow mounted his counter-attack, and at last the Gendarmerie started to recoil.

The Elector of Bavaria was nearby at this juncture. 'Is that the Gendarmerie running away?' the conceited general wanted to know. 'Is it possible? Go, Messieurs, tell them that I am now here. Rally them, let them return to the charge!'[4]

Acting on the Elector's orders, Baron de Montigney-Langost rode to the head of the Gendarmerie. 'While setting upon an English squadron,' he wrote, 'I received two sabre cuts on the head, a sword thrust through the arm, a blow from a musket ball on the leg, and my horse was wounded. Being surrounded on all sides I was captured by an officer, who, taking away my pistols, said, "I give you quarter, follow me and I will see your wounds dressed," but what a disappointment to witness the English cavalry, which had been repulsed, returning to the charge and again routing our Gendarmerie . . . under cover of so ominous a movement all the cavalry of their [the Allies'] left were already crossing the stream and taking possession of our terrain.'[5] The Allies' cavaliers succeeded in scattering the highly reputed Gendarmerie. Subsequently an ever-increasing number of enemy reserve units were fed into the already overcrowded village of Blenheim, owing to a serious blunder committed by General the Marquis de Clérambault, who commanded at that point. Mérode-Westerloo describes the scene in Blenheim:

The men were so crowded in upon one another that they could not even fire, let alone receive or carry out any orders. Not a single shot of the enemy missed its mark, whilst only those few of our men at the front could return the fire, and soon many of those were unable to shoot owing to exhaustion or their muskets exploding from constant use. Those drawn up in the rear were mown down without firing a shot at the enemy; if they wanted to reply they could only fire at their own comrades or indiscriminately without aiming.[6]

The enemy having been dealt that blow, General Lumley, commanding the cavalry on the left wing, was now ordered to lead his squadrons to the centre. Marlborough's newly-devised, mutually-supporting cavalry-and-infantry formation was now put into execution. It was composed of two lines of Horse in the fore, followed by two lines of Foot, with more Horse behind, intervals separating the companies of Foot, between which the Horse could withdraw if hard-pressed. These tactics soon showed up the ineffectiveness of the Franco-Bavarian cavalry in defence.

Eugène, leading the Allies' right wing, was in the thick of the fighting now. And, by late afternoon Marlborough, commanding at the centre, had established several infantry bridgeheads over the miry Nebel and had many cannons manhandled across the pioneers' causeways. Three cavalry generals had managed to pass the majority of their troops to the firm foothold of the far bank and beyond. Henry Lumley with the British squadrons on the left, Count Hompesch and the German cavalry in the centre and the Duke of Würtemberg, leading the Danish Horse on the right, all of them, riders and mounts, bathed and splashed with black slime. They reached the far side weary, but, in general, in far better condition than their opponents.

The time had come for the Allies' 'general advance'. The Captain General drew his sword, Cadogan rode to the head of his regiment, the Allies' trumpets and drums sounded the order, Blood's guns fired terrifying grape shot, and 15,000 men and 8,000 horses quickened their pace on the 2,000-yard frontage of the Allies' centre. But, as the triumphant Allied Horse reached the top of the stubble beyond the Nebel they were greeted by volleys of musketry, the advance being checked by a hail of fire. The Scottish earl, General Lord Orkney

Deployments at
the Battle of Blenheim

North

Schwenenbach

Wolperstetten

Eugene

Weilheim

Allies

Nebel

Unterglau

CUTTS

Marsin and Elector

Franco-Bavarian Army

Lutzingen

Oberglau

Tallard

Schwananbach

Sonderheim

Blenheim

Prince Eugene
of Savoy
(After von Schuppen)

John Churchill
Duke of Marlborough
(After Kneller)

Brunnen

River Danube

Höchstädt

Pulver Bach

Danube

Franco Bavarian		Allies	
	Infantry		Infantry
	Cavalry		Cavalry
	Artillery		Artillery

0   yards   2000

Lord Cutts of Gowran
He was nicknamed *The Salamander* after
the mythical reptile, which was said to
always be found in the hottest parts of
the fire, but never burnt. Cutts also earned
a reputation for braving himself to fire,
but remaining unscathed.
*(Artist uncertain. Probably either
Kneller or Thomas Murray)*

Maréchal Comte de Tallard
(Artist uncertain)

Sidney, Earl Godolphin
During Godolphin's tenure as Lord Treasurer
Cadogan could always be sure that the army
received substantial financial backing
(After Kneller)

59

(husband of the beautiful and witty Elizabeth Villiers) wrote 'By this time I had gott over with what Foot was left with me, and marched straight to Sustean our Horse, whom I found in some confusion . . . and calling out for Foot I went to several Esquadrons and gott them to rally and maike a front till I enterlined them with Foot.'[7]

'At last our men renewed the charge,' Sergeant Millner recalled, 'and that with such Vigour and Success that they broke and routed the Enemy's Horse, and the Ten Battalions who were abandoned by them were entirely cut in Pieces, none escaping but a few who threw themselves on the ground as dead, to save their Lives.'[8]

Tallard was asking his cavalry to make one final effort, but both the French troopers and their horses – many of them sick with farcy – were exhausted. And his grey-coated recruit battalions, brave as young lions, but unsupported, died where they stood in their defensive squares. Tallard's reserve infantry being – most unwisely – locked up in Blenheim village Mérode-Westerloo went to fetch them: 'I rode over to Blenheim wanting to bring out a dozen battalions (which they certainly did not need there) to form a line on the edge of the stream supported by the cannons . . . The brigades of Saint-Simon [not the author of that name] and Montfort were setting out when M. de Clérambault in person [the commander in Blenheim] countermanded the move, and, shouting and swearing, drove them back into the village.'[9]

The Danes under Eugène's command now cut off the village of Lutzingen while his Prussian Foot captured the guns emplaced there. The pursuit – notwithstanding the weariness of the Allies' horses – went as far as Höchstädt, three miles on. Clérambault, deeply ashamed of having let his country down, galloped his horse into the Danube and drowned. When the 9,000 survivors in the village garrison surrendered the men of the ancient Régiment de Navarre burnt their Colours with tears of shame and rage.

Some 30 squadrons of French Horse, jammed knee-to-knee, were driven headlong over a 15-foot drop into the river. Mérode-Westerloo, caught up in the stampede, tells us that 'so tight was the press that my horse was carried along some three hundred paces without putting hoof to the ground, right to the edge of a deep ravine; down we plunged a good twenty feet.' As Tallard (whose son had been mortally wounded at his side)[10] attempted to escape, he was recognized by his Order of the Saint-Esprit and captured along with his staff. Marsin and the Elector, leading the ragged and forlorn 16,000 survivors of the battle, trudged northwards to the Rhine where Villeroi met and fed them before they continued their sorry journey back to France.[11] The threat to the Austro-Hungarian empire was a thing of the past, the French had been dismissed from Bavaria and King Louis and the flower of his land forces were severely humbled. No one dared hand the Blenheim dispatch to Louis except Madame de Maintenon who crisply informed him that he was no longer invincible. 'It can be guessed,' wrote Saint- Simon, 'what was the anguish of the King, who had held the Emperor's fate in his hands, and who, with this ignominy and loss, saw himself reduced to defending his own lands.'[12] Yet the question still remained: would the Hapsburgs or the Bourbons dominate the Continent of Europe?

Meanwhile the Captain General, using the back of a 'bill of tavern expences', a stump of pencil and his saddle to rest the paper on, jotted a note to his Duchess (the first lady of Queen Anne's household): 'Aug 13, 1704. I have not time to say more, but to beg you will give my duty to the Queen, and let her know Her Army has had a Glorious Victory. Mons. Tallard and two other Generals are in my coach and I am following the rest; the bearer my Aide de Camp Coll Parke will give her an account of what has pass'd. I shall doe it in a day or two by another more att large.'[13]

Writing of the aspirations of France on the eve of Blenheim

and those of the French King after the battle, Winston Churchill noted that:

> All this glittering fabric fell with a crash. From the moment when Louis XIV realized, as he was the first to realize, the new values and proportions which had been established on August 13, he decided to have done with war. Although long years of bloodshed lay before him, his object henceforward was only to find a convenient and dignified exit from the arena in which he had so long stalked triumphant. His ambition was no longer to gain a glorious Dominion, but only to preserve the usurpation which he regarded as his lawful right, and in the end this again was to shrink to no more than a desperate resolve to preserve the bedrock of France.[14]

Cadogan's work – returning to his role as Quartermaster General in the aftermath of the Battle of Blenheim – was far from finished. There were the wounded to be directed to the surgeons, graves to be dug, spaces allotted for men and horses for the night, prisoners to be guarded (there were 14,000 of them) and bread to be distributed. But the problem of rations was somewhat alleviated by loot. For the Franco-Bavarian tents were 'so full of loaf and cabbage', said an officer, 'that one could not but wonder where the men lay'. One historian has written that 'the success of the Blenheim campaign was largely due to the skilful arrangements of the Quartermaster General'.[15] Although that must have been overstating the case Cadogan's services were duly recognized with promotion to brigadier general in the field.[16] He did rather well financially, too (considering that money in Queen Anne's day should be multiplied by more than 50 to bring it level with today's value) – £90 in arrears for his promotion, £60 as Quartermaster General and £120 as Colonel of a regiment of Horse.[17] (Incidentally his regiment of dragoons played distinguished roles, not only during the march to the Danube and at the Schellenberg, but also during the final charge of the enemy centre at Blenheim.)[18]

Notes

1 Journal, *op cit*, 114
2 Cutts was so called because – like the mythical reptile which was reputed to be impermeable to fire – he was usually to be found where the action was hottest.
3 Chandler, *op cit*, 166–67
4 Pelet and de Vault, 584
5 *Ibid*, 585
6 Chandler, *op cit*, 173
7 From *Letters of the First Lord Orkney* (in the English Historical Review, 1904)
8 Journal, *op cit*, 118
9 Chandler, *op cit*, 172
10 According to Saint-Simon, Tallard's eldest son, Vicomte Labaume, was severely wounded, and died in a few days. (*Memoires*, II, 194)
11 Sgt Millner put the number of enemy survivors at 21,391, but does not mention the authority for his precise figure (Journal, 126)
12 The French King's dismal reaction to the news of Blenheim is described in Saint-Simon, *op cit*, 194–99
13 Coxe, I, 206 (The original is now on display at Blenheim Palace)
14 WSC II, 882
15 A. S. Turbeville, *English Men and Manners in the 18th Century*, 478
16 Treasury Papers xciii, 79.
17 Scouller, 148
18 The events of the Blenheim campaign are more largely described in Coxe, I, 169–217; WSC, II, 785–868; and GMT, I, 354–401

7

Cavalry Commander in Brabant

(1705)

Brigadier General Cadogan must have felt very gratified for the highly significant part he had played in the Allies' triumphs of 1704. Not only were the French dismissed from Bavaria and their land forces crippled, but, under Admiral Rooke's leadership, the English navy captured Gibraltar and inflicted a severe defeat of the enemy fleet off Malaga, victories which at once gave Allied warships supremacy in the Mediterranean and relieved the pressure on the Duke of Savoy's army fighting in Italy.

Although the Margrave of Baden conducted a half-hearted siege at Landau, its citadel surrendered on 8 November 1704. The Captain General then made successful diplomatic missions to Berlin, Hanover and Amsterdam, gaining promises of more troops, horses and guns for the 1705 campaign, while Cadogan saw to the immediate administrative details, the army being poised in the Moselle valley, ready in the spring to launch an offensive into France. At home, all – with the exception of the

Tory politicians – indulged in Blenheim euphoria, as described by Bishop Burnet:

> England was full of joy, and addresses of congratulation were sent from all parts of the nation; but it was very visible that, in many places, the tories went into these very coldly, and perhaps that made the whigs the more jealous and affectionate.[1]

However, the offensive planned for the Moselle valley, with a view to bringing France well and truly to her knees, was thwarted. The early summer of 1705 was at least as wet and cold as it had been in 1704, prompting Marlborough to write to Godolphin on 12 June that 'we have every night very hard frosts which does hurt both to our men and horses. This weather, joined with some wants, makes a great many men [mercenaries] desert.'

Secondly, the Palatine and Prussian princes failed to produce their promised reinforcements. Nor, to make Cadogan's task that much more difficult, were certain supplies forthcoming. 'I may assure you that no one thing – neither for the troops nor for the subsistence of the army – that was promised me has been performed,' the Duke added.[2] Thirdly, the Margrave of Baden, who received a considerable *douceur* from King Louis to delay his link-up with the army of the Moselle, and who needed the money for a palace he was building himself at Rastadt[3], made a long detour to effect that delay and earn his bribe.

The Captain General had arrived at Trèves on 26 May 1705, to be informed by Cadogan, who had carried out a reconnaissance in force, that Villars had occupied an exceptionally strong position at Sierck. Cadogan also went in search of Baden, only to find that the treacherous Margrave, instead of proceeding directly from Landau to Trèves, had sent his army on a long northwards detour via Kreuznach, with another general in command, while Baden himself had retired to 'take the waters' – to relieve an injury to his foot incurred at the Schellenberg.[4]

He had been relieved by the Comte de Frise who, in the words of Winston Churchill, 'manifested no zeal. He moved sluggishly forward. It was certain he would not arrive, if he could help it, before the 20th [of June].[5]

To cap all these setbacks, in Flanders Villeroi launched a new offensive against Overkirk and threatened Liège, movements dictated to him from Versailles, the objects of which were to draw the Allied army away from the Moselle (a ploy that was to have its desired effect).[6] Outnumbered, Overkirk withdrew to Maastricht, from where he sent word to the Captain General requesting a reinforcement of 30 battalions and 30 squadrons. And Marlborough felt obliged to comply. In the heavy rain of the night of 17–18 June the Allied army of the Moselle struck camp, to begin their muddy trek northeastwards, a march masterminded by Cadogan.

By the time they joined Overkirk at Maastricht Villeroi had consolidated his forces within the Lines of Brabant, a string of fortifications and waterways stretching from Antwerp to Namur, the purpose of which was not only to defend Brabant, but also to restrict the Allies' movements, particularly their cavalry and artillery. To hold the Lines Villeroi was constrained, to a great extent, to dissipate his main strength, to deploy, so to speak, in 'penny packets'. So it was difficult for him to adopt flexible tactics. With the advent of the Allies the French *maréchal* withdrew his siege contingent from Liège, and the Allies wasted no time in recapturing Huy.

The Captain General then planned to pierce and turn the Lines of Brabant, without informing the over-cautious States General or their Field Deputies or generals, with the exception of Overkirk ('He dared not offer to persuade the Deputies of the State', as Doctor Hare expressed it, 'but perfectly bubbled them into it as you manage children.'[7]) Marlborough's cover plan was one of the most ingenious ruses of his military career. To put it in a nutshell he made a feint at the weakest point in the Lines (which prompted Villeroi to reinforce the place) then intended to attack it at the strongest point.

On the evening of 17 June, having had pontoons put across the river Mehaigne (a tributary of the Meuse) the Captain General sent Overkirk's army across, then withdrew them under cover of darkness by crossing-places further north, at the point where the Lines were joined by the marshy stream of the Geet. The enemy were caught unawares. Before first light between Orsmael, Elixem and Wangé the Anglo-Dutch battalions and squadrons led by Lord Orkney waded over the fords to force Villeroi's Lines. By 5 am at least 5,000 men were inside the French position. But it was after 6.30 before the French

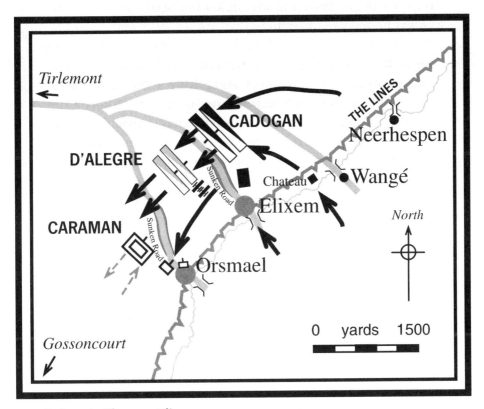

Cadogan's Charge at Elixem

maréchal, having been thus tricked, arrived in person to face the Anglo-Dutch invaders.

Then came the cavalry action at Elixem, one of the most dramatic moments in Cadogan's career. The enemy lieutenant general of Horse, Marquis d'Alègre, mounted 33 squadrons of Bavarian, Spanish, Cologne and French cavalry and sent for Comte Caraman's infantry division, which was supported by France's much vaunted and newly-invented three-barrelled field guns, each of which could fire triple salvoes or three shots in quick succession. But those were not brought into action on this occasion. For the seven regiments of British Horse, lined up to face d'Alègre's cavalry, charged before Caraman's division and its supporting artillery had time to link up with their mounted comrades, let alone deploy for battle.

Lord Orkney, approaching the bridges, says that

> By the time I came to the river, I could see two good lines of the enemy, very well formed, coming down upon our people, a line of foot following them. We were in a very good condition to receive them, and we outwinged them, and still more troops coming over the pass. As I got over the foot guards, I saw the shock begin.[8]

Cadogan rode to the head of his own heavy dragoons, drew his sword, shortened his reins and, giving the order to charge, brought his lower leg and spurs against his horse's flanks. He led his men, who were riding almost knee to knee, at an awesome trot, oblivious of the cannon and musket shot that flew past his head. And, says the eyewitness, 'drove the Bavarian Horse Grenadiers off the field'.[9] Cadogan never failed to emulate Marlborough, who, when upbraided by his Duchess for exposing himself at Elixem, replied, 'as I would deserve and keep the kindnesse of this army I must let them see that when I expose them, I would not exempt myself'.[10] Lord Orkney tells us that, at Elixhem, 'My Lord Marlborough in person was

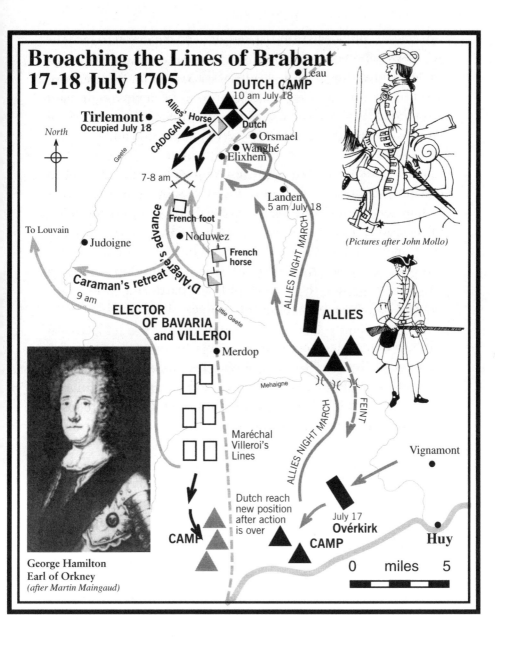

Broaching the Lines of Brabant 17-18 July 1705

Tirlemont •
Occupied July 18

North

Geete

Allies' Horse

CADOGAN

• Leau

DUTCH CAMP
10 am July 18

Dutch

• Orsmael

• Wanghé

• Elixhem

7-8 am ✕

French foot

• Noduwez

D'Allegre's advance

Caraman's retreat
9 am

ELECTOR OF BAVARIA and VILLEROI

To Louvain

• Judoigne

Little Geete

French horse

Landen
5 am July 18

ALLIES NIGHT MARCH

(Pictures after John Mollo)

• Merdop

Mehaigne

ALLIES

ⱦ)Ⱦ(Ɇ

FEINT

Maréchal Villeroi's Lines

ALLIES NIGHT MARCH

Dutch reach new position after action is over

Vignamont •

July 17
Ovérkirk
CAMP

Huy •

CAMP

George Hamilton
Earl of Orkney
(after Martin Maingaud)

0   miles   5

everywhere, and escaped very narrowly . . . a fellow came to him and thought to have sabred him to the ground, and struck at him with that force; and, missing his stroke he [the enemy trooper] fell off his horse. I asked my Lord if it was so; he said it was absolutely so. See what a happy man he is . . . I believe this pleases him as much as Hogstet [Blenheim] did.'[11]

It must have been about the same for his Quartermaster General. Anyhow the main result of the victory was that more than 50 miles of the Brabant Lines, between Aershot and Namur, were now in Allied hands, with 6,000 troops in occupation. Quite apart from the fact that Villeroi's army suffered over 5,000 casualties at little cost to the Allies.

August found the Anglo-Dutch army close to Waterloo and poised in inflict another blow, a blow that would surely have ended French domination of the Spanish Netherlands. However, when the Captain General broached the subject with the Dutch States-General, of bringing Villeroi to battle again, he received the preposterous reply that he was permitted to 'make three marches' and was to do nothing more without the consent of the Field Deputies. Marlborough's army succeeded in forcing the French contingent bestriding the road through Waterloo to withdraw. The Allies then manoeuvred Villeroi (who was by then numerically and morally inferior) into a weak position on the River Yssche.

The Captain General was naturally eager to attack, but was frustrated by the Field Deputies and Dutch generals, in particular by the touchy, jealous and devious General Slangenberg, who was foremost in forbidding any further action. Marlborough and Cadogan were at their wit's end. Heated complaints were sent to the States General and Slangenberg's dismissal demanded. The Dutch people, too, were furious at their leaders' faint-heartedness. The disgraced Slangenberg opted for early retirement.

In that same month Marlborough and Godolphin (the Duumvirs, as they were known) insisted to Heinsius that there could be 'no peace without Spain' – the war must not end before Spain and her dominions were won in the name of the Austrian claimant, Charles. They were strengthened in that resolve when Peterborough stormed and took Barcelona and turned his eyes towards Madrid, while Galway began his march towards the Spanish capital from Portugal.

During the third week of January 1706 Cadogan wrote from London to someone he refers to, frequently, as 'dear Judge', the Deputy Judge Advocate, Henry Watkins, who was clearly a close friend. 'I am sure I need not assure you,' Cadogan told him, 'I value and esteem you as much as I despise the worthy Generous Gentleman that was pleased to be angry with you aboard the yatch [yacht]. Dear Judge I hope you will never want my services, but I protest there is no body I would be more willing to serve than you, or more willingly hurt than him. I have dined with Mr St John and am pretty warm, and therefore hope you will excuse this however ill put together . . . [He adds a postscript]. I write at ten att night, and I shall make no apology for being clear att that time since I am well and Mr St John's wine is come safe.'[12]

Meanwhile Cadogan had stood, at the Captain General's behest, as Whig candidate for Woodstock, in Oxfordshire (the town closest to where Blenheim Palace was to be built). And the 33-year-old Brigadier General was duly elected, the Whigs winning a substantial majority in the Commons again. The name of Cadogan was to be conjured with at home as well now as with the field army of the Netherlands.

Notes

1 Burnet, V, 154
2 WSC II, 936
3 De la Colonie, *op cit*, 293–94
4 WSC II, 934–35
5 *Ibid*, 935
6 *Ibid*, 934–35
7 GMT II, 53

8 From *Letters of the First Lord Orkney.*
9 Coxe, I, 297; DNB, *op cit*
10 WSC II, 965
11 Orkney, *op cit*; WSC II, 953–54
12 By kind permission of Lord Cadogan.

8

Ramillies

(1706)

When, in the autumn of 1705, the Captain General proceeded on another round of diplomatic visits, Cadogan was left to see the army of the south Netherlands into winter quarters and to make arrangements for their sustenance and training during the winter months. Doubtless, too, he enjoyed some periods of leave with his beloved Margaretta.

While Cadogan proceeded on diplomatic trips to Hanover and Vienna Marlborough spent the early spring of 1706 in England where, with Godolphin, he put together, and got passed through Parliament, the Regency Act whereby, when the Queen either died or became incapacitated, a body of Lords Justices would rule England until the heiress apparent, the Electress of Hanover, and her son (the future George I) arrived in London, thus endorsing the 1701 Act and reaffirming the Protestant succession.

Cadogan had been taught by the Captain General to think globally. The situation looked rather bleak for the Alliance in the spring of 1706. The French military resurgence following their defeats at Blenheim and on the Lines of Brabant proved just how resilient that nation was. For Louis and his ministers had refilled the gaps in their military machine with astonishing promptitude. The French armies were soon strong and proud again. In Spain, while ineffectual Peterborough dilly-dallied in Valencia, Galway, marching from Portugal towards Madrid, was in danger of being outnumbered and outgeneralled, as well as being cut off from the line of communication with his base, Marlborough's nephew, the gifted Duke of Berwick, having the French command in Spain. In Italy Maréchal Comte de Vendôme scored a crushing defeat over the Imperialists at Calcinato and, soon afterwards, Villars made a vigorous offensive against the Margrave of Baden's forces, pushing him in headlong retreat across the Rhine, an event which put paid to a scheme of the Captain General's for joining Eugène in Italy.

Marlborough saw little prospect at this time of luring Villeroi into a fight. What he did not know, however, was that both King Louis and his Minister of War and Finance, Chamillart, had written to their Netherlands *maréchal* exhorting him not to shirk a pitched battle. (According to Saint-Simon, Villeroi 'had the feeling that the King doubted his courage . . . He resolved to put all at stake to satisfy him, and to prove that he did not deserve such harsh suspicions'.[1]

It was at this stage that Cadogan's astonishing insight and diligence as the Allies' intelligence chief first became apparent. In two remarkable articles Patricia Dickson summed up his role. Having read the relevant papers in the Sunderland archives I feel that I cannot do better than quote directly from her. 'At this time [May 1706],' she wrote, 'the French forces were becoming mobile for the start of a new campaign. In the third week of May Cadogan's intelligence department informed Marlborough that, after crossing the River Dyle, Marshal Villeroi's Army lay close to Tirlemont on the Great Geete. To Marlborough, familiar with the topography of the area, this surprise indicated that the enemy had designs upon the strategic position of Ramillies.'[2]

On 22 May Villeroi and the Elector of Bavaria, with 60,000

men under command, plus a recent reinforcement of cavalry from Marsin, duly emerged from behind the Dyle to occupy, on a four-mile front, the plateau of Ramillies, the watershed standing between the sources of the Mehaigne and the Great and Little Geete. The Allied army was less than 20 miles away. Colonel de la Colonie, then commanding a Bavarian brigade, was as confident of victory as Villeroi himself:

> The army had but just entered on the campaign, weather and fatigue had hardly yet had time to dim its brilliancy, and it was inspired with a courage born of confidence. The late Marquis de Goudrin, with whom I had the honour to ride during the march [to Ramillies], remarked to me that France had surpassed herself in the quality of these troops; he believed that the enemy had no chance whatever of breaking them in the coming conflict; if defeated now we could never again hope to withstand them . When the leading battalions of our columns arrived near the marsh on our right their direction was changed a quarter left, followed by those in rear, with the immediate result that the army found itself in battle array two lines in depth parallel to the position of the enemy who were now in range of our artillery.[3]

Before first light on 23 May Brigadier General Cadogan started out from the Allied camp through dense fog with the advance guard, comprised of six cavalry squadrons (which included the crack Danish cavalry who had just arrived in the Allies' camp). Of course Cadogan knew exactly where to find the French. He was a little way past Merdorp (in the demolished Lines of Brabant) when he came into contact with some vedettes, mounted standing patrols, parties of French hussars, who fled at the sight of his squadrons. At about 8 am the fog cleared to reveal the enemy's position beyond the Geete.

Villeroi had disposed his army in an inverted crescent shape, his left flank being hinged upon the village of Autréglise, his right on the Mehaigne at Taviers. A mile or so north-north-west of Taviers lay the village of Ramillies. The hamlet of Francquenée was half a mile to the east of Taviers. Confident that the Allies' Captain General would advance to meet him, there was no doubt in Villeroi's mind of a sure victory. He had good reason to feel assured. He had deployed in a fine position; he believed it to be an impregnable one. It was well known for its strategical importance as a watershed between the rivers, and had often before been surveyed by generals for that significance. Meanwhile reinforcements, under command of

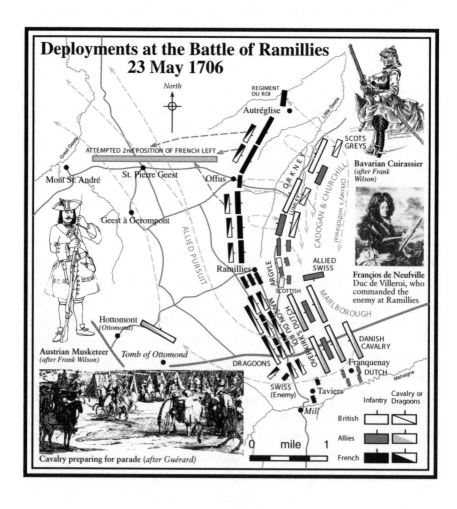

Deployments at the Battle of Ramillies 23 May 1706

North

REGIMENT DU ROI

Autréglise

Little Geete

Great Geete

SCOTS GREYS

ATTEMPTED 2nd POSITION OF FRENCH LEFT

St. Pierre Geest

Offus

ORKNE

Mont St. André

LUMLEY

Okney's withdrawal

Bavarian Cuirassier
(after Frank Wilson)

Geest à Gerompont

CADOGAN & CHURCHILL

ALLIED PURSUIT

ALLIED SWISS

Ramillies

ARGYLE

François de Neufville Duc de Villeroi, who commanded the enemy at Ramillies

SCOTTISH

MARLBOROUGH

Hottomont *(Ottomond)*

MAISON DU ROI DUTCH

OVERKIRKS DUTCH

DANISH CAVALRY

Austrian Musketeer
(after Frank Wilson)

Tomb of Ottomond

DRAGOONS

Franquenay

DUTCH

Mehaigne

SWISS *(Enemy)*

Taviers

Mill

Cavalry or Dragoons

Infantry

British

Allies

0   mile   1

French

Cavalry preparing for parade *(after Guérard)*

Maréchal Marsin, were getting close to hand and racing to join him.

By the time Cadogan's report reached Marlborough the Allies' main army had just crossed the old Brabant lines in eight columns. Marlborough deployed in two lines, a little under a mile east of Ramillies. Orkney's infantry division, supported by cavalry under Lumley, was sent north to attack across the marshes of the Geete opposite Autréglise, the Captain General's aim being to draw off as much of Villeroi's strength as possible to that sector before launching the main effort in the south, betweenTaviers and Ramillies. Eyewitness Captain Parker sets the scene after the eight main columns had deployed into line:

> We drew up in two lines opposite them, having rising ground on our right, whereon a great part of our British troops were drawn up. From hence the Duke had a fair view of the enemy, and saw, evidently, that the stress of the battle must be on the plain, where they were drawn up in a formidable manner. He saw also that things must go hard with him unless he could oblige them to break the dispositon they had made on the plain. On this occasion his Grace showed a genius vastly superior to the French generals; for although he knew the ground along the Geet was not passable yet he ordered our right wing to march down in great order, with pontoons to lay bridges, as if he designed to attack them in their weak part.'[4]

The galaxy and diversity of regimental colours in both armies was now half-hidden, and the jingle of weapons, equipment and horse furniture silenced by the roar and blaze and smoke of artillery fire, a cannonade for which the Allies showed a marked superiority in both numbers of guns and calibre and tactical positioning. The splendid Danish cavalry were present, but not the infantry promised by the King of Prussia. On 21 May Marlborough wrote this caustic complaint to Raby, the English envoy at Berlin: 'If it should please God to give us a victory over the enemy, the Allies will be little obliged to the King [of Prussia] for the success: and if, on the other hand, we should have any disadvantage, I know not how he will be able to excuse himself.'

Villeroi ordered de la Colonie to lead his troops over to the Franco-Bavarian extreme right, by the banks of the Mehaigne, behind Taviers. De la Colonie relates the move:

> I noticed, when passing the Maison du Roi, that there were large intervals between the squadrons and that their formation was disproportionately extended. This made me think that the principal attack was to be made here ... when these gentlemen saw us pass the head of their squadrons they evidently thought that we were coming to support their right on the marsh, and by the graceful applause with which they greeted my grenadiers this semed to give them some pleasure; they recalled the action of Schellenberg, and made known to us how much they counted on our valour in the coming engagement; but they soon found that they could hardly reckon upon us as we continued our march and crossed the swamp.[5]

Soon after this, on the Allies' left, four battalions of the Dutch Guard drove the enemy from Franquenée and the village of Taviers. And there was a shock there for de la Colonie. The Swiss infantry and dragoons who were sent to recapture Taviers, he recalls, 'came tumbling on my battalions in full flight, just at the time I was re-forming my men ... They brought such alarm and confusion in their train that my own fellows turned about and fled along with them.'[6]

At 2.30 pm the Captain General ordered the central force of Allied infantry, which were commanded by his brother Charles, to attack between Ramillies and Offus, while the Allied Horse of the left wing, Danish and Dutch cavalry led by Overkirk, advanced towards the open country to the right of Taviers, in the direction where 82 French squadrons, fronted by the Maison du Roi, stood, sabres drawn, to receive them.

On the right Lord Orkney led his division across the Geete marshes and its rivulet, his scarlet columns of English Foot splashing through the reed beds and braving the Geete current, while many of Lumley's cavalry managed to cross too, leading their mounts. Villeroi, astonished to see the English redcoats in such a positon as to seriously threaten his garrisons at Autréglise and Offus, realized that they also put his potential line of withdrawal to Louvain in jeopardy. The French therefore switched every unit he could spare northwards, which was

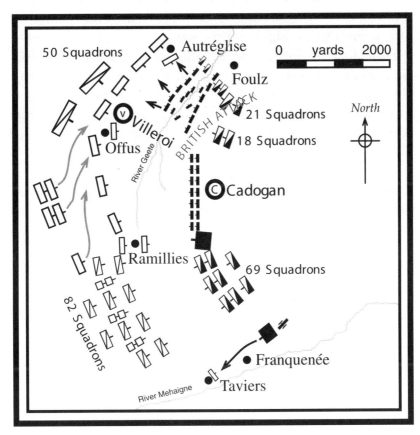

Ramillies: The British Attack on the Right Flank.

just the course of action Marlborough had prompted and anticipated.

While Villeroi and the Elector of Bavaria focused their attention on the northern flank the Captain General and Cadogan, astride their chargers opposite Ramillies, were rather more interested in Overkirk's Dutch and Danish squadrons which had now clashed with the French cavalry near Taviers. The Captain General, having successfully drawn off so much of the Franco-Bavarian strength to the north, intended to break through their defences in the centre and to outflank them in the south. The Allies' left flank must be reinforced. First Marlborough sent for Lumley's cavalry, ordering them to cross the four miles that separated Orkney's wing and Overkirk's Dutch and Danish Horse on the left.

The Captain General then attempted to bring Orkney's division over to the centre. But the gallant Scots general had not been informed that his attack between Offus and Autréglise had been predetermined as a feint – perhaps because his Chief feared that such an offensive might not otherwise be pressed with sufficient determination to convince Villeroi that it was of genuine intent. Orkney, having led his soldiers over the Geete and its bogs with great effort, hazard and courage, and now believing the enemy in that sector to be at his mercy, refused to take on trust the orders relayed by the succession of ten ADCs whom Cadogan sent ordering him to withdraw and advance south.

Even when Cadogan himself rode over with the same message Orkney at first thought that the Chief of Staff must be acting on his own initiative, that he could not be conversant with the master plan. But, being at last persuaded by Cadogan, he withdrew his brave infantrymen – the First Guards and Royal Scots covered their retirement – and marched them across the two miles – of 'dead ground', thus unseen by the enemy – to the centre, leaving behind one line of troops, by Foulz, to further deceive the enemy. 'Cadogan came and told me it was impossible I could be sustained by the horse if I went on then,' wrote Orkney, 'and since my Lord could not attack everywhere, he would make the grand attack in the centre, which I bless God, succeeded.'[7] G. M. Trevelyan makes an apt comment of the feint:

> The manoeuvre of the false attack, by which the enemy was deceived, sounds a simple device. A schoolboy might think of it. But it required a great general and a fine army to carry it out. The honours must be divided between Marlborough and his men. Orkney, in particular, must be praised for keeping his head and temper at a moment of confusion, peril and sharp disappiontment, when some of his subordinates were so angry that they swore Cadogan had invented the orders to retreat.[8]

A massive mounted engagement, involving some 25,000 cavaliers, was now raging between Taviers and Ramillies – it is counted as one of the largest-ever horsed cavalry fights in the history of war – with the Allies enjoying a 5:3 superiority. While Cadogan was left with General Churchill, to coordinate the action from the centre, their Captain General was in the thick of the mounted battle on that left flank, being seen to lead at least two charges by blue-and- grey-coated Dutch cavalry-men in person. At one point Marlborough was thrown and lost his horse. Seeing him in danger of being cut down by one of the heavy troopers of the Maison du Roi, a Captain Molesworth handed him his own. A senior ADC, Colonel Bringfield, holding firm the stirrup for his chief to mount, had his head carried off by a cannon-ball. Lord Orkney adds that another cannon-ball 'passed through Marlborough's legs'.[9]

Villeroi and the Elector, surveying the battle from an eminence behind Offus, having been preoccupied with the scene on the Geet to the north, now turned their glasses on to their southern flank, and were duly flabbergasted to witness their hitherto beautifully arrayed 82 squadrons, headed by the

Maison du Roi, routed and in flight, the Danish and Dutch cavalry hot on their tails. At around the same time the Allies, given a fresh preponderance of infantry betwen Offus and Ramillies, and with deadly volleys of musketry and flashing, menacing bayonets, smashed the Franco-Bavarian centre. As Sergeant Millner recorded:

> The Elector of Bavaria and Marshal Villeroi made a Motion with their Left to assist their Right; the which the Duke observing, put a sudden stop thereto, by causing our English and Danes

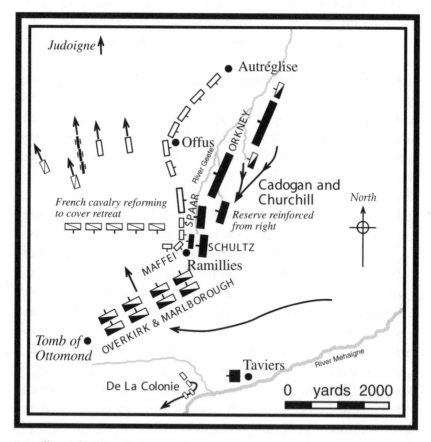

Ramillies: The New Front.

Squadrons from our Right wing and body of Reserve to sustain our Left which had shrunk back . . . and attack'd that Part of the enemy with such Courage . . . that, in short, in about half an Hour . . . they quite broke the Enemies Right Wing of Horse, and then fell upon their Foot and Centre.[10]

The Captain General then ordered his left wing to swing right-handed and face north, and his brother, Charles, to bring his force onto the right of the left wing. This new deployment was completed at about 6 pm, directly after which time the Allies began advancing against the retreating enemy, who fled north-west until, eventually their survivors put the Scheldt and the Dender between themselves and the Allies, some taking refuge at Courtrai on the Lys. Apart from the fact that 7,000 French and Bavarians were killed and 5,000 enemy were taken prisoner, Villeroi's entire artillery and baggage fell into the Allies' hands. So ended the Battle of Ramillies – with Villeroi pushed behind the French frontier and the southern Netherlands almost won for Charles of Austria. Let an Irish soldier in the French service have the last word:

We had not got forty yards in our retreat when by some means I know not the word sauve qui peut, fly that can, went through [a] great part if not the whole army and put all in confusion. Then might be seen whole brigades running in disorder, the enemy [Allies] pursuing almost close at our heels and with regularity. Thus circumstanced we went on till we came to a small rivulet, which was a ford, in passing nearer some grenadiers poured several platoons [fire] in amongst us, which we returned in the best manner we were able. . . . Having waded the ford we contrived our march pretty fast up a gradual descent. Though the enemy appeared no more that night yet we never halted till break of day, near Louvain, when we crossed the river dispirited and weary, having been on our feet twenty-four hours without the least rest. It was indeed a sight truly shocking to see the miserable remains of this mighty army, which the day before consisted of 70,000 men, reduced to a handful; such havoc does the ambition of princes make.[11]

At the end of that night of 23–24 May Cadogan, along with his chief, having been over 19 hours in the saddle, reached a spot some 12 miles north of Ramillies to lie under their cloaks in the open. But Marlborough continued to lean heavily on his overworked chief of staff. 'I have sent Brigadier Cadogan with six squadrons of horse, to offer terms to the town and citadel of Antwerp,' he was writing to Godolphin on 3 June.[12]

Madame de Maintenon compared the tribulations of the Sun King to those of Job: 'God wants to give him the same patience,' she said. Anyhow Louis recalled Villeroi, transferring Vendôme from Italy to take over the beaten army (now at Courtrai), which the King proceeded to rebuild with drafts from the Rhine, the Moselle and Italy. Maréchal Villars, being wise after the event, wrote somewhat immodestly to Madame de Maintenon that Ramillies was 'the most shameful, humiliating and disastrous of events. How many misfortunes would have been avoided if I had been allowed to act.'[13]

On 5 August, 1706, Vendôme having taken command in the Netherlands, reported to Chamillart, the French Minister of War, unhappily:

With regard to the troops in the Spanish service no one can answer for them; but that grieves me far less than the sadness and dejection that appears in the French army. I will do my best to restore their spirit. But it will be no light matter for me to do so, for every one here is ready to take off his hat at the mere name of Marlborough. [*Toute le monde ici est pret d'oter son chapeau quand on nomme le nom de Marlborough*].[14]

84

Notes

1 Coxe I, 375
2 Dickson, *Lieutenant General William Cadogan's Intelligence Service*, in *The Army Quarterly*, January and April, 1979, Pt I, 161
3 De la Colonie *op cit*, 305
4 Chandler, *op cit*, 61
5 De la Colonie, *op cit*, 308
6 *Ibid.*, 309
7 Orkney, *op cit*. Colonel Cranstoun, commanding the Cameronians, afterwards wrote a letter to a friend in London complaining about Orkney's withdrawal. But, to quote Winston Churchill, 'Cranstoun imagined that Cadogan had given the order out of jealousy or ignorance, and had not had Marlborough's sanction . . .' WSC, III, 185
8 GMT II. 110
9 Orkney, *op cit*
10 Millner, *op cit*, 173
11 Drake, *Amiable Renegade*, 79–80
12 Coxe, I, 371
13 Coxe, I, 419
14 GMT II, 128. For a fuller account of the Ramillies campaign see Coxe I, 407–22; GMT II, 103–20; WSC III, 95–118

9

Prisoner of War

(1706–1707)

Once that dour and devout Presbyterian, Major Blackadder of the Cameronians, was clear of the grim battlefield of Ramillies and the immediate path of the French retreat – with their dead and wounded, anguished men and horses, their burning villages and refugees – he became quite ecstatic in his diary, notwithstanding the blasphemous oaths of his Lowlands soldiery:

> May 26. They have abandoned Brussels and all Brabant. The Lord has taken heart and hand and spirit from our enemies. May 27. Passing the canal [of Brussels] at Vilvoord. No resistance from the enemy, though we thought happen what might, they would have defended the canal. May 30. A fatiguing march this Sabbath. All day I met with what I hate in this trade, viz. cursing, swearing, filthy language, etc, yet though it was all around me, I bless the Lord there was a heaven within. We are still pursuing our victory, and they are still fleeing before us. There is certainly something in this affair beyond human working. June 4. Marching still forward crossing the Lys above Ghent. Still no enemy to be seen. Bruges, Antwerp and in short all Brabant and

Flanders almost yielded, what the French got in a night by stealth, at the King of Spain's death, they have lost again in a day. That old tyrant who wasted God's church is about to be wasted himself.[1]

Antwerp having surrendered to Cadogan, he and his chief were 'received with one piece of ceremony which was odd enough, the magistracy of the town marching before [them] with lighted flambeaux, which is looked upon as the greatest mark of honour they can show, which they seldom, or ever, have bestowed on their Dukes of Brabant'.[2] One by one their great fortresses of the southern Netherlands fell to the Allies, their provinces all declaring for the Emperor's brother, 'Charles III'. (Flanders and Brabant were to remain Austrian for the next three generations, which is to say until 1830 when the Spanish Netherlands became the independent nation of Belgium.)

Following Antwerp's surrender in the first days of June, 1706, says Patricia Dickson,

Cadogan turned his attention to the reconstruction of roads and bridges in the Oudenarde district. Consequently, he took measures to tighten his Intelligence Service. With the collaboration of a certain Monsieur Chanclos[3], reliable agents were sent out to keep the route of Mons under strict surveillance and to report every movement direct to Marlborough ... Over the next two years Cadogan organised an espionage network with such efficiency that few moves made by the French passed undetected. He took care to have trustworthy agents posted at the principal sea-ports, and the result was a flow of accurate information.[4]

The capture of Ostend on 6 July was a godsend to the Quartermaster General, for it meant a useful shortening of communications with the English ports, in fact a direct line of supply between England and her front-line army. The Allies were then able to besiege and capture Nieuport and Dunkirk, both of them nests of those French privateers, pirates so dreaded by English merchants, and from whom Cadogan had suffered personally three years previously. During the next three months Menin, Tournai, Ypres, Courtrai, Charleroi, Namur, Dendermonde and, finally, Ath, succumbed to the Allies. All of them were fruits plucked from the tree of Ramillies.

While reconnoitring the approachs to Menin the Captain General dropped a glove. He asked Cadogan to dismount and pick it up for him. Recalling the incident back at the Allies' base camp at Helchin, Marlborough told his chief of staff, quartermaster general and master spy that he wanted a battery of guns positioned on that spot. Cadogan replied that he had already given the order, explaining that he knew his supremo to be too much of a gentleman to have made such a request as to pick up a glove for him (an ADC or a groom could have done that) without good reason. And he had guessed what it was.[5] It is a good example of the understanding existing between the two soldiers. On a less happy note, on 23 August the Captain General wrote to his Duchess from Tournai as follows:

> An officer has just come to me to give me an account of the forage we have made this day, and he tells me that poor Cadogan is taken prisoner or killed which gives me a great deal of uneasiness, for he loved me, and I could rely on him. I am now sending a trumpet to the Governor of Tournai to know if he be alive; for the horse [the enemy cavalry patrol] that beat him came from that garrison. I have ordered the trumpet to return this night, for I shall not be quiet till I know his fate.[6]

One of Cadogan's perpetual concerns was to find a sufficient supply of fodder for the army's many thousands of horses.

This is what happened. During the siege of Tournai he was on an expedition reconnoitring for pasture when he became detached from his party and its escort and got captured close to the walls of the fortress. His friend Raby (up from Berlin to offer himself as a volunteer with Marlborough's army) was with Cadogan at the time of the arrest, but escaped capture. Raby managed to get a letter to Cadogan who replied from his place of detention in the fortress:

> I received with all the pleasure imaginable the honour of your Lordship's obliging letter. I assure your Lordship the greatest pain I had when I was taken, was my apprehension for your Lordship's safety, which I was not assured of till my trumpet came in the evening. I was thrust by the croud. I endeavoured to step into a Ditch on the right of the way we passed, with great difficulty I got out of it, and with greater good Fortune escaped falling into the Hussars hands who first came up with me ... it made us fall to the share of the French Carabiniers, who followed their Hussars and Dragoons from whom I met with Quarter and Civility, save their taking my watch and money ... My Lord Duke has been so extremely kind as to propose exchanging the Marquis de Croissy for me, so I hope my prison will not be of very long continuance.[7]

It was in fact not de Croissy but Baron Pallavicini, a lieutenant general captured at Ramillies, for whom the indispensable Cadogan was exchanged. 'Vendôme, knowing how high Cadogan stood in Marlborough's affection', as Winston Churchill put it, 'released him at once on parole as an act of personal courtesy to his adversary'.[8] On 24 October the appreciative Captain General wrote as follows to Godolphin:

> I find by your last letter that applications are made by Mr Mordaunt and others for my brother's place in the Tower.[9] I beg he will not be engaged, and that the Queen will gratify me on

this occasion. I would not have this place disposed of as yet; but when I shall think it a proper time, I would then beg the Queen would be pleased to let Brigadier Cadogan have it, since it will be provison for him in time of peace. As I would put my life in his hands, so I will be answerable for his faithfulness and duty to the Queen. I have for the Queen's service obliged him this war to expose his life very often, so that in justice I owe him this good office.[10]

In December Cadogan was duly appointed Lieutenant of the Tower of London, a usefully paid sinecure and one that gave him access to the Office of Ordnance, which controlled the making and issue of firearms and trials of all weapons.

Meanwhile, on 6 September 1706, at the time that Cadogan was on duty at the siege of Ath, the first of his and Margaretta's two daughters, Sarah, had been baptised at the Church of St Jacobskerk at the Hague. He was not able to join his wife and child until November, by which time the Captain General had held an end-of-season review of his army. Cadogan then supervised the return of the various Allied units to their winter quarters.

He was always at great pains to be impartial in his distribution of quarters, rations, forage and grazing to each Allied contingent, a principle which was perhaps largely in emulation of his mentor, his fair-minded Chief. In recognition of Cadogan's faithful service King Frederick bestowed on him the Prussian Order of Generosity. Raby was sceptical:

I should not think it worth your acceptance unless it had a good Diamond fixed in it, which I wish it had on that presumption I wish you joy, tho I wonder neither you nor Cardonnel writ me one word of it; you have heard the storry without doubt that formerly when the King was going to give the same order to my Lord Lexington he bow'd with a resolution to refuse it, but in his bow observed the diamond glitter and instead of refusing made a great compliment of thanks and took it . . . I hear the Duke is now at Brussels, where I don't doubt but you are with him . . . When I was at Brussels I found the Dutch pushed their pretensions too high . . . What I was piqued at was the little regard they had to the Queen & not much to the Duke of Marlb, as if neither had had the least hand in the recovery of those countrys the irreverence with which they used to express themselves of those two . . . made me think it was necessary that the Duke should . . . soon assume the Government himself.[11]

Their letters crossed. Cadogan, writing from the Hague on 12 November in terms of somewhat false modesty emphasized how well all the German contingents had done by his administration:

The affair of the winter quarters for the troops of Prussia is very near setled; we shall give half the bread and the agio [the charge for changing one currency into another, a charge from which Cadogan frequently made a personal profit] in these Places where the German mony is not currant and agree with the Country to furnish all the forrage for which the Queen and the States will be answerable. I believe I have been very serviceable to the Prussian Troops in the whole course of this affair . . . this I suppose procurred me the Order of Generosity which was a greater surprise to me then to any body else when Cromshaw [General Grumbkow, Prussian attaché] brought it me. I was so far from desiring it that I never thought of it. However I received it with all the Deference and Respect Imaginable and my Lord Duke has writt to the Queen for leave for me to wear it. I am told there is a thousand Ducats designed for me to buy a Jewel as soon as the affair of the Winter Quarters if fully regulated . . . there is hardly any of the little Princes in Germany who have Troops here, who have not acknowledged much more considerably the Services I have done them in the business of the Winter Quarters.[12]

The Queen and 'my Lord Duke', too, fully acknowledged his services. For on 1 January 1707 he was promoted, at 34, to major general.

During the siege of Ath news came through that Eugène had captured Turin, an event which marked the end of French domination in Italy. This was a great triumph for the Alliance and, in one respect, especially for England, in that a large proportion of Eugène's army was made up of German troops paid for from the English exchequer. (But most observers, especially among the Tories, would have concurred with Mérode-Westerloo who commented of this time 'I don't believe that the Duke of Marlborough and Cadogan had any desire to make peace so soon'.[13])

Cadogan, who expected to settle in England once a peace was signed, was concerned about how thinking minds at home regarded the conflict. For the majority of English men and women – those not involved, those without loved ones in the armed forces, for example, or merchants whose ships or cargoes were not in danger of being sunk or captured – the war must have seemed very remote. Even for those paying the Land Tax, which largely supported the campaigns, it did not give much cause for complaint. Of course England's triumphs were duly applauded, but, for the most part Britons – as the English were sometimes to be called since the Union with Scotland – had more mundane things on their mind.

In the early months of 1707 Cadogan spent some time in England. During March he bought an estate in Oxfordshire, the Manor of Okeley (Oakley), a 17th century house, with a little over 370 acres. It was only 20 miles from Woodstock, his parliamentary constituency. He paid £9,450 for the property.[14] Cadogan, being fairly unscrupulous in money matters, much of that sum was almost certainly ill-gained.[15]

While in London he must have been struck by the atmosphere of detachment from the conflicts raging on the

Continent. What were Londoners talking about? Apart from the daily exchange of family news and other gossip, for the gentry there were, for example, the latest fashions in the Strand to be discussed; the plays of Vanbrugh and Steele; the portraits of Godfrey Kneller; the writings in the recently introduced *Tatler*; the journeyings of Addison and Defoe; Congreve's affair with the actress, Mrs Bracegirdle; the marriage of Marlborough's old paramour, the Duchess of Cleveland (now in her 60s) to 'Beau' Fielding (a man over ten years her junior, who transpired to be a bigamist). Perhaps Cadogan put in a visit to the Italian opera which was performed when he was in London. Old Lady Wentworth, the mother of his confidant Raby, wrote to her son in Berlin that:

Our famous Nicolini got 800 guineas for his day, and 'tis thought Mrs Tofts whose turn is on Tuesday next, will get a vast deal. She was on Sunday last at the Duke of Somerset's where there was about thirty gentlemen, and every kiss a guinea; some took three, others four, others five at that rate. The Dutchis of Molbery [Marlborough] had gott the Etallian to sing and he sent an excuse, but the Dutchis of Shrosberry [the Duchess of Shrewsbury was also Italian] made him com, brought him in her coach; but Mrs Taufs huft and would not sing because he had first put it off . . . Lady Derringwater's new husband coms every day to the coffy house in his fyne coach and twoe footmen to wait on him' and the coach waits at the Coffy house and all elc hear walk to it, so he is laught at for it . . . [She goes on to regale her son with accounts of her animals] I am sure could you see my fyer side you would laugh hartely to see Fubs [her dog] upon a cushin, the cat of another, and Pug [her monkey] of another, lapt up, all but her face in a blanket.[16]

Cadogan, back at the Hague towards the end of March, had more pressing matters to relate to Lord Raby on 15 April 1707:

I have been here about ten days my Lord Duke of Marlborough having thought it necessary to send me some little time before him to acquaint the States with his opinion and sentiments for the opening the Campagne, and to settle with the undertakers of Bread and Forrage every thing in order to it. I find they are more in earnest here for the War now than they have been all the winter . . . [Cadogan then refers to the peace negotiations with which he was to be deeply involved] The ? of Roterdam who was sent some time since into France, being returned without such an answer as they expected, France offering little more than what had been refused by this State at the end of the last campagne.[17]

The Order of Generosity was still a matter for his correspondence with Raby. 'I shall be glad to hear that you have the diamond to your Cross,' Raby was writing on 31 May. All Europe then being electrified by the grave tidings from the Spanish front, the envoy ends his letter on a less trivial note. 'I am afraid the ill news from Spain increases every post . . . I am doubly uneasy for my poor Regt which I doubly wish had staid with you.'[18]

The War of the Spanish Succession might well be termed the first worldwide conflict. For the struggle between France and the Grand Alliance was fought not only in the Mediterranean and on five European land fronts, but also reached across the Atlantic to the Spanish possessions in the West Indies and South America. The year 1707 augured well for the Alliance, with the chance of good peace terms in sight. It transpired, however, to be an extremely disappointing year. The Captain General returned to his army's base camp at the end of April – from diplomatic visits to Charles XII, Sweden's fiery and aggressive young soldier-King, Frederick of Prussia and the Elector of Hanover – to be greeted with the news of the crippling defeat of Lord Galway's Anglo-Portuguese army by Berwick's superior force at Almanza on 25 April, an event which dashed almost every hope of putting Charles of Austria on the Spanish throne.

(The Austro-Hungarian Emperor, having made a secret and treacherous pact with France, whereby the French garrisons in Italy were permitted to leave unmolested, Berwick had an unexpected 8,000 extra troops under command.) 'I am mighty glad my Regt escaped being at the fatal Battle of Almanza,' wrote Raby to Cadogan on 25 June.[19]

A plan for Eugène to follow up his capture of Turin by marching over the maritime Alps and along the Mediterranean coast to besiege the French naval base of Toulon also ended in failure. The court in Vienna were lukewarm about the expedition, which started out from Turin much too late (in the summer, not the spring as it should have done). Eugène's army reached Toulon and was well supported by the Anglo-Dutch fleet, under Sir Cloudesley Shovell's command, but the Toulon garrison proved too strong (a proportion of the French troops from Italy had joined it) and the Allied forces were obliged to withdraw along their approach route, many of them stricken with disease. The siege was raised in mid-August.

There were other French successes, too. During May Villars made a daring raid en masse, overrunning the Rhine and the Lines of Stollhofen (where the ineffectual Margrave of Bayreuth commanded) and spreading into Bavaria. In the southern Netherlands, where the summer weather was again appalling, the Duc de Vendôme kept slipping his army away and out of contact whenever the Allies attempted to confront him.

The Captain General would have been more aggressive had it not been for the continuing timidity and undue caution of the States General and their Field Deputies, as Cadogan, writing from Meldert, on July 7, told Raby:

The answers he [Marlborough] received were *qu'il ne faut rien risquer il faut agir avec Precaution*, in time the substance is they would have us doe nothing but guard Brussels this summer notwithstanding the considerable superiority wee have. [In the same letter he boasts once more of his kindness to the Prussian

95

contingent] I am as useful here to the Prussian Troops as tis possible in all the little matters in my Province. I hope Count Lottum does me the Justice to give an account of it. I assure your Lordship that for Waggons, Quarters, Forrage and Carriages for their Sick they have had more douceurs by my means than any Troops in the army and I shall continue to act on the same foot notwithstanding tis uneasy to be always persecuted by unreasonable demands by People that think I am under an obligation to help them in every thing.[20]

Cadogan organized the return of Marlborough's army to Helchin in October. Thus ended the campaigning season of 1707, which proved to be as frustrating for him as for anyone (although, as we shall see, he had been busy enriching himself at the expense of others).

Notes

1   Blackadder, *op cit*, 280–82
2   GMT II, 125–26
3   Chanclos was the governor of Ath; WSC III, 351
4   Dickson, *op cit*, Pt I,161
5   DNB, *op cit*, 183
6   Coxe,III, 5–6
7   BL Add MS 22196, *op cit*, f 33
8   WSC, III, 179
9   General Charles Churchill had been appointed to the Governorship of Guernsey
10 Coxe, III, 6–7
11 BL add MS 22196, *op cit*, f 37
12 *Ibid*, f 45
13 Chandler *op cit*, 198
14 PRO C/54/498
15 see Chapter Nine
16 GMT II, 312–13
17 BL Add MS 22196, *op cit*, f 59
18 *Ibid*, f 76
19 *Ibid*, f 81
20 *Ibid*, ff 85–88; cf Stowe MS, 58

10

Envoy Extraordinary

(1707–1708)

The Treaty for the Union of England and Scotland ('North Britain') was signed as early as July 1706, although the statute confirming the merging of the two countries, the consolidating of Great Britain, was not ratified until May 1707. In Scotland there was a great deal of opposition to the amalgamation, coming mostly from the people of Edinburgh and Glasgow, from those in particular who feared for the liberties of both the Catholic and Presbyterian religions, and, of course, from dyed-in-the-wool Jacobites of any religious persuasion. Those men denounced the 1701 Act of Succession, which provided for the Hanoverians, a Protestant succession.

King Louis and his protégé, the English Pretender, Prince James Edward Stuart (the Chevalier St George as he was known in France) and other Jacobites believed that British opposition to Hanover, amounting to a willingness to rebel, was far greater than was the case. The Sun King, at once a cynic and a realist, saw that, if he put Scotland under an invasion threat, Marlborough would be obliged to subtract a high proportion of his army of the Netherlands to meet it. He therefore gave his blessing to the formation of a fleet of thirty sail, 6,000

French infantry and an assortment of Scottish and Irish Jacobites, under the 20-year-old Prince's nominal command, but in reality led by Admiral Comte Forbin.

Despite French attempts to keep the preparations secret, agents employed by the Allies' director of intelligence, General William Cadogan, were made quickly aware that the bustle at the ports was for something rather greater than piracy or naval contingency. Throughout this war, whenever the Captain General had occasion, as we have seen, to delegate a task of vital importance, Cadogan, whom he recognized as both the 'Jack and the master of all trades', was invariably the officer to whom it was assigned. To meet the Franco-Jacobite invasion threat Marlborough signalled Cadogan from London, on 17 February 1708, saying:

> Upon what you wrote the last post to Mr Cardonnel, and the advices come from other parts of the preparations making at Dunkirk, HM has thought fit that, upon receipt thereof, you forthwith repair to Flanders and by all possible means to inform yourself of the enemy's designs and . . . that there be a proportionable number of her Majesty's foot-forces, not only kept in readiness to embark immediately, but . . . if the enemy should embark with the intention of landing in Great Britain, before you have any other orders from hence, that then you put H. M.'s troops on shipboard with all possible speed, either at Ostend or in Zeeland, and come yourself with them, to the first convenient port you can make.[1]

On 10 March 1708 Cadogan wrote to the Secretary of State (foreign affairs), from Brussels, as follows:

> I came hither from the Hague on Wednesday last . . . to be more at hand to find out the real design of the Enemy's Preparations at Dunkirk . . . I goe tomorrow to Ostend to the immediate putting aboard ten of Her Majesty's Battalions . . . at Sluys and

at Zeeland . . . Two small Ostend privateers [spy ships] are already sent to lye as close to the Harbour of Dunkirk as possibly they can to observe the Enemy's Squadron, and to carry notice of all they can learn to the Commanding Officer of Her Majesty's Fleet.

The invasion had been designed for February, but, since the Pretender then lay sick at Dunkirk, with measles, Forbin's fleet did not set sail until 20 March, which was the precise date given for its departure by Cadogan's agent at the port. Cadogan promptly dispatched a sloop, escorted by a gunship, to carry the news to Admiral Sir George Byng, who was ready to intercept the enemy fleet. Cadogan also 'made everything ready to embark his ten battalions of British and Dutch troops as soon as a convoy arrived.'[2] In the event Byng's squadron of thirty-two ships caught Forbin's fleet in the Firth of Forth and had them fleeing northwards, the French armada returning to Dunkirk via Britain's west coast; and, by the end of the month the scare was over.[3]

Meanwhile Cadogan was involved in a more lasting commitment. Following the victory of Ramillies and the Allies' occupation of Flanders and Brabant, Prince Charles of Austria having been declared Charles III of Spain, and thus King of the Spanish Netherlands, an Anglo-Dutch Condominium was set up in Brussels to govern in his name. This ruling body was composed ot two representatives from the States-General, Johan van den Bergh and F. A. van Reede, Baron of Renswoude, along with Marlborough and George Stepney, who had been transferred from his ambassadorial post at Vienna (because he had offended the Imperialists by his constant demands that they should come to terms with the Hungarian rebels). When Stepney died, in 1707, Cadogan was appointed to replace him in the Condominium with the title Envoy Extraordinary to the Southern Netherlands. He had been on diplomatic missions to Vienna, Hanover, Berlin, Brussels and the Hague. Now he was an Envoy Extraordinary as well as a 'soldier extraordinary'. His diplomatic experience was burgeoning fast. The Jacobite Earl of Aylesbury, who had lived in the Netherlands for several years, had this comment on the work of the Condominium:

> I cannot say their [the Belgian people's] laws were violated, but their purse paid well, and great sums were laid upon pretence of giving safeguards, and contributions were exacted, and for three years the fields and meadows were as bare as the high road by continued foraging for to make the armies subsist . . . And to give them their due they [the Belgians] loved the English officers and soldiers, but not the hoarders up of mony.[4]

Which was, presumably, a dig at Cadogan among others, as will be revealed more fully in the next chapter. And the Dutch opinion of the English element of the Condominium was even less flattering. According to Professor A. J. Veenendaal, citing documents in the Hague archives,[5] the Captain General 'in January, 1708 . . . sent his confidant, William Cadogan, to the Hague to propose evacuating Brussels in the next campaign, to be better able to use his troops in Flanders and elsewhere.'

The Professor goes on to state that 'of the two Dutch representatives on the governing body . . . van den Bergh, burgomaster of Leiden, was the stronger figure, and proved himself a match for the powerful personalities of Marlborough and Cadogan . . . Van den Bergh, who could not understand why the English wished to abandon Brussels and to move the government in his departments and the archives to Antwerp, was joined in his dissent by Overkirk and all the other Dutch generals.'[6]

Van den Bergh, objecting to Marlborough's plan, pointed out, in a letter to Heinsius, that an evacuation of Brussels would eventually lead to the abandonment to the French of the whole of Brabant, the province most favourably disposed to the Allies; that a large proportion of the army would be robbed of its maintenance, and that Holland itself would be exposed to the enemy. Whilst at the Hague the Captain General wrote to Heinsius saying, 'I could not leave this place without begging again of you to lose no time in sending the necessary orders to your Deputys at Brussels for the removing of the Archives it being absolutely necessary for the good success of this campaign.'[7] But no leading British writer on the war has so much as mentioned the plot to give up Brussels in 1708.

In the event the Captain General's scheme was abandoned when Vendôme took Ghent and Bruges. Veenendaal, whose verdict is in contrast to the principal British versions (eg. as presented by G. M. Trevelyan and Winston Churchill[8]) tells us that a projected attack by the French on Antwerp, failed owing to the vigilance of the Dutch deputies, who were alerted to the conspiracy. The raid on Ghent – the key to all the waterways of Flanders – was mounted on 4 July, taking place the following evening. This was led by a group of Frenchmen pretending to be deserters, under command of the renegade Colonel F. H. de la Faille, formerly Grand Bailiff of the town, whose cavalry rushed the gate. Major General Robert Murray, who was posted with his brigade nearby, had his troops on the move as soon as he heard of the French attack, but was too late to save Ghent. At about the same time Bruges was also assaulted and over-whelmed. By its loss the direct line of communication with England was surrendered. Veenendaal writes, in the same article that

the treachery of his [Marlborough's] favourite town [Ghent] which all the time had an English garrison, was no doubt a heavy blow to [him] . . . how [he] was surprised by Ghent becomes clear only when it is known he intended to leave Brussels and Brabant to the French, after which the waterways of Flanders would have formed his only connection with Holland. For the intended siege of Lille these waterways were essential . . . his insufficient care to protect Ghent was a serious mistake.[9]

101

Cadogan was not only a man of colossal courage and ability he was also someone who was very gregarious, who formed close friendships, who knew how to relax and enjoy himself, who loved a bit of gossip. Clearly, he and Raby had enjoyed one another's company enormously when they cavorted together in Dublin during the 1680s. In February 1708 Raby wrote to him saying, 'I don't believe you divert yourself half so well at the Hague as at Brussels which to me seems the much more agreeable place'.[10] A month earlier Cadogan had written to Watkins urging him as follows: 'I hope during the Carnival you will doe your Friends the Favour to let them see you here, you know the wine is good, and I can assure the women are sound, I shall only therefore add that no body living can be more welcome to me than your self, and that I am, my Dear Judge . . . etc.'[11]

Apart from helping to govern the southern Netherlands, running missions for the Captain General and fiddling the books, Cadogan filled Raby in that winter with complaints concerning the Dutch and also some local gossip, which must, for him, have put those far-off Dublin days in mind again:

December 8, 1707. The people are generally dissatisfied . . . The Dutch grow more and more oppressive to them and unreasonable and our business is to keep these two extremes from breaking out into very unhappy Consequences, tis a hard task, and I already feel myself unequal to it, and heartily wish for the Campagne to relieve me . . . January 19, 1708. I will give you in a few words the description of Brussels. Count Corneille is the Principal Trickster and [?] Oxenstein the Top Wit. My Lord Ailesbury a shining Beau, and his Lady a celebrated [?]. Toast not a woman as puts on so much Red as my Lady Falkland and is as Coquette as our former Friend my Lady S---n. They play Deep and pay ill, and in short there is a tolerable deal of Scandal, but no F-----g thoe to do the women justice tis not their fault.[12]

One may well imagine lascivious, gossip-loving Raby reading that last sentence and thinking, 'Just so; the wives would like to commit adultery, but are kept so vigilantly under the eyes of their husbands that they dare not wander astray.'

Notes

1. Marlborough, *Dispatches III*, 680
2. Dickson, *op cit*, Pt I, 161–62
3. GMT, II, 337–47; WSC III, 317–21; cf *Marlborough Dispatches*, III, 662–95
4. Aylesbury, *Memoirs*, Roxburghe II, 602
5. Veenendaal, *History*, February and June, 1950, 34–48
6. Veenendaal, *op cit*, 35
7. Veenendaal quotes A R Archief Heinsius, 83 (April, 1708)
8. GMT II, 37; WSC III, 342–5 (Churchill states, on page 342, that 'the hatred that the Dutch occupation had aroused, in the two years since Ramillies, had made the former French yoke light by contrast'. One wonders whether the English occupation was much more, if at all, popular).
9. Veenendaal quotes *Het Engels Nederlands Condominium*, 16–40, 54–62
10. BL Add MS 22, 196, *op cit*, f 139
11. By kind permission of Lord Cadogan
12. BL Add MS 22, 196, *op cit*, ff 111–12

11

Sleaze

(1707–1708)

There is ample proof that William Cadogan, the gallant soldier, the brilliant military administrator, intelligence chief and inspiring leader of men, was also a crafty swindler, an extortionist, a brazen army profiteer. He had met, and rubbed shoulders with, a considerable number of very rich young men during his army career. Having worked his way up, with almost unparalleled success, through the officer grades to general rank, he seemed to take the view that it was a well-merited perquisite, if not a right, to make a bit on the side, to give himself wealth commensurate with his exalted military status. It should be added, however, that this was an age in which officers of all nationalities and all ranks were inclined to rationalize that they were entitled to take whatever perquisites were available – and the more senior they were the greater the prizes. So perhaps neither Cadogan nor Marlborough should be criticized too harshly.

Cadogan ought, he reckoned, to be a man of property and he must have substantial capital to endow upon his growing family. And Marlborough, who doubtless condoned such of the murky activities of his Quartermaster General of which he was aware, set an iniquitous example. In a letter dated 21 March 1709, Van den Bergh told Heinsius that:

> I learned from a very reliable source that in the time of three months before his departure for England the Duke of Marlborough had six hundred thousand rixdollars or 15 tons of gold transferred to England by Antwerp bankers; so that the safeguards, the marches, the orders for winter quarters, and more things of that kind, no doubt bring in nice profits.[1]

As for Cadogan, after being appointed to succeed Stepney in the southern Netherlands Condominium, he proceeded to fill his own pockets with a proportion of the tax levied on the unfortunate war-torn people. It seems, at the time, that it was only the Dutch who found him out. Professor Veenendaal says that 'Cadogan looked after the interests of England (and his own) so keenly and so unscrupulously and moreover treated the States of Brabant with such insolence that Van den Bergh complained seriously about his behaviour in his letters home . . . The man who most of all was guilty of exaction was the Quartermaster-General of the English troops and plenipotentiary at Brussels, William Cadogan. His colleague in the Brussels conference, Van den Bergh, called him 'the greatest thief of the whole army', and this opinion completely tallies with that of Cardinal Alberoni in 1718: *Cadogan, insigne voleur, fripon acheve, qui avoit enleve de Flandre plus de deux cents mille pistoles, independamment des autres vols ignore.* It also corresponds with the opinion of the four nobiliary members of the southern Netherlands council of state, who, after Cadogan's dismissal as envoy at Brussels, lodged with the English government a formal complaint against him.[2]

'The Deputies of Ghent wrote to the Queen of Great Britain [asking her] to deliver them from the infamous and contribution-thirsty thieves, the Lord Duke and Cadogan.'[3] They also 'continually urged Marlborough to spare the country districts from billeting. In 1706 they drafted a *Reglement* which was meant to "put an end to the excessive corruption in the levying of the subsidies . . .". In 1707 they drafted new regulations for the prevention of the many excesses committed by the generals while stationed in the winter quarters.'[4]

Evidence of Marlborough's duplicity and avarice is well documented and has often been exposed by British authors. We cannot know quite what was in the Captain General's mind when he wrote to Stepney during the winter of 1706–07 saying that:

> our chief aim ought to be to satisfy the people and make them easy under the present administration, so that the collecting at present a little money more or less, ought not, in my opinion, to come in competition in a matter of this moment, especially considering when we take the field, we shall be able to leave but small garrisons in the great towns, and must depend in some measure on the faithfulness of the inhabitants.[5]

Yet Marlborough was quite prepared to take a percentage of their dues for his own purse. As for Cadogan we have witnessed his annoyance at receiving only a small diamond in his Prussian Order of Generosity. He was also an addictive gambler. (Raby wrote to him on 1 November, 1707 saying, 'I could scold at you for loosing mony at play as I hear you have lately don, I thought you had shook off that passion . . . in Ireland you gave me [? good] reason for playing so much there'[6].) James Brydges wrote to Cadogan on 18 October 1707, saying, 'this is chiefly to congratulate you on two peices of good that ye town is full of, one that you have won six thousand pistoles at play, the other that you are to reside at ye Hague or Brussels in ye room of Mr Stepney'.[7] Perhaps Cadogan required funds beyond his army pay, his sinecures and emoluments to pay off gaming debts? And, although his aristocratic Dutch wife was a rich woman, with extensive estates, he needed capital for his anticipated settlement in England after the war.

Some of the correspondence between Cadogan and James Brydges (later 1st Duke of Chandos), Paymaster of the Forces Abroad, reveals very clearly how the old Westminster school friends speculated and profited most unscrupulously from the military finances.[8] One method was to use Cadogan's position to secure inside information on the next move of the army, in any particular campaign (having opened a betting book on the subject) or to buy and sell stocks as the prospects of peace looked promising, or adverse as the case might be. Or they took advantage of the different rates of exchange – from place to place and from time to time – in the Netherlands. They bought up coin at a cheap rate and, to their considerable advantage, paid the army at a higher one.

They managed to pull the wool over the eyes of Lieutenant General Lumley, along with the various commanding officers, and Benjamin Sweet, the Deputy Paymaster to the Army in the Low Countries. In letters to Cadogan from Brydges in the spring of 1707 there are references to an attempt to make money out of the forage consumed by the Prussian cavalry (about whom the Quartermaster General boasted to Raby that he looked after so well). Cadogan is told that Brydges had 'informed Benjamin Sweet not to settle one particular account but to leave it to Cardonnel or Cadogan himself'. ('I added his [Cardonnel's] name,' said Brydges, 'that Sweet might not suspect there was any bargain made by you alone for it'[9].) Goslinga remarked in 1707 that 'Cadogan had the same interest as others in prolonging the war'.[10]

At about the same time Cadogan managed to persuade Brigadier General Palmes and others to receive pay for their regiments at the same rates (in 1707) as for the previous year. Then he made a bargain with a 'Jew' to supply him with 6,000 louis d'or at a more favourable rate than he would give the regimental commanding officers. 'I am persuaded this matter is so settled,' he told Brydges, 'that we shall turn fifteen or sixteen thousand pounds a month at 2 per cent, clear of all charges. I would not indicate a greater sum for these two reasons. First, I could not conveniently manage it; and in the second place too great a sum would alarm . . . Sweet.'[11]

Cadogan suggested that the money be sent to his wife rather than to Sweet. He added that he would agree to any method of remitting the money provided Sweet, 'on whom there is no depending', was not employed. Brydges concurred and promised to remit to Mrs Cadogan, 'but the bill must be drawn payable to Captain Cartwright (paymaster at Antwerp) in current money of Holland and endorsed by him to Mrs Cadogan (which he shall have private orders constantly to do) by which means it will appear in our books to be upon his account and no other name but his [Cartwright's] will be seen'.[12]

It is not easy to say just when Cadogan began his nefarious financial activity. As early as October 1706 he sent to Sweet this fishy note:

> I believe you will be surprised at receiving this letter by ye hand of Mr Cartwright, more soe when you know he is going to settle at Antwerp. Sir Hy Furnese hath perswaded my Ld Treas that yr Exchg, may be made upon a more advantageous foot to Antwerp, ye Army may likewise better be served by having one under me there than to continue yr payments upon ye foot they are at present whereby ye charges commission reckoned by Bankers who supply them may in a great measure be saved.[13]

Presumably he had always been ready to make a bit on the side, and in his old friend James Brydges he found a faithfully like-minded colleague. On 31 May 1707 Brydges told him that:

> I . . . wrote to Mr Sweet not to pay the Prussian commissary any thing on account of forrage . . . and that you or Mr Cardonnel

1. Louis Laguerre's portrait of Cadogan as a major general. *(National Portrait Gallery)*

6. Kneller's portrait of the Countess Cadogan (née Munster).
(Reproduced by kind permission of the Trustees of Goodwood House)

7. The Cadogans' elder daughter, Lady Sarah (by Enoch Seeman). She became the 2nd Duchess of Richmond.
(Reproduced by kind permission of the Trustees of Goodwood House)

8. A 19th-century image of the Battle of Blenheim (13 August 1704): the Earl of Derby's Regiment of Foot (later the Bedfordshire) attacking the village. *(After the watercolour by Richard Simkin.)* Cadogan acted as Chief of Staff during the fighting.

9. Prince Eugene leading the attack against the French left wing at Blenheim. *(Detail from Louis Laguerre's oil sketch of the battle)*

10. The attack on the French right at Blenheim. *(Detail from Louis Laguerre's oil sketch)*

11. Interior of a French tent. Puysegur's contemporary demonstration of the way in which nine men might occupy the floor space.

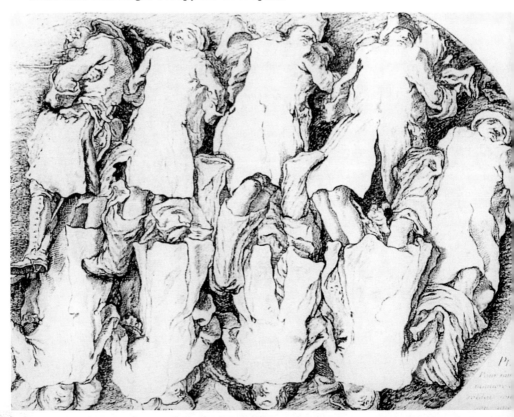

12. Kneller's portrait of John Churchill, Duke of Marlborough, as Captain General. Marlborough could not have won the Spanish Succession War in north-west Europe without the services of Cadogan. *(National Portrait Gallery)*

13. Marlborough receiving Marshal Tallard's surrender at Blenheim, with Cadogan riding behind the Duke. *(From the tapestry woven by De Vos after L. de Hondt. By kind permission of his Grace the Duke of Marlborough)*

14. Dutch caricature
of Prince Louis
of Baden, in
1705.

15. Fortress warfare: Dutch engineers
building a bastion salient towards the
end of the 17th century.

16. Forcing the Lines of Brabant, 17-18 July 1705, showing the village and bridge at Elixhem and, in the centre, the castle of Wangen. *(Detail from the tapestry woven by De Vos, after L. de Hondt. By kind permission of his Grace the Duke of Marlborough)*

21. The battle of Oudenarde, 11 July, 1708, showing the climax of the fighting.
(After the line engraving by J. Huchtenburg)

22. Baggage wagons at Wynendael, 28 September, 1708. *(From the tapestry woven by De Vos, after L. de Hondt. By kind permission of his Grace the Duke of Marlborough)* Cadogan's last-minute intervention probably saved the day for General Webb and his convoy of supplies for the Lille besiegers.

23. The Siege of
    Tournai, June-July
    1709. *(From an
    engraving after
    Louis Laguerre's
    sketch)*

24. English troops dismantling logs, chained together by the French, at Malplaquet,
    11 September 1709. *(From the oil sketch by Louis Laguerre)*

29. 'The Old Pretender', the Chevalier de St George, son of James II. *(From the collection of the Duke of Alba. Artist unknown)*. His invasion of Scotland, in 1715, was finally defeated by troops under Cadogan's command.

30. George I of England and Elector of Hanover. *(Artist unknown)*. Cadogan was not only his commander-in-chief, but also his favourite Englishman.

would take care to pay it. I added his name that Sweet might not suspect there was any bargain made by you alone for it . . . I'll send him word in a letter . . . that I desire he'll follow our directions either by paying ye Deputies himself or by furnishing you with mony to do it, but then you'll please remember . . . ye voucher necessary for me to have to produce to ye Auditor . . . Pray don't forget to speak to ye Duke of Wirtemburg. I understand he is very uneasy [about Cadogan's transactions apropos forage for the Danish cavalry] and intends to complain to my Lord Duke . . . Ye notice you give me of ye intended Measures would be of advantage if one could guess ye time that ye town would be taken . . . [This refers to bets on a tactical matter] be at your liberty to take what share (if you have a mind to be concerned) you please.'[14]

Three weeks later Brydges informed Cadogan that:

I am now fully convinced that Mr Sweet will obstruct – not withstanding what I wrote you formerly – as much as he possibly can our design and therefore to prevent his being able to do it [I] have remitted Mr Romswinkle by ye hand of Captain Cartwright £50000 and by ye hands of Mr Chitty near £15000.[15]

And so the evidence piles up. In the autumn of 1707 Cadogan borrowed money from his father-in-law, Jan Munter, in order to buy up pistoles, which he sold to the army at a substantially higher rate. Brydges arranged for up to £14,000 to be provided well in advance of the time payments were due. The two profiteers thus reckoned to make as much as 25,000 guilders pure gain.[16] Cadogan spent a good deal of time each winter buying gold and then selling it at a profit.[17]

What an extraordinary person he was – highly intelligent and practical, charismatic, supremely imposing and self-confident, extremely industrious, both physically and morally courageous, he was content to expose himself to mortal danger

109

during each campaigning season; then craftily, and mostly by illicit means, to spend much of the 'off-season' amassing money to himself. Let us give him the benefit of the doubt, however, and suggest that, in his dishonest dealings, his motive was largely to provide for his family in case he was killled. But it is once again in his nobler role that we see him next.

Notes

1   Veenendaal, *The Opening Phase of Marlborough's Campaign of 1708 in the Netherlands*, in *History*, February, 1950, p45. Quoting Heinsius, 1383
2   *Ibid*, 46; cf BL Add MSS 37209, ff 301–05
3   PRO, SP, 77/ 60
4   Veenendaal, *op cit*, 46
5   BL Add MS 7058, ff 65–66
6   BL Add MS 22196, *op cit*, ff 99–100
7   Huntington, no 248
8   The correspondence is contained in HMC Stowe MS 57 and 58; cf *The Seamy Side of Marlborough's War* by Godfrey Davies, in *the Huntington Library Quarterly*, November 1951
9   Huntington, *op cit*
10 WSC III, p 384
11 Huntington, 26. The letter is dated April 28, 1707
12 *Ibid*, exchange of letters, June, 1707
13 *Ibid*, 37
14 *Ibid*, 159, 11A
15 *Ibid*, 159
16 *Ibid*, Cadogan to Brydges, November 28, 1707
17 *Ibid*, November 12, 1707

12

Hero of Oudenarde

(1708)

The Allies' general strategy for 1708 was for General James Stanhope, still commanding in Spain, to continue his holding operation and for the Elector of Hanover (the future George I) to act as Imperial generalissimo on the Rhine in a similar role, while the Army of the Netherlands was to make a push through the frontier fortresses into France, assisted by an amphibious operation from the Isle of Wight against the French Channel ports. Marlborough, having failed to persuade the Emperor to send Prince Eugène and his army – who were watching the Moselle front – to reinforce Stanhope in Spain, hatched a secret plot with Eugène whereby the two old comrades-in-arms should cooperate in the Netherlands, leaving a token force on the Moselle. Eugène's coaches and escort of Hungarian hussars set forth on the 150-mile journey from Coblenz on 29 June, his army following several days' march behind him.

While Eugène drove northwards Cadogan, who had been delayed at Ostend, on intelligence work in connection with further reports of Franco-Jacobite intentions, was also on his way to join the Captain General and his army, which was concentrated eight miles north-west of Brussels at Assche. 'Marlborough . . . was very glad to have Cadogan back from Ostend,' wrote Winston Churchill; 'he had notably missed his Quartermaster-General and Intelligence Chief during these exhausting days.'[1] It was during the march to Assche that the Captain General received the devastating news of the fall of Ghent and Bruges. Melodramatic events were to pass during the next couple of days.

On 9 July Marlborough was writing to Godolphin that:

the Treachery of Ghent, continual marching and some letters I have received from England [from the Queen and Sarah] have so vexed me that I was yesterday in so great a fever that the doctor would have persuaded me to have gone to Brussels; but I thank God I am now better . . . The States [Dutch government] have used this country so ill that I no ways doubt that all the towns in this country will play us the same trick as Ghent has done.'[2]

The French army of the southern Netherlands was now nominally under command of Louis' grandson, the Duc de Burgundy, but the King had ordered the youth to defer to the decisions of the veteran *maréchal*, the Duc de Vendôme, an illegitimate great grandson of Henri IV, a tough, rough soldier's soldier with a hot temper. Vendôme, having surprised and captured Ghent and Bruges, held his forces for the moment behind the canal linking those two crucial towns. Burgundy, who was accompanied by his brother, the Duc de Berri, and the English Pretender, the Chevalier de St George, gave the opinion that their next objective should be Menin. Vendôme disagreed. He decided on Lessines – in order to hold the Allies east of the River Dender – with a view to taking the Scheldt town of Oudenarde. He was aware that, if he could be first over the Scheldt, he might not only protect his communications with France but would also be in a position to threaten Brussels and the Allies' communications with Holland. He would then take the precaution of investing Oudenarde.

Meanwhile the Duke of Berwick's army was marching north to join him. (Berwick had left the Elector of Bavaria to face the Elector of Hanover on the Rhine front.) Fortunately for the Allies the States-General, to make amends for the failures of the 1707 campaign, had instructed their Field Deputies to give Marlborough a free hand. The 'Two Princes', as he and Eugène were known in the army, put their heads together on 9 July and decided to strike west over the Dender to the Scheldt. Their next objective (like that of Vendôme) was to be Lessines – with a view to marching on Oudenarde. Their other aim was, in the words of Private Deane, of the Foot Guards, 'to force them to a battel, although on great unequallety, they being 21 Battalions of Foot and 24 Squadrons of Horse more than we att this juncture'.[3]

Dependable Cadogan was duly sent ahead with the advance guard of 16 battalions, eight squadrons of Hanoverian cavalry, 32 guns and a team of engineers and pioneers carrying the pontoon train – to mend the road, lay bridges over the Dender, occupy Lessines, push on to Oudenarde and fix crossing-places there, too. Cadogan left his outpost at Herfelingen at four o'clock in the afternoon and by 11 pm had not only reached Lessines but had also crossed the Dender. His men spent the remainder of the night of 9–10 July and much of the following day repairing the road and building more pontoon bridges for the main army, which having enjoyed a brief rest at Herfelingen, was not far behind.

Although Cadogan and his men were very short of sleep they set off from Lessines at one o'clock on the night of 10–11 July towards Oudenarde, which was another 13 miles to the west. The soldiers marched with a quick lively spirit, born of an impatient desire to fight and to take revenge for the loss of Ghent and Bruges; born, too, of implicit faith in this tall, burly general, William Cadogan. He had never let them down. He was the efficient administrative officer who ensured that their rations, their pay and their new shoes were up on time; who knew as much about pontoons as the pioneers and engineers laying them; and who was always ready to fight alongside with the best of the troops. The French had no conception of the astonishing speed at which those soldiers under Cadogan's command could march.

When Vendôme heard that Cadogan had reached Lessines before him, he cursed. The French *maréchal* doubled his regiments back, making for Gavre and ordering the siege of Oudenarde to be suspended. There was no doubt in Vendôme's mind that he would be first over the Scheldt, first too at Oudenarde. But he was wrong. Cadogan was at Oudenarde before him. G. M. Trevelyan describes Cadogan's arrival on the Scheldt very nicely:

[The Vanguard] reached the edge of the hills above Eename . . . and suddenly saw below them the Schelde (sic) winding through its marshes, and on the further bank the pretty fortress town of Oudenarde. Above its houses rose the tower and high-pitched narrow roof of the church, and the gorgeous architectural fantasies of the Hotel de Ville. But that morning Cadogan had no eyes for such matters his gaze was turned northward.[4]

By about 9.30 am, on 11 July Cadogan, accompanied by the Hanoverian squadrons, had reached Eename which topped the high ground south-east of the river. Putting his spyglass to his eye he saw, six miles or so to the north, the white coats of the French advance guard at Gavre preparing their pontoons. He returned to the river. A little later, his own pontoon train having caught up with him, he gave orders for five bridges to be laid across the Scheldt, hard by Oudenarde, a town with two stone bridges of its own. In all seven bridges for 80,000 men.

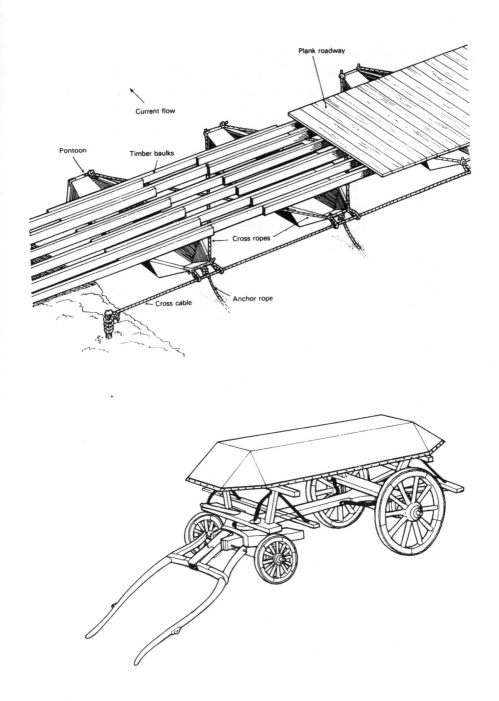

Bridging Equipment and Transport

Marlborough and Eugène set an equally lively pace for the main army whose column was out on the Lessines-Oudenarde road by 7 am. 'It was no longer a march,' as the Dutch field deputy, Goslinga, recalled, 'but a run'. The men whistled and sang as they trotted along the dusty track. (Major Blackadder, of the Cameronians, was among the mute: 'My thoughts were much on the 103rd psalm, which I sang, in my heart, frequently upon the march'.[5]

At Gavre, too, there was progress, and Vendôme ordered the Marquis de Biron, with four battalions of Swiss infantry and six squadrons of French cavalry to advance and seize Eyne on the Gavre-Oudenarde road. At about the same time Cadogan sent General von Rantzau and the Hanoverian Horse over the river, and northwards, in the role of reconnaissance in force. Leaving four battalions to guard the pontoons, Cadogan then led 12 battalions, including Brigadier General Joseph Sabine's Guards Brigade, forward to back up von Rantzau. As those redcoats marched northwards de Biron climbed the steps of the wind-mill at Eyne and, reaching the top, took out his glass. What he saw appalled him. The French *général* was faced not only with the picture of Cadogan's troops coming in strength straight for him, but also the entire Allied army snaking along the Lessines-Oudenarde road, their leading units already beginning to debouch from Cadogan's pontoons. This was incredible: Marlborough's army was last reported, only two days before, at Assche, nearly 50 miles away. They had covered the distance in 40 hours!

The devastating news was relayed to Vendôme while he lunched with the Royal princes at the riverside. 'If they are there,' the *maréchal* exclaimed, 'the devil must have carried them. Such marching is impossible!' Vendôme rode to the top of a hillock to see for himself and promptly sent an ADC to order his divisional commanders to form up a mile north-west-wards, behind the Norken rivulet around the hamlet of Mullem. (The battlefield of Oudenarde was mainly concen-

116

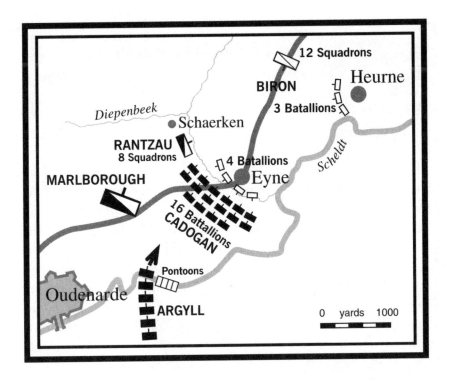

trated on two other rivulets, the Marollebeek, a tributary of the
Scheldt flowing through Eyne, and its branch stream, the
Diepenbeek, which runs through Schaerken.)

Cadogan's advance guard contained the pick of the English
infantry. These battalions advanced on Eyne in line, with
shouldered muskets, never firing a shot or even bringing their
bayonets to the charge till they were in musket and pistol shot
of the Swiss mountain troops, which were among the best
troops the French fielded. When Cadogan's infantiers had
advanced within 50 yards of the Swiss they brought their
musket-butts into their shoulders and saluted them with an
almighty volley. The survivors of three Swiss battalions gave
themselves up. The fourth battalion, attempting to flee to the
refuge of their main army, were mostly cut down by von
Rantzau's cavaliers. Cadogan, looking left and seeing de Biron's
cavalry on the plain south of the Norken, ordered Rantzau to

117

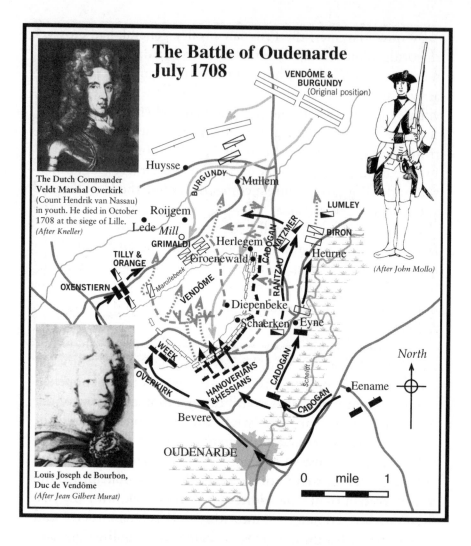

The Battle of Oudenarde July 1708

VENDÔME & BURGUNDY
(Original position)

The Dutch Commander Veldt Marshal Overkirk (Count Hendrik van Nassau) in youth. He died in October 1708 at the siege of Lille.
(After Kneller)

Huysse

BURGUNDY

Mullem

LUMLEY

Roijgem

Lede Mill
GRIMALDI
Herlegem
KATZMER
CADOGAN
RANTZAU
BIRON

TILLY & ORANGE
Groenewald
Heurne

OXENSTIERN
Marollebeek
VENDÔME
(After John Mollo)

Diepenbeke

Schaerken
Eyne

North

WEEK
CADOGAN
Scheldt
Eename

OVERKIRK
HANOVERIANS & HESSIANS
CADOGAN

Bevere

OUDENARDE

Louis Joseph de Bourbon, Duc de Vendôme
(After Jean Gilbert Murat)

0   mile   1

charge again. The Hanoverian Horse, having broken up those squadrons, cantered on and were soon in the thick of a fight with the main French Horse. But von Rantzau managed to extricate them. Among the Hanoverian casualties was the charger ridden by Prince George, son of Hanover's Elector. The squadron leader beside whom the future George II of England was riding, Colonel Loseke, surrendered his own horse, but was killed helping the prince to mount.[6]

118

By now Natzmer, the Prussian cavalry general, had crossed the bridges and was up with the advance guard. He wrote in his memoirs that 'Cadogan himself came to me in great joy at our arrival and at my coming up in his support. I traversed the village of Eyne, where the fighting had just ended.' He added that his squadrons met a great many prisoners coming back from Cadogan's attack.[7] At about 4 pm Vendôme advanced the French main army – with the exception of their left wing, which was under Burgundy's direct comand – to line the Marollebeek and Diepenbeek streams. The country thereabouts was very close, being filled by small hedge-bordered groves, thickets, farm enclosures and swamps. Vendôme instructed Burgundy to bring his formations up on the left. But the young Prince, being informed by one of his *générals* that the ground was too soft for horses, declined and remained out of action behind the Norken rivulet.

Oudenarde would be no set-piece battle but an encounter engagement with the 'Two Princes', Eugène and Marlborough, directing their units up into the battle line as they debouched from the pontoon bridges. Marlborough took command of the Allies' 80,000-strong army's left wing, composed mainly of Hessian and Hanoverian regiments, along the Diepenbeek, with Lumley's cavalry protecting the extreme left. Eugène (whose own corps had not yet arrived from Coblenz) led the largely British right wing along the Marollebeek, with Argyll's division hinged on the junction of the Diepenbeek and Marollebeek, Cadogan's division being on Argyll's right and the Prussian and Hanoverian cavalry guarding the right flank. There was a battery of guns on the hill behind Schaerken. Eyewitness Sergeant Millner of the Royal Irish gives a fitting description of the deployment:

the Duke, on this Occasion, having no Time to give exact Dispositions for attacking the enemy, order'd what was up as they were, to begin the attack, and the rest as they came up to fall in accordingly; whereupon all that was up, which was a little above the Half of our Army, immediately advanced on with undaunted Courage, and vigorously attacked.[8]

No body of men fought with greater 'undaunted courage' or attacked more 'vigorously' than Cadogan's division whose position that afternoon was in the greatest peril. 'No one can pretend to measure,' as Winston Churchill justly stated, 'what would have happened had Cadogan been driven, as he surely would have been, back upon Eyne, by the concerted onslaught of overwhelming numbers . . . Another mortal danger confronted the heroic Cadogan. Overweighted in front, his right flank in the condition we have described, he was now momentarily being overlapped by the advance of the French right wing. This alone rendered his situation desperate.'[9]

By 4.30 pm Cadogan's men were fighting with their bayonets, or hand-to-hand, being pushed back across the Diepenbeke by the sheer weight of superior numbers, the gallant Cadogan, prominent astride his heavyweight charger in the mêlée, prominent not only for his general's crimson coat, probably much torn by now, and the Prussian Order of Generosity gleaming on his chest, but also for his gigantic figure and customary *sang-froid* as he cheered his soldiers to ever greater ferocity. But just when the situation was at its most critical 'the Duke of Argyll with twenty battalions of British infantry advancing in perfect order', to quote Churchill again, 'came into line on his left, and met foursquare the masses of French infantry who assaulted along the whole front from Herlegem to Schaerken'.[10]

Vendôme sent another ADC requesting Burgundy to lead the French left wing (30,000 soldiers) up in support, but the officer was killed as he galloped back. ('I cannot comprehend,' as Vendôme was to remonstrate in his report to King Louis, 'how 50 battalions and 190 squadrons could be satisfied with observing us engaged for six hours, and merely looking at us as though watching the opera from a third-tier box.') Thus over a third of Vendôme's army took no part in the battle. Vendôme himself was, quite wrongly, not directing the action but in the thick of the infantry battle, halberd in hand.

Meanwhile a great enveloping operation was in process, the main task on the left being given to the Dutch and Danish corps under command of the veteran Veldtmarshal Overkirk, via Oudenarde's bridges, one of which gave way, and there was a long delay while it was repaired. Notwithstanding that mishap the Prince of Orange, commanding Overkirk's cavalry advance guard, raced on to Oyck. Orange swung his troopers right-handed to sever the enemy's communications, while General Week's brigade cut in behind the French right wing by Bronwaan castle. Meanwhile the enemy found themselves surrounded on their left flank by General Natzmer's blue-coated sabre-wielding Prussian gens d'armes and cuirassiers.

The intensity of the musketry fire was said to have surpassed all previous experience. Cadogan's redcoats and their German allies were having the better of the fight now. The British method of regimental firing was never more effective than at Oudenarde. The commanding officer's orders, 'first (or second, etc) firing – take care!' rang out while the tapping ruffles of the drummers sounded amid the din of battle; and the sergeants, with their halbards and half-pikes, knocked the redcoats' barrels level to point, supposedly, at the enemies' chests. The front rank knelt, the second crouched and the rear rank stood upright. While platoons reloaded their neighbours advanced or fired. They were not very accurate, but their drill and fire discipline was much better than that of the French. In places of honour, on the right of each battalion, were the hand-picked grenadier companies, well known for their height, courage and superior weapon handling. Private Deane, fighting with Brigadier General Sabine's Foot Guards under Cadogan's command, wrote that:

the fight was very desperate on both sides and continued from 5 in the evening as long as there was any light ... in which time the enemy was beate from hedge to hedge and breastwork to breastwork, from trench to trench ... and one would have thought it impossible for them to have lost the battle, they having had so much time for to secure themselves as they always do of good strong ground ... getting into villages, possessing themselves of houses, and making ... every quickset hedge a slight wall that we might not see them. So that if God Almightys Providence had not protected us and caused there contrivance to be of noe effect, they might, one would have thought, cutt off the one halfe of our army ... About 7 in the evening it began somewhat hott upon the right, and our two Battalions of Guards, together with the two brigades of English ffoote wch were come up, advanced up on the enemy who boldly bore down towards us, and having recd there fire with out much damage we gave them a merry salute, firing into there verry faces.[11]

While the French kept bringing up reinforcements to reach around the Allies left, troops were still pouring across the Oudenarde pontoons to meet them. Count Lottum's Hessians and Hanoverians, having made a successful counter-attack across the Diepenbeek, were switched to the right flank to support hard-pressed Cadogan, whose men were thus able to drive the enemy from Groenewald and Herlegem.

On the extreme right Natzmer's Prussian Horse fought the Maison du Roi ('rich in scarlet with silver facings', said Natzmer in his memoirs.[12]) Survivors from the Prussians' twenty squadrons, which had been met not only by the slashing sabres of the Maison du Roi, but also from deadly musket fire, found refuge behind Cadogan's battalions. It was not until dark when the Allies' encirclement movement was complete that the enemy, admitting defeat, began to slink away, through heavy rain, towards Ghent.

122

Huguenots in the Allies' ranks, haters of Louis XIV's France, played good tricks on their erstwhile persecutors. Their drummers marched about beating the French retreat, while their officers cried aloud the names of opposing regiments, such as *A moi Picardie!* or *A moi Roussillon!* until groups of bewildered French soldiers ran through the darkness to those familiar summons and were captured.[13]

Cadogan and his soldiers, worn out along with all the victors, slept on their arms or beside their exhausted horses, in the rain. Dawn revealed the ghastly scene, a battlefield marked by the slain and the wounded, the dejected, rain-soaked prisoners and their sleepy guards, fields of blood and mud, swirls of gunsmoke still in the air. There were countless heroes of Oudenarde. Perhaps the chief of them all was big General Cadogan. For his contributions as leader of the vanguard, both as administrative organizer and fighting commander, were exceptional. (In a later age he would surely have been an outstanding candidate for the Victoria Cross. Certainly, by this point in the war, he would have had his KCB and a third DSO.[14])

Meanwhile he had become the father of a second daughter, who was to carry the same name as Mrs Cadogan – Margaretta.

Notes

1   WSC III, 349
2   Coxe II, 133–34
3   Journal, *op cit*, 318–19
4   GMT II, 357
5   Blackadder *op cit*, 318–19
6   Prince George, who, as George II was the last British King to take part in a battle as monarch (Dettingen, 1743) was always immensely proud of the fact that he had been at Oudenarde
7   WSC III, 365 (Quoting from *Das General Feldmarshalls Dubislav, G von Natzmer Leben und Kriegsthaten* (1838)
8   Journal, *op cit*, 216
9   WSC III, 368
10   *Ibid*

11 Journal, *op cit*, 59–60
12 WSC III, 374 (Quoting Natzmer, 292)
13 GMT II, 364; WSC III, 380
14 More comprehensive accounts of the battle are to be found in Coxe, II, 247–69; GMT II, 353–66; WSC III, 356–82

13

Saviour of the Convoys

(1708)

The Captain General, while giving the bulk of his army a well-earned period of recuperation following their arduous marches, their struggle at Oudenarde and the effects of foul weather, sent Count Lottum to superintend the levelling of the defensive earthworks which the French had constructed between Ypres and the Lys fortress of Warneton. Lottum beat Berwick's army, which had just arrived in Flanders from the Rhine, to the objective, in a close finish. Burgundy, Vendôme and Berwick now boasted, between them, a force of some 110,000 troops. Shrewd Berwick, judging that Marlborough and Eugène would next target the capital of French Flanders, Lille, the greatest masterpiece of Vauban's engineering skill, visited both that city and Douai, and supplied the two fortresses with all the ammunition and provisions he could muster. It was after this that he lost the race to the Ypres-Warneton earthworks. Lottum's men having pulled those earthworks down, the Captain General wrote to Godolphin saying, 'We are now masters of marching where we please'.

Sicco van Goslinga, the principal Dutch deputy, disagreed with the strategy of 'the Two Princes' immediately after

Oudenarde, saying that the next move should be to blockade Burgundy and the French army at Ghent and Bruges. In his memoirs Goslinga offers some cynical reasons why nearly everyone went along with Marlborough and Eugène and not with him. 'Cadogan and Dopff [one of the Deputies],' he concluded, 'also followed the Princes, *the first because he had the same interest as others in prolonging the war*' (author's italics)[2]

The Allies' strength in the southern Netherlands was now more than 100,000. The Captain General had a mind to finish the war by the close of 1708 by invading France with the help of the planned seaborne attack from the Isle of Wight. But there were many problems involved, and the project was vetoed by Eugène, who argued that it was essential, just as Berwick had predicted, to besiege and capture Lille and to secure it as a

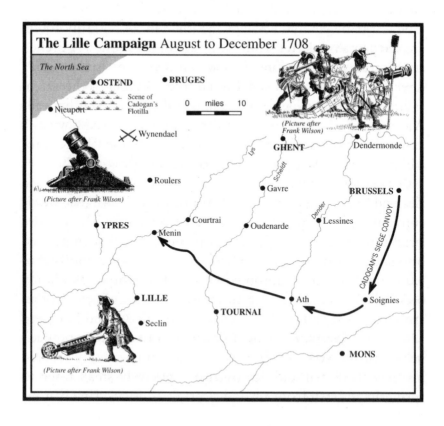

launching-pad for the invasion. Vendôme ridiculed the idea of the Allies' bid to attack such a powerful fortress town, defended as it was by 16,000 troops under the veteran Maréchal Boufflers, particularly considering the tenuous nature of the Allies' supply routes. But, in assessing that factor, Vendôme had not taken Cadogan's ingenuity into account.

The Allies' first major problem was how to bring the great siege-train up from Holland. The direct route being blocked by the enemy, from the vicinity of Ghent, a detour must be made via Brussels. That implied – for the convoy of 100 gigantic siege guns, 60 mortars and 3,000 wagons, involving no fewer than 16,000 horses (including those of the escort)) – a journey of 70 miles, during which the entire train would occupy as much as 15 miles of road. Not surprisingly the task of ensuring the safe conduct of this essential cargo was delegated to Cadogan. ('For God's sake be sure you do not risk the cannon,' Marlborough enjoined him in a letter from Warwick on 3 August.[3]) A French attempt to intercept the train was foiled. Under Cadogan's direction the convoy was delivered from Brussels to Menin in as little as six days, and the siege of Lille duly began in mid-August. It was conducted by Eugène's army with a circumvallation radius of nine miles, while Marlborough organized the covering operations and the re-supply convoys.

Provisions from England to Lille were now delivered via Zeeland and Ostend, a difficult route considering the enemy controlled all the waterways in the Ostend area. There was a large and vital convoy, due towards the end of September, led by Major General John Webb, whose escort was comprised of 6,000 Foot and a squadron of Horse. The Duc de Burgundy ordered General La Motte to intercept that convoy with an army composed of no fewer than 24,000 Horse and Foot and 12 cannons. When Webb became aware of La Motte's approach he was close to the village of Wynendael and he wisely ordered his men to lie flat and deployed his relatively small force to spring an ambush from a wood clearing, thus ensuring that his flanks were well covered and that his opponents must make a frontal attack. Saint-Simon gave, in his memoirs, a less than accurate account of the Wynendael affair, a version which doubtless reflected the universal French view of the action:

The enemy had formed an entrenched post at Winendal to cover the advance of their immense convoy. La Motte could think of nothing better than to attack this post, and did so with vigour; but Cadogan's defence was more vigorous still. La Motte's troops gave way; Cadogan sallied out and attacked in his turn; and, though his troops were not more than half so numerous as La Motte's, he beat him completely and drove him back in confusion. In the meantime the convoy arrived safely in Prince Eugène's camp, to the great joy of the besiegers, who were destitute of everything.[4]

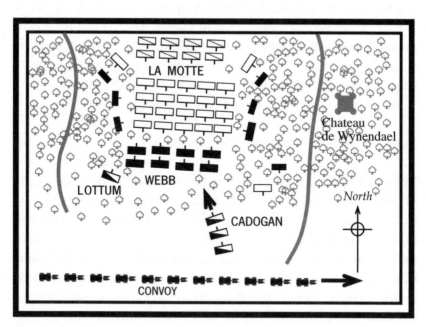

The Action at Wynendael

However, although it was Cadogan's intervention that ultimately saved the day, the major part of the glory should go to Webb and his men as that sound military observer, Captain Robert Parker, describes the action:

La Motte drew up his foot in nine lines and his horse in rear of them, and began to cannonade; this however did little execution, as Webb had ordered his men to lie flat on the ground while the cannon were firing. La Motte's foot advanced several times but were repulsed with considerable loss. The Duke, being informed of La Motte's design, ordered Major-General Cadogan to march with a good body of horse to reinforce Webb; he [Cadogan] upon hearing La Motte's cannon, hastened his march, and La Motte, on the first sight of his [Cadogan's] squadrons, immediately drew off with great precipitation, leaving all his cannon and a great many men killed and wounded behind him. In consequence of this action that great convoy arrived safe; and this in effect was the taking of Lille. Webb very deservedly acquired great honour and reputation by this gallant action; but then he spoyled all by making it the subject of his conversation on all occasions. This he should have left to fame which . . . does him infinitely greater honour than all his own vain boasting. And, after all, had not Cadogan come up with his squadrons it would be hard to say what might have been the consequence.[5]

Webb's touchiness was the cause of some embarrassment. Marlborough wrote to Godolphin, on 1 October, saying 'Webb and Cadogan have on this occasion, as they always will do, behaved themselves extremely well . . . If they had not succeeded, and our convoy had been lost the consequence must have been the raising of the siege next day.'[6] The unfortunate political postscript to the Wynendael episode was caused by a notice in *The London Gazette*, which gave all the credit for the salvation of the convoy to Cadogan.

Webb, who was jealous of both Marlborough and Cadogan, fed the Captain General's Tory opponents with the fabrication that the Captain General had deliberately put it about that Cadogan had been the only hero of the day. Marlborough, ever the diplomatic superior, and quick to recognize what damage such malice might provoke, wrote a warm letter of congratulation to Webb, had a paragraph to that effect inserted in his official dispatches,and recommended Webb to the Queen for promotion to Lieutenant General, which was immediately granted. Marlborough's letter to Webb told him that 'Mr Cadogan has just now arrived and has acquainted me with the success of the action you had yesterday in the afternoon against the body of troops commanded by M. de la Motte at Wynendael, which must be attributed chiefly to your conduct and resolution. You may assure yourself I shall do you justice at home.'[7] A masterpiece of tact! However, the Tories continued to make political capital out of the 'Cadogan accolade'.[8]

Although the victory of Wynendael and the safe arrival of Webb's convoy allowed the siege of Lille to continue, Parker cannot have meant to say, by that achievement, that the fortress was captured. Its ramparts were the most formidable of all, while there were no more gallant defenders than Boufflers' staunch division.There was still a long way to go.

The French response to the Allies' Portsmouth-Zeeland-Ostend route was to have the dykes cut and the land flooded around Ostend. However, the imaginative and ingenious Cadogan promptly had the fresh supplies of ammunition, and food etc, from England, packed in skins. He formed a fleet of flat-bottomed boats to carry those parcels to the besieging forces across the flooded land. He had several consignments delivered by that means. However, eventually the French responded by letting in more water and launching a flotilla of galleys, mounted with cannons, from which to attack Cadogan's supply boats. But that failed to stop further convoys. Coxe sums up the episode:

Communications from the
coast to Lille

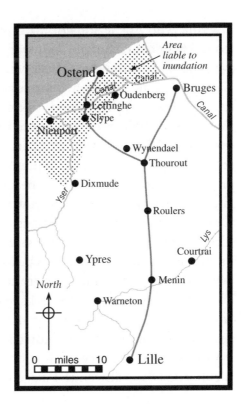

The ammunition was packed in skins, and conveyed in flat boats from Ostend to Leffingham, where it was received by carriages, mounted on high wheels, and conveyed to the camp. In this difficult task Cadogan distinguished himself, as he did on every occasion which required extraordinary diligence and activity, and the convoys were brought to safety, in spite of the hostile batteries and the incessant attacks of armed gallies.[9]

However, thereafter the unfortunate soldiers had to make do with four-days bread ration to last six days, and, of course, the programme of bombardment had to be reduced.The Allies began to dispatch parties to secure food from the already ransacked neighbouring Artois farms rather than let the army starve. (*'Nous avons ordonné a l'ordre ce matin, que les quatre jours de pain qui se livrent aujourd'hui aient a servir pour six jours,'* wrote the Captain General, *'et que l'officier ait soin de payer les deux autres jours en argent.'*[10])

Eugène, who had been wounded during the siege, was back in action by late September. Under his skilful direction the Allies took the town of Lille on 3 October forcing Boufflers into the citadel. A couple of weeks later the French prepared to draw off a proportion of the besiegers by moving against Brussels. But the attacking force, under command of the Elector of Bavaria, was badly mauled by a detachment from Lille, led by Cadogan, and the Elector was obliged to retreat. The citadel of Lille surrendered on 9 December, and, notwithstanding the fact that the European winter of 1708–09 was the severest for over a hundred years, the Allies went on to re-capture Ghent and Bruges early in the New Year.[10] 'Without them,' the Captain General had written, 'we can neither be quiet in our winter quarters or open with advantage the next campaign'.[11]

As at Oudenarde so at Lille surely no officer contributed more to the Allies' successes than William Cadogan. On 1 January 1709 he was promoted to lieutenant general. At 36 he must have been one of the youngest ever non-Royal officers to reach that rank.

Cadogan was probably aware of the approximate extent of the Captain General's cupidity. It must, indeed, have been the setting of that example of avarice by the greatest man in Europe that mainly encouraged Cadogan to extract whatever financial gain might be had from the war. But how soon did Marlborough's deputy know, one wonders, that, while the terms for the capitulation of Lille were negotiated, the Captain General wrote to his nephew, Berwick, suggesting that King Louis should be persuaded to ask for an armistice? The Captain General added that he would pledge his support for such a request on the understanding that he would receive a *douceur* of two million livres.[12] In London the Tories soon heard of this suggestion by their arch-enemy of a huge private bribe for himself. They were hell-bent on destroying Marlborough. Cadogan must have known that, if that happened, he would also be entirely reduced – at least temporarily.

Notes

1   Marlborough-Godolphin corres, no. 1033
2   WSC III, 384 (quoting from Goslinga's Memoirs)
3   Marlborough, Dispatches, IV, 144
4   Saint-Simon, *op cit*, III, 158
5   Chandler, *op cit*, 79–80; cf Coxe II, 318–20
6   GMT II, 372
7   Marlborough-Godolphin corres; Coxe II, 321
8   Thackeray, in his novel *The History of Henry Esmond*, has Tory Esmond as Webb's ADC; and, through him, gives boastful Webb a shining reputation, while portraying Marlborough as the villain of the episode. During the reign of George I Webb, being found guilty of militant Jacobitism, was dismissed from the army.
9   Coxe II, 322
10 Marlborough to the Comte de Rechteren, October 16, 1708; *Dispatches* IV, 263
11 GMT II, 373; The siege of Lille is described in Coxe II, 298–337; GMT, II, 368–73; WSC, III, 424–40
12 Berwick records this instance of his uncle's bid for a *douceur* in his *Memoires*, II, 34–35

14

Spying at Malplaquet

(1709)

It was not only in the southern Netherlands that 1708 proved a triumphant year for the Grand Alliance. Stanhope scored sucesses in Spain, and Victor Amadeus, Duke of Savoy, in Italy, while the Royal Navy captured Minorca and Sardinia. But, on England's home front the situation, in 1708–1709, was rather less happy. The Captain General's Duchess, who ruled the Queen's household, was now irredeemably unpopular with Anne, and that did nothing to help Marlborough, who also blotted his copybook by applying for the Captain Generalcy for life, a request that convinced many of the Tories more strongly than ever that he was making a bid to be dictator of Britain. The Queen, who had become increasingly disenchanted with the Whigs, even with her old friend Godolphin, refused Marlborough's request. Anne's cry on hearing of the victory of Oudenarde – 'Oh, my God, when will this bloodshed cease?' – was echoed by her people, who had grown cynical about the tax burden and the press gangs, many British citizens being even disgusted by the sight of a soldier's red coat. The nation was war-weary, a situation that did not suit ambitious Cadogan at all.

Of all the nations wanting peace France longed for that day most of all. Not only was her war machine in a state of exhaustion and her armies crippled, but the severe winter of 1708-1709 left most of the country's cattle frozen to death, her seed corn congealed in the ground and many thousands of her people dead or drastically reduced by famine and hypothermia. It was in these circumstances that, in March 1709, Louis sent a representative to discuss peace 'preliminaries' at the Hague, Cadogan being among the representatives of the Alliance. The French monarch thought, with his habitual duplicity, that he might deal with the Allies separately, but none of them would submit to having wedges driven between them by their common enemy. The March talks broke down but, watched closely by Cadogan, were reopened in May.

For Britain there was then a French undertaking to recognize both Anne as Queen and the Electress of Hanover as her successor, while Louis agreed to exile the Pretender, the Chevalier St George (but had little intention of doing so). The fortifications of Dunkirk were to be destroyed and British sovereignty of Newfoundland and Hudson Bay admitted. The French also agreed to the Hapsburg claimant to Spain as 'Charles III', and gave the Dutch generous terms apropos the border fortresses. There was, however, one article to which Louis would not consent. It was that Philip of Anjou should be removed from Spain. How, asked de Torcy, Louis' chief representative at the Hague 'preliminaries', could the King of France be expected to dismiss a grandson who now loved Spain and was loved by the Spanish people, who were fighting a war on his behalf? To which the deputies from the Allies enquired, in so many words, 'What is the good of your master agreeing to relinquish Spain to Charles of Austria if Philip, supported by an army, remains on the throne in Madrid?'

'Very well, if war there must be,' replied Louis, notwithstanding the plight of his country and his armed forces, despite the superiority of the Grand Alliance in numbers, weapons, equipment, sustenance and morale, 'I would prefer to wage it against my enemies than against my children!' (In fact it may well have been Madame de Maintenon, who now ruled the King, heart and mind, who made the decision.) Anyhow Louis dispatched Maréchal Villars as commander-in-chief to the Netherlands frontier, while thousands of young Frenchmen, on the point of starvation, flocked to the regimental colours and thus to the bread wagons that followed them. But that bread was all oat and rye and a very limited amount of that; there was practically no wheat available. There was now a growing mood of rebellion against the dictatorship of France, the joint dictatorship of Louis and Madame de Maintenon. As for the Allies they would live to regret that lost opportunity of a favourable peace, a peace for which they had also fervently yearned.[1]

The Royal Navy, being in command of both the Channel and the Mediterranean, succeeded in blockading the French ports.The Grand Alliance was now intent upon marching to Paris and dictating terms at Versailles. And, in the words of Sergeant Millner, the Allies 'therefore vigorously prosecuted or proceeded on with the War, to bring the French to that with Force of Arms that they could not do otherwise by Fair Means and Terms; and for that end the Duke and Prince Eugène instantly caused the Allied Troops ... to assemble and took the Field about Gaver [Gavre] on the West Side of the Scheld, opposite to, and near unto Oudenard'.[2]

Maréchal Claude-Louis-Hector, Duc de Villars, a rough and tough braggart and liar, poseur and bully, but also a resourceful and energetic commander and brilliant tactician, one beloved by his troops (of whom there were soon 80,000) set about preparing his lines of defence between St Venant and Douai, the 'Lines of La Bassée'. Was it not better to die for France, the veterans as well as the new recruits were asking, than from starvation?

In opposition to the Captain General, who favoured a

northern route (via Ypres) into France, Eugène and the Dutch Deputies opted for the southern way, via Tournai and Mons. The Allies duly invested Tournai in the last week of June and the siege opened on 10 July, Cadogan's corps being part of the attacking force. (He was, as usual, also responsible for provisioning the whole army.) Not content with that, Cadogan 'traversed at the peril of his life, disguised as a labourer, a large section of Villars' front'.[3] Given another wet summer, following the harsh winter, 1709 was not a happy campaigining year. Marlborough wrote home during the siege to say that

> All the wheat is killed everywhere that we have seen or heard of. It grieves my heart to see the sad condition all the poor country people are in for want of bread; they have not the same countenances they had in other years . . . It is not to be imagined the ill weather we have, insomuch that the poor soldiers are up to their knees in dirt which gives me the spleen to a degree that makes me very uneasy and consequently makes me languish for retirement . . . in all likelihood we shall not find forage to enable us to make a long campaign and that is what I fear the French know as well as we.

The town of Tournai gave in on 28 July, but the citadel did not surrender so easily, chiefly on account of the mine-filled tunnels surrounding it. 'There is not a foot of ground,' wrote Colonel Revett of the First Guards (and soon to be killed), 'that is not undermined and casemated,'[5] while the Cameronians' second-in-command, Major Blackadder, reported that 'our siege goes on slowly and in the dark, underground'.[6] Private Deane thought that 'there is as yet but little Signe of surrendering for the mines are so invincible strong that the Place seems . . . to be impregnable'.[7] One day Corporal Bishop saw, from his trench 'a prodigious Blaze, and it ascended up into the air like into a Cloud. We could distinguish they had sprung one of their grand mines . . . At our return I found there was almost a whole Regiment of Scotch Hollanders[8] blown up. There was likewise a kind of report spread through all our army that it was their intention to blow us all up.'[9] The citadel did not surrender until 3 September.[10] The Allies then turned their attention to Mons.

That same day, 3 September, Orkney with twenty squadrons and a unit of grenadiers set forth to seize Saint-Ghislain, which proved too stoutly defended for them. However, Prince Frederick of Hesse-Cassel was sent 10 miles further east to surround Mons. Cadogan followed him after dark at the head of forty squadrons and, within three days, Mons was invested. Cadogan then rejoined the main army.

Villars, anticipating that the Allies' offensive would indeed steer via Mons, concentrated his main effort astride the Trouée [gap] d'Aulnois, just north-east of the village of Malplaquet, 12 miles south-west of Mons. The Trouée was flanked on the French left by the Forêt de Laignières, with the Bois de Taisnières adjacent to the gap on that side, and the Bois de Laignières on the right of the gap. Villars filled the open ground, the Trouée, with mutually supporting redans, batteries of field guns and mortars being hidden on either side of it. His woodland defences were composed of trenchs dug in triple depth, with well constructed parapets and *abbatis*, trees stripped of their foliage, the trunks and branches sharpened and facing the enemy. More cannons were sited to sweep the open plain ahead. The French cavalry, which were boosted by an extra 30 squadrons sent up from the Rhine, were deployed behind the redans, in front of Malplaquet. Old Maréchal Boufflers was up from Paris to command the right wing.

Marlborough and Eugène, with 90,000 under command, poised at the gateway to France, had reason to feel confident. They imagined the French would finally be reduced by famine. Leaving Mons blockaded by 30,000 troops, they marched south-westwards. On 11 September 'the Two Princes' climbed the windmill at Sart and took out their spyglasses. First the Germans, Imperialists and British would attack on the right under Eugène. Half an hour later the Dutch, with their attached Highland brigade, would assault on the left, into the Bois de Laignières. Then, when the French had reinforced their (duly subdued, so it was imagined) woodland wings from their formidable central redans, Lord Orkney would sweep across the Trouée d'Aulnois with his 15 battalions and six squadrons. The day before the battle Cadogan had a dialogue with the French, as recounted by Saint-Simon:

A few officers, apparently of no high rank, but probably well selected, approached our entrenchments and entered in conversation with the outposts. They told our officers that General Cadogan was not far off, and would be glad to speak to one of our generals. The Marquis de Charost . . . declined and sent word to the officers to withdraw; but, at this moment, Albergotti came up, and showed himself less punctilious. He allowed Cadogan to advance up to a certain point, where he met him, each [of them being] accompanied by a few officers. Cadogan, after many compliments, began talking about the prospects of peace; Albergotti replied that he was sorry Villars was not there as he would have been glad to discuss the subject . . . The rumour that terms of peace were being discussed spread rapidly through our lines, and came to the ears of Villars, who was much displeased at a conference of this sort being held without his orders, and sent word to Albergotti to put an end to it. The enemy's officers, however, lingered so long that some cannon-shot had to be fired over them before they would retire. During this ridiculous colloquy some of them had been busy examining our position and taking sketches of different parts of our entrenchments; and, next day, they profited only too well by the knowledge thus acquired. We heard of this artifice after the battle from some prisoners of war.[11]

Cadogan next galloped back and forth, ensuring that the replenishments of ammunition were brought forward, that aides-de-camps were apportioned, that guns were sited in their ordained places, that formation commanders were sure of their orders (in the confusion of several languages). The commanders of his regimental scouts, sent forward to test the defences, now reported back to him. Cadogan relayed their findings to the Captain General, then he went forth on foot, dressed in his enthusiasm once again as a peasant, in order to take a closer look.

The Allies formed up, that fatal morning of 11 September, concealed by a thick mist. At about seven the sun came through to reveal their multinational, multicoloured host, the battalions and squadrons of those several nations in their symmetrical ranks, bayonets and swords flashing in the early light, regimental standards, pennants and other flags held colourfully and proudly aloft, horses whinnying nervously, orders shouted, some gun crews limbering their field-pieces, some already in action. For, as soon as the gunners of both sides (the Allied artillery being now under command of Colonel Armstrong) could aim with precision, the cannonade began in earnest. Graphic Colonel de la Colonie was a witness for the enemy:

> As soon as this dense column [the division commanded by Count Lottum] appeared in the avenue [the Trouée] fourteen guns were promptly brought up in front our brigade, almost in line with the regiment of Garde Francaise. The fire of this battery was terrific, and hardly a shot missed its mark . . . The cannon-shot plunged into the enemy's infantry and carried off whole ranks at a time.[12]

The Allies' right wing began their advance through the Bois de Taisnières and were soon engaged in a fierce fire-fight against young soldiers pathetically undernourished but willing to sell

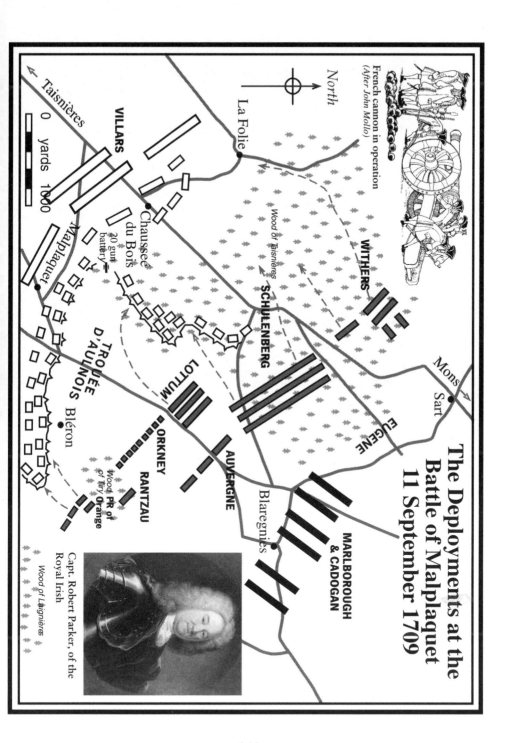

The Deployments at the Battle of Malplaquet 11 September 1709

North

French cannon in operation
(After John Mollo)

Taisnières

0   yards   1000

VILLARS

La Folie

Malplaquet

Chaussée du Bois

20 gun battery

WITHERS

Wood of Taisnières

SCHULENBERG

Mons

Sart

EUGENE

LOTTUM

TROUÉE D'AULNOIS

Bléron

ORKNEY

RANTZAU

AUVERGNE

Wood PR of of Tiry Orange

Blaregnies

MARLBOROUGH
& CADOGAN

Capt. Robert Parker, of the
Royal Irish

Wood of Laignières

141

their lives dearly for the love of France. *Vive le Roi! Vive le Maréchal de Villars!* they shouted[13] as they aimed their muskets across their trenches' parapets and hewn trees fashioned into *abbatis*. A smoking inferno ensued, thunderous cannon and musket fire in the thick woodland, men killed, men grievously wounded.

On the left wing where the Dutch and Highlanders next marched forth the casualty rate was even higher, whole ranks being torn down by the French cannons' grape and ball before they had even reached the Bois de Laignières. When the young Prince of Orange's horse fell dead he cheered his musketeers forward on foot. In the space of 30 minutes the Dutch and their Highland brigade lost 5,000 soldiers, until the Prince of Hesse and his squadrons drove back a French counter-attack. The Captain General then sent Cadogan to order the Dutch general, Count Tilly, to retire and re-form.

Corporal Matthew Bishop, a member of Argyll's division on the right wing, recalled that the French

> returned our volley with great success. I may say it for my Right and Left hand Men were shot Dead, and in falling had almost thrown me down, for I could scarce prevent my falling among the dead Men. Then I said to the second rank: 'Come my Boys, make Good the Front'. With that they drew up. Then I said: 'Never Fear, We shall have better Luck the next Throw'. But I just saved my Word for my Right Hand Man was shot through the Head and the Man who followed me was shot through the groin, and I escaped All, though nothing but the Providence of God could protect Me.'[14]

Inside that wood, where Bishop commanded his section and where the fighting was thickest, some 7,000 soldiers now lay dead, or so badly wounded they could not walk. Eugène received a musket-ball close to his ear, but would not have the wound tended. 'If we are to die here,' he exclaimed 'it is not worth dressing. If we win there will be time tonight.'[15]

As 'the Two Princes' had predicted, Villars, (who was now painfully wounded in the knee) had been extracting more and more units from the Trouée and its closely guarded redans to reinforce his faltering woodland wings. It was at this juncture that old Boufflers assumed command. Now was the moment for Cadogan to give the word for General Withers to lead his division (which had arrived on the scene late, from Tournai) through the western edge of the Forêt de Taisnières, to outflank the French left as its horn withdrew. The Cameronians were advancing in the Trouée with Lord Orkney's division which was now signalled forward by Cadogan. Major Blackadder, the Cameronians' second-in-command, wrote that

> It was the most deliberate, solemn and well-ordered Battle I ever saw, a Noble and fine Disposition and as nobly executed ... I never had a more pleasant Day in my Life. I was kept in perfect Peace; my Mind stayed trusting in God. Every man was at his Post, and I never saw troops engage with more Cheerfulness ... Providence ordered that our Regiment was not further engaged than being cannonaded which was, indeed, the most severe that ever our Regiment suffered.[16]

Cranstoun, the Cameronians' commanding officer being killed by a round shot on his chest, Blackadder assumed command. For the most part Orkney's battalions occupied the front trenches in the Trouée d'Aulnois which had been held by the recently withdrawn French infantry, while Cadogan ordered cannons to be advanced to take on the mass of enemy cavalry. Then the Allies' Horse galloped between and around the redans and a furious contest between the respective *armes blanches* ensued. By this time Withers' division was grappling with the French units on the enemy's extreme left. In this context Captain Parker, of Ireland's

Royal Regiment, gives a description of battalion firearms tactics:

> Colonel Kane, who was then at the head of the Regiment having drawn us up, and formed our platoons, advanced gently towards [the enemy], with the six platoons of our first fire made ready. When we had advanced within a hundred paces of them they gave us a fire of one of their Ranks: whereupon we halted, and returned them the Fire of our Six Platoons at once; and immediately made ready the six Platoons of our second Fire, and advanced upon them again. They then gave us the Fire of another Rank, and we returned them a Second Fire, which made them shrink; however they gave us the Fire of a third Rank after a scattering manner, and then retired into the Wood in great Disorder: on which we sent our third Fire after them, and saw them no more.[17]

Parker goes on to explain the reasons for the British superiority. First, the weight of the ammunition: whereas the French muskets carried ball-shot of 24 to the pound, the British firelocks' ball was 16 to the pound. Secondly, the British inflicted much greater execution with their well-drilled platoon firing as opposed to the French practice of firing by ranks. By remarkable coincidence, Parker's opponents, in the incident he describes, were the men of the French Royal Irish Regiment (some of the 'Wild Geese').[18]

Meanwhile the cavalry battle was fought – mostly between the redans and the villages of Malplaquet and Taisnières – on very even terms, with 65-year-old Boufflers commanding the Maison du Roi in person, until, late in the afternoon, the French cavaliers were scattered and Boufflers led his defeated army, unmolested, south-westwards to camps at Le Quesnoy and Valenciennes.

But Malplaquet was no more than a technical victory for the Allies, in that they finished the battle in occupation of the ground previously occupied by the enemy. They were too exhausted and crippled for pursuit. They suffered far more casualties than their opponents (about 17,000 as against the French 11,000). The commanding officer of the (Allies') Royal Irish described Malplaquet as 'the most desperate and bloody attack and battle that had been fought in the memory of men'.[19] Blackadder (who was to be accorded substantive command of the Cameronians in October) wrote that 'in all my life I have not seen the Dead lie so thick as they were in some Places about the Retrenchments . . . The Dutch have suffered most in the Battle of any . . . It is a Wonder to me the British escape so cheap, who are the most heaven-daring Sinners in this army. But God's judgements are a great depth.'[20] (The British casualties were no more than 600.)

The Imperialist officer, Count Mérode-Westerloo (who had changed sides after Ramillies), explained that the delay in waiting for the division under command of General Withers to come up from Tournai was the cause of the French getting off relatively lightly: 'All . . . might have gone well had this [the Allies' attack] been executed at the right moment, but in order to permit a reinforcement to reach us we afforded M Villars and Marshal Boufflers . . . three whole days in which to entrench themselves to the teeth in an almost impregnable position, thus enabling him to make the best dispositions and manoeuvres possible.'[21]

Cadogan, who had been in the full heat of the battle from start to finish, now returned to his administrative roles. He had the men's rations brought from Brussels to Enghein, where they were distributed to the regimental wagons. He then had the empty transport used to evacuate those wounded who were fit enough to withstand the jolting journey. Regarding the enemy wounded the Captain General wrote to Secretary of State Henry Boyle that 'Upon viewing the field of battle on Thursday, and finding great numbers of French Officers and Soldiers who had crept into the neighbouring Houses and in the Woods, wounded in a miserable Condition, for want of Assistance, I wrote to both the Marshals [Villars and Boufflers] to acquaint them with it, that they might send a number of Waggons to fetch them away, and told them I would order Lieutenant-General Cadogan, with two hundred horse, to Bavay to meet such Officer as they should send with the like number of Men to agree on the manner of carrying them off. Accordingly the Chevalier de Luxembourg, a lieutenant-general, came yesterday morning, and they having concerted together we left commisssaries to take account of all that should be found for which two days are allowed them and they are agreed to be our Prisoners of War.[22]

One of those killed at Malplaquet was Cadogan's brother-in-law, Lt Colonel Sir Thomas Prendergast (who had married William's sister, Penelope). Eighteen months after the battle Cadogan's mother (née Bridget Waller) wrote a long and furious letter to Marlborough, who had not, apparently supported her claim to a pension for her daughter. There were, of course, no official pensions in those days. The following extracts throw some light on the influence required to gain compensation for widows and their children:

> I did not think itt posible a person your Graces goodnes cld so easily give up yr charitable solicitation to the Queen in the behalf of so faithfull a servants sister as Mr Cadogan's who I am sure wld sacrifice his life and fortune to yr Graces comands: the hopes of seeing my son here being over compleats our misfortune . . . he being exeycutor to Sir Thomas Prendergast itt was absolutely necessary for him to have com to take care, in the selling the estate which is now doing to pay debts and in his absence my dauter hath no frend to assist or defend her from the injustice of Sir Thomas's bro who resents her no doubt, so that she and her six children are not only left begars, but harassed . . . yr Grace had never used any officer as poor Sir

Thomas Prendergasts family ... I am yr Graces miserable unfortunate faithful obedient Humble servant. B Cadogan.[23]

The siege of Mons began towards the end of September. Cadogan, who reverted to the role of formation commander for that operation and 'whose duties took him always into the most dangerous places' (as Winston Churchill observed)[24] was wounded again.[25] In a letter re-emphasizing how strongly the Captain General leaned upon the talent and energy of the sturdy young man who combined the roles of Chief of Staff, Quartermaster General, Director of Intelligence and formation commander, Marlborough wrote to Sarah on the 26th saying that

> After a greate deal of trouble we have at last gott some Part of our Artillerie from Bruxelles so that we open'd last Night the Trenches where poor Cadogan was wounded in the neck. I hope he will do well, but til he recovers it will oblige me to do many Things, by which I shall have but little Rest. I was with him this morning when they drest his wound. As he is very fatt [heavily built] there greatest aprehension is growing feaverish. We must have patience for two or three dressings before the Surjeans can give their Judgment. I hope in God he will do well, for I can intierly depend upon him.[26]

The Captain General's right-hand man made a speedy recovery and Mons capitulated on 20 October. Meanwhile James Brydges told Cadogan that he hoped 'it will prove a Warning to you how you expose yourself on such like occasions again'. Be that as it may, he and Brydges now resumed their nefarious monetary dealings. Cadogan was also back in harness as Intelligence Chief as this message from the Hague to the Whigs' representative at the peace negotiations, Lord Townshend, indicates:

December 9, 1709. I have to send your Excellency copies of two Intercepted Letters which may to give you some light into the State of Affairs and present Disposition of the French Court. I am afraid that the Person who passed lately by this Place under the name (?) à Jourdière was Monsr de Puisiquex, but I have not been able to learn who it was who came from Holland to meet him at Antwerp. There is no manner of news here, everything is very quiet on the Frontier and great Numbers of Deserters come in dayly.[27]

Next, a respite with his family was, as Cadogan tells Brydges, interrupted by 'my Lord Duke sending me back with the greatest haste, to take care of forwarding our preparations for the [1710] campaign'.[28]

Notes

1 Coxe II, 363–416; GMT II, 396–404; WSC IV, 494–557
2 Journal, *op cit*, 258
3 WSC, IV, 569
4 *Ibid*, 576–77
5 GMT III, 7
6 Blackadder, *op cit*, 343
7 Deane, *op cit*
8 A Scots brigade was attached to the Dutch corps
9 Bishop, 80–81; cf WSC IV, 579–80
10 Coxe II, 417–27
11 Saint-Simon, *op cit*, III, pp 341–42
12 De la Colonie *op cit*, 338
13 Coxe III, *op cit*
14 Bishop, *op cit*, 211
15 WSC IV, 613; cf Nicholas Henderson, *Prince Eugène of Savoy*, 173
16 Blackadder, *op cit*, 350; WSC IV, 619–20
17 Chandler, *op cit*, 88–89
18 *Ibid*, 89. 'Among the latter [wounded]', said Parker, 'was one Lieutenant O'Sullivan who told us the battalion we engaged was the Royal Regiment of Ireland'.
19 Kane, *op cit*, 851
20 Blackadder, *op cit*, 350–51

21 Chandler, *op cit*, 215
22 Marlborough, *Dispatches IV*, 599–600
23 These extracts are printed by kind permission of Lord Cadogan
24 WSC IV, 635
25 His ADC, Colonel Thomas Foxon, was killed in the same action
26 WSC IV, 635–36
27 BL Add MS 38500, f 144.
28 Huntington, *op cit*, 22

15

Perfidious Albion[1]

(1709–1711)

Now cannon smoke fills all the sky,
And through the gloomy wood,
From every Trench the bougres fly,
Besmear'd with Dust and Blood,
While valour's Palm is ours in fight,
And Mons to terms we bring,
Let bragging Boufflers vainly write
False wonder to the King.

Monsieur, Monsieur, leave off Spain.
To think to hold it is in Vain,
Thy Warriors are too few.
Then without more ado
Be Wise and Strait
Call home little Anjou.[2]

Following the bloodbath of Malplaquet those verses were set to music and chanted by sanguine Whigs, who, in stating the British case in the peace negotiations, were still, when the talks re-opened at Geertruidenberg in March 1710, insistent upon their preposterous Article 37, by which Louis would be obliged to send a French army to remove Philip of Anjou from Spain. As for Cadogan, who had a place at that table, he imagined that one more successful campaign would compel Louis to make peace on the Allies' terms (and that the continued fighting would further assist his shady financial dealings). He wrote to James Brydges on 26 March as follows:

> I received the honour of yours . . . at the Hague. Which I had not time to acknowledge from thence. My Lord Duke sending me back with the greatest haste, to take care of forwarding our preparations for the Campaign, that are so advanced as everything will be ready against the 13th of April next. The troops have orders to march out of garrison at that time and the whole army will be formed the 18th. . . . Before leaving the Hague, I took measures with Mr Cardonnel for his writing to you early . . . what passes in relation to the Peace . . . if the negotiations should ever be continued, yet the Army's taking the field, and all the wars going on, will, I am persuaded, *occasion the falling of the best funds, and in my opinion that will be the time to employ one's money* [author's italics]. For undoubtedly such is the condition of France that we must have a Peace on our own terms before the end of the campaign, or we shall pierce into Champagne and Picardy, which is an extremity the King of France will hardly wait for. There is but one town of consequence to stop us [Douai] and we shall begin with the siege of it, before the enemy, for want of magazines can bring together such a body of troops as may be able to oppose our undertaking, or disturb us by a diversion.[3]

Cadogan's days at the Hague were temporarily over. He was replaced, in his diplomatic functions there, by Lord Orrery[4], presumably to placate the Dutch, and was soon once again in the thick of siege warfare. The Army of the Netherlands took the French frontier fortress of Douai at the end of June and went on to capture Béthune, Aire and St Venant between August and November, but they could not bring the French to open battle, Louis' commander-in-chief, on that front, Villars, playing an evasive game, otherwise contenting himself with harrassing the Allies' communications. The Allies' losses in this campaign were very heavy and the conditions deplorable, 'the trenches being so verry dirty and miserable for the men, who could neither sitt nor lye to rest themselves,' said Private Deane of the siege of Aire, 'but was obleidged to stand all ways come life or death.'[5]

Cadogan's optimism in 1710 regarding the prospect of another great victory, along with his hope of a triumphant peace, proved to be ill-founded. Nor was any of the news from London good for his aspirations. Everything now augured well for the Tories, whose leader, Robert Harley, 'Robin the Trickster', saw himself on the path to power. The Queen no longer trusted Godolphin, nor the Marlboroughs. Her Tory-inclined Bedchamber Woman, Abigail Masham (née Hill) foreseeing Sarah Marlborough's downfall, was (like Abigail's cousin Harley) waiting in the wings. The nation was largely fed up with what the Tories now called 'the Whigs' War', weary of the tax burden, the seemingly interminable recruiting, the rolls of dead and wounded, the exorbitant food prices.

Another harbinger of Whig defeat was a crypto-Jacobite Tory parson called Henry Sacheverell, who, for a sermon before the Lord Mayor of London, delivered on the anniversary of the Gunpowder Plot in 1709, took as his text 'In perils among false bretheren' implicating, in particular, Godolphin, who, according to Sacheverell, had betrayed the Church. At the same time the parson denounced the Revolution of 1688 along with the 1701 Act of Settlement. The Whig Government impeached and thus, unwittingly, martyred him and made him a national hero. The Commons found Sacheverell guilty by 69 votes to 52 on 23 March 1710. He received a derisory sentence, which made the Whigs look ridiculous. Brydges, in a letter dated 7 April, informed Cadogan that 'This last prosecution of Sacheverell . . . hath raised a very great ferment in the Kingdom, set all pens pro and con at work and fetched up addresses from all parts of the kingdom. There is one to be presented on Thursday next to the Queen from the City of London which we are much surprised at.' [Brydges and his Whig friends fondly believed the City to be largely Whiggish]. Brydges goes on to tell Cadogan that 'his Grace, the Duke of Argyle hath had the Garter given him,'[6] which was perhaps a further snub for Marlborough by the Queen. For, although Argyll[7] was a competent general, he was no friend of the Captain General's, whom Argyll believed to be prolonging the war for his own benefit. And he hated Cadogan. Argyll was soon to be appointed to the Spanish command.

On 13 April the Tory Duke of Shrewsbury replaced the Marquis of Kent as Lord Chamberlain. Brydges wrote to Cadogan on 18 April that 'The Tories are very high upon it and give out that 'tis but the first step of what the Queen intends and that there's to be a new Parliament . . . 'tis industriously given out that my Lord Treasurer [Godolphin] knew nothing of it, till an express from the Queen brought him a letter on the road, as he was returning from Newmarket.'[8]. Brydges wrote to Cadogan again on 20 May with the news that Marlborough's son-in-law, Sunderland, a *bête noire* of the Queen's, was about to be dismissed as Secretary of State. 'People's expectations are very great what course our friends will take in this ticklish point . . . But if they continue in, they must quit the Junto, or act not in concert with the rest of the Queen's ministry,' he adds.[9]

Marlborough was well aware that the new parliament would be overwhelmingly Tory and was anxious that Cadogan should retain Woodstock. On 16 August he wrote a coded letter to his duchess:

I beg there may be no alteration made at the election of Woodstock; for I intend Cadogan shall come to England with me. 39 [Marlborough] shall expect more assistance in 87 [Parliament] from 197 [Cadogan] and 202 [Macartney] than any other members, for they have both honesty and courage to speak the truth; so that I do earnestly desire that these two men may be chose preferable to all others, with which I desire you will lose no time in acquainting 38 [Godolphin] and that I beg if of him as a particular favour that he would take care of securing an election for 202, for 39 does think it absolutely necessary to have him early in 108 [England] this winter, of which he will take care,[10]

Although Lieutenant General Cadogan was almost totally preoccupied either with organizing the administrative needs of the 90,000-strong myriad army or with holding down substantial commands at the various sieges, he must have been duly shaken by these unwelcome omens, none of which were to prove false or unfounded. In June Secretary of State Sunderland was sacked. In August the Queen dismissed Godolphin, giving his place to Harley and, in September Cardonnel was replaced as Secretary-at-War. The general election in December resulted in a Tory landslide. Harley and St John were now solidly at the helm (the first as Lord Treasurer, the second as Secretary of State). In January 1711 Sarah Marlborough lost her appointment as the Queen's Groom of the Stole and First Lady of the Bedchamber to the Duchess of Somerset, while Abigail Masham was made keeper of the Privy Purse. Colonel Kane did not mince his words:

> The Queen, soon after the death of her honest Bosom-friend, the Prince of Denmark, was so infatuated as to change her old trusty Ministry, and brought in a set of vile Creatures, entirely in the Pretender's Interest, who overturned all that had hitherto been doing: and tho' France was reduced to her last Extremity, and not able to hold out another Campagne, yet these perfidious Men prevailed so far on the silly [gullible] Queen, as

to court France for a Peace, to bring in their beloved Chevalier.[11]

In Spain in December Stanhope suffered a resounding defeat at Brihuega at the hands of Vendôme, which gave France dominion over most of the country, including all Castile. There was no removing 'little Anjou' now. Cadogan would have resigned himself to the fact that the Tories were bound to reduce the Whigs' previous peace demands drastically, to the benefit of France. Meanwhile the mischievous cleric Jonathan Swift was writing in his newly-founded, Tory-backed *Examiner*, of the Captain General's 'gross avarice', and that, too, must have struck an unpleasant chord with William Cadogan, the embezzler. His anxiety is reflected in the following sentences penned to 'Dear Judge' from Brussels on 12 January 1711, 'I shall be infinitly glad . . . if my Lord Dukes presence in England has the effect his Friends desire and the Publiq wants, but I am afraid the Disease is too far gone for a cure, as to my self I am endeavouring to grow insensible and resolve to be for the future as unconcerned as a Stoick, and as resigned as a Passive Obedience man. I hope to wait on you very soon at the Hague.'[12]

Alas 'the disease' was indeed already 'too far gone' and the Grand Alliance army of the Netherlands suffered two serious setbacks before the start of the 1711 campaign. Secretary of State St John had five battalions removed from the Netherlands command for a hare-brained scheme for the capture of Quebec. And when the Austrian Emperor Joseph died of smallpox in April, his heir being his brother Charles (the Hapsburg pretender to the Spanish throne), the authorities in Vienna envisaged potential unrest and, perhaps, a French invasion. They recalled Eugène and his army. Those reductions rendered the French army under Villars, on the Franco-Flanders border, superior by over 15,000 men.

Villars, arguably France's finest tactician and most

155

resourceful general since Turenne, occupied a particularly formidable defensive line in 1711. It was based, just within the French border, on canals, earthworks, swamps and acres of inundation, linked by the Rivers Canche, Scarpe, Sensée and Scheldt, and reaching from the English Channel eastwards to Valenciennes and Condé on the Scheldt. As though to mock Marlborough, Villars called these lines *Ne Plus Ultra*. (That had been the Captain General's reported remark when shown a new scarlet coat, which, in his opinion could not be surpassed in elegance.) The French *maréchal's* aim was to lure the Allies onto these lines, which bristled with cannon and behind which, at the most vulnerable points, his infantry were well dug in. Villars even wrote a letter to Louis, for which he was later mocked, saying that he had enticed the Allies onto the *Non Plus Ultra* lines and was about to smash them. It was early July 1711. The Allies were determined to seize the Scheldt fortress of Bouchain; and, from that base, to march down the road to Paris and then dictate peace terms. To achieve that they must cross the Sensée in complete secrecy, for, as the Captain General was well aware, such an operation was unlikely to secure the sanction of the Dutch Deputies. No officer below the rank of lieutenant general would be informed of the real intentions. There was a causeway over the marshy Sensée which was guarded by the well defended fort of Arleux. If the Allies were to take and demolish Arleux clearly Villars would shift the emphasis of his superior defences to that point and the element of surprise would be lost. The Captain General decided, therefore, to trick Villars into demolishing it. On 6 July he sent a detachment to seize and occupy the fort, leaving only a skeleton party to defend it.

By now it seemed clear to the *maréchal* that Arleux was of the greatest importance to the Allies, that Marlborough wanted the fortress in order to prevent a French incursion there. So Villars dispatched a force under the Duc de Montesquiou to retake it, which they did on 22 July. Meanwhile the Captain General, by

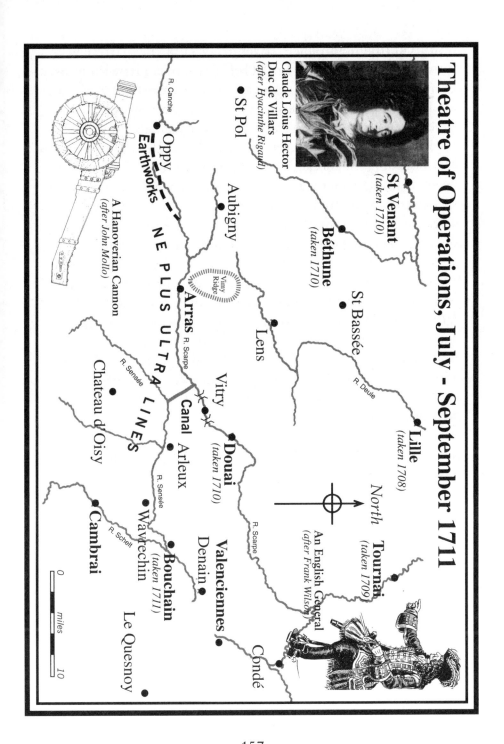

Theatre of Operations, July – September 1711

Claude Loius Hector
Duc de Villars
(after Hyacinthe Rigaud)

St Venant
(taken 1710)

R. Canche

St Pol

Oppy
Earthworks

A Hanoverian Cannon
(after John Mollo)

Aubigny

Béthune
(taken 1710)

Viry
Ridge

St Bassée

N E   P L U S   U L T R A   L I N E S

Arras R. Scarpe

Lens

R. Deule

Lille
(taken 1708)

R. Sensée

Vitry

Chateau d'Oisy

Canal

Arleux

R. Sensée

Douai
(taken 1710)

North
(after Frank Wilson)

An English General

R. Scarpe

Tournai
(taken 1709)

Cambrai

R. Schelt

Wavrechin

Denain

Valenciennes

Bouchain
(taken 1711)

Le Quesnoy

Condé

0   miles   10

157

way of further deception, led his army 25 miles westwards, to a point near Arras. As usual Cadogan was allotted the most important roles in this campaign, the first being to lead 30 squadrons and a contingent of grenadiers to rescue the Arleux garrison. But, deliberately, he arrived too late.[13] Villars now did what Marlborough intended. Because the Allies had greatly strengthened the Arleux fortifications Villars dismantled them (and was duly mystified by the Allies' westward march).

Bolstering his cover plan Marlborough put on a morose face and hazy eyes, which took in the French when reported by their spies, as well as his own side. They all attributed this strange demeanour as being a softness in the head, or a fury, owing to the treatment he had received from the Queen and Tories, along with dismay at the dismissal of his Duchess and the loss of Eugène and of the British battalions of which St John had deprived them. Villars, having hastened to keep parallel with the Allies, eventually concentrated his main strength west of Arras, within cannon-shot of the Allies, who were now convinced that their chief would lead them into a bloodbath far worse than Malplaquet.

As though to endorse their worst fears the Captain General next deployed his army for battle and, attended by his divisional commanders, rode to the front of the regimental lines, pointing ostentatiously every now and then at the enemy positions which, eyewitness Captain Parker informs us, 'were very strong and high and crowded and men and cannon . . . My Lord Marlborough still continued in a sullen, dissatisfied humour, and, nothwithstanding that Villars was so strongly posted, he seemed determined to attack him'.[14] To quote Coxe, the Captain General 'explained to the several commanders the direction of the columns which each was to lead to the intended attack'.[15] Kane was one of those commanders. He wrote:

'This he [Marlborough] spoke openly in the hearing of all about him, and, as it were, with a confidence of success; when at the same time, everyone with him was surprised at this rash and dangerous undertaking, and believed it proceeded from the affront which Villars had put upon him, and the ill-treatment he had of late from the Queen and the Ministry, which had now made him desperate.[16]

'The Duke's countenance was now cleared up [Parker takes up the narrative] and . . . he pointed out to the army general officers the manner in which the army was to be drawn up . . . In short he talked more than his friends about him thought was discreet, considering that Villars had spyes at his very elbow . . . Soon after the Duke returned to Camp, he gave orders that the army should prepare for Battle.'[17]

Triumphant Villars sent an express to Louis to say that he had at last brought the Allies to battle on the *Ne Plus Ultra*, another claim for which he was to be severely ridiculed. 'However, the Duke was no sooner returned to camp [recalls Kane] but Cadogan slipt privately away taking with him only forty Hussars . . . At length Tattoo beats, and before it had done, Orders came to strike our Tents immediately, and in less than half an Hour the whole army was on their March to the Left . . . with a full Moon and fair Weather . . . About break of Day the Duke received an Express from Cadogan that he and Lieutenant General Hompesch had, a little before One, passed the Causey [Causeway] of Arleux without Opposition, and were actually in Possession of the Enemy Lines. When Villars's spyes told him of our Army being on their march to the Left he believed it to be a feint of the Duke's to draw him off from the Post he was in and did not stir from thence 'til he heard of Cadogan's passing the Lines at Arleux . . .'[18]

The Anglo-Dutch force thus won the race, their main army arriving easily in time to reinforce Cadogan and Hompesch. When Villars himself eventually arrived on the scene he very narrowly escaped arrest, all his escort being captured. To achieve their mission the Anglo-Dutch army covered 39 miles, intersected by several marshy streams, in 10 hours which, especially considering the weights carried by the Foot – their accoutrements, together with their flintlocks and ammunition weighed some 60 lb – was an astonishing feat. It could only have been accomplished by a force imbued with outstanding *esprit de corps*, a morale based on high degrees of physical fitness, discipline and training under leaders approaching the calibre of officers such as Cadogan.

Bouchain was now in the Allies' grip, yet as the Master Gunner observed, 'everybody almost except my Lord Duke and Cadogan are against this siege'.[19] Cadogan found time on 17 August to jot his 'Dear Judge' a line (although he told him that 'I will write with one Foot in the Stirrup'.) He sent 'a short account of what was done last night', adding that 'I hope everything that relates to the cutting of the Enemys communication will be perfected tomorrow morning, and that I shall have the pleasure to acquaint you then of matters being finished so that even my Lord Orkney will be convinced wee may make the siege.'[20] Anyhow, when the siege-train arrived from Tournai the Anglo-Dutch army proceeded to reduce Bouchain in the face of the superior French force which they kept at bay with well entrenched lines of circumvallation. Villars had placed a brigade under the Chevalier d'Albegotti at Wavrechin close on Bouchain's south-west corner. However, the Dutch General Dopff was sent to deal with it. 'Dopf (*sic*) was reinforced during the night of the 8th [August] by sixteen battalions under [Baron] Fagel,' says Winston Churchill, 'and Cadogan, that trusted Eye, went with him.'[21] After a month the stronghold fell and 2,500 defenders marched out and into captivity.

Here Kane relates an incident throwing further light on Cadogan's personality. A certain French brigadier

> was desperately wounded and taken prisoner, and most of his men cut to Pieces. Villars, with the rest of his shattered Squadrons, scoured back as fast as they could. This brigadier, when Vendôme commanded, had taken Cadogan Prisoner on a

Foraging Command, and treated him with great Civility; now Cadogan, having it in his Power made a suitable return; he sent him in his Coach to his own Quarters, had all possible Care taken of him till he was cured of his wounds and then sent back.[22]

The Allies were eager to end the campaign by taking Le Quesnoy, which was the only obstacle lying on the path to Paris. But neither the authorities in England nor in Holland would produce the necessary supplies. The double-dealing Harley, who had been in secret negotiations with the French since the summer of 1710, had resolved that France had been sufficiently humiliated for the treacherous peace he had in mind. To allow the army to advance on Paris would prejudice the private accord which the Tories had agreed with Louis.[23]

The Tory ministers had decided, by the autumn of 1710, that Philip of Anjou, should, as Philip V, keep Spain and the Indies and that, in return, Britain should receive extensive commercial advantages in both Europe and the Americas. Those perfidious Tories would scrap the 1709 Anglo-Dutch Barrier treaty, replacing it with an Anglo-French agreement, thus playing traitor to Heinsius and his people. Although the Dutch had contributed as much as any of the Allies to the war effort (losing more of their soldiers than any, too) the Tories hated them. They proposed, step by step, to dismantle the Anglo-Dutch union, that of the 'Maritime Powers'. Their terms were also largely detrimental to the Austrians and the German states, which was why the Emperor, the Prussian monarch and the German princes were very much on the side of Marlborough and the Whigs. The Queen, whose mind was firmly set on a Hanoverian succession, was blissfully unaware that the first principle of Harley's peace plan was the recognition of her half-brother, James the Pretender, as her heir.

As Cadogan became increasingly aware – since the Captain General knew that peace on Harley's terms would be at once dishonourable to the Allies and that he would therefore be against it – Harley felt he had to make Marlborough redundant. The Tories decided that, in order to be rid of the Duke, evidence must be found to disgrace him. During October, while Cadogan was busy organizing the army in their winter quarters, his Chief, arriving at the Hague, found himself accused of fraud, embezzlement and extortion (accusations that were at least as applicable to Cadogan as to himself).

There were two main charges brought against Marlborough by the commissioners appointed by Parliament. Sir Solomon Medina, the contractor for the Allies' bread, testified that, between 1702 and 1711, he had paid the Duke over £63,000 in commissions from the rations and transport contractors in the Netherlands, which had not been properly accounted for. The second charge was that Marlborough had taken 2½ per cent, amounting to £280,000, from the pay of the foreign troops hired by the government. The Duke answered, when faced with these accusations in London, that it was customary for a commander-in-chief to take a commission to pay for his secret intelligence, and that, in the case of the 2½ per cent, he had a document, signed by the Queen, to prove it. Regarding the sum from Medina he said he had no proof of how the money was spent except for the celebrated efficiency of Cadogan's spy network, through whom the war had, in great measure, been won.

There are too many examples of the Captain General's monetary acquisitiveness for that aspect of his personality to be whitewashed. And we have seen that he was not past asking for very substantial *douceurs*. He had an expensive wife and family to maintain and was ambitious that Blenheim should outrival, in size and splendour, any other house in England, the expenses being largely met, at this stage, from his own purse. Cadogan had spent more than a decade emulating his chief and hero. Cadogan, too, aspired to substantial estates – perhaps partly to match his wife's Dutch properties. Oakley House was small fry. In June 1709, when Brydges, his old Westminster school friend, had written to him enquiring whether the Captain General would soon be in a position to compel Louis to make peace, he mentioned, *inter alia*, Cadogan's forthcoming purchase of a grand estate, near Reading, called Caversham:

> Most of what I have done consisting of having secured the refusal of some matters at a fixed price at the end of three and six months. If there was any probability of the negotiations being renewed in that time I should be a considerable gainer (besides it would not be amiss to secure a larger parcel while they [stocks] are at such low rates if there are such hopes). On the contrary, if there's no likelihood of it, the best thing I can do will be to get rid of what I have engaged for . . . I have given directions for your bill of 6000£ to be paid. I think you are very much in the right to lay it out in the Bank, since as they divide 9, if not 10 per cent per annum they are (whether peace or war) intrinsically worth 150 per cent. I think I may give you joy by this time of your new purchase of Caussum [Caversham]. 'Tis a very sweet place, and I think not dear but the properest thing for you in the whole kingdom.[24]

Towards the end of 1709 Cadogan sent Brydges an account of their joint gains, adding that 'the last year was wholly lost and the profit arising in the enclosed specification is only the product of the year before. You may judge by this what an opportunity has been neglected and how future occasions may be improved'. Anyhow Cadogan was able to invest £6,100 (probably over £300,000 in today's money) in Bank of England stock and thus to buy and maintain the Caversham estate. The 'enclosed specification', the net fraudulent profit from 1708, to be divided between himself and Brydges, amounted to £67,173.17.[25]

Little wonder therefore that Wassenaer van Duivenvoorde, a member of the Dutch government and nobility, found occasion to write to his compatriot in London, the old Earl of Portland, as follows

> *On pardonne ce que fait l'avarice* [of Marlborough] *mais on ne scauroit la superiorite que prend le favori* [Cadogan], *sa manière hautaine et brutale et les dispositions qu'il fait au prejudice des troupes et au profit de sa bourse.*[26] (One can [perhaps] excuse [Marlborough's] avarice, but one cannot forgive the arrogance shown by his favourite [Cadogan] nor [that officer's] haughty, coarse manner [coupled with] his dishonest conduct, which is to the prejudice of the soldiers and to the profit of his own purse.)

It is apparent that William Cadogan could, at times, be very overbearing, especially when he was on the defensive.

Notes

1 *Albion*, the Roman name for England taken from *albus* (white) referring to the sea cliffs of Sussex and Kent. 'Perfidious Albion' was used by several nations which had been outwitted, or tricked, by English, or British, governments. The controversial French cleric, Padre J.B. Boussuet (1627–1704) was, apparently, the first to express it. 'L'Angleterre!' he exclaimed, 'ah! La Perfide Angleterre!'
2 GMT III, 21
3 Huntington, *op cit*, 42
4 WSC IV, 829
5 Deane, *op cit*, 120
6 Huntington, *op cit*, 43
7 'Argyll' was then 'Argyle'
8 Huntington, *op cit*, 44
9 *Ibid*
10 WSC IV, 757(n). General Macartney, along with two other generals, was to be cashiered in October, 1710, for 'drinking to the health of the Duke of Marlborough in camp, and confusion to the new Government and Mr Harley' (*Ibid*, 772–73)
11 Kane, *op cit*, 81
12 By kind permission of Lord Cadogan

13 Lediard, *op cit*, 289–90; WSC IV, 843
14 Chandler, *op cit* 100
15 Coxe III, 226
16 Kane, *op cit*, 84
17 Chandler, *op cit*, 100–101
18 Kane, *op cit*, 86
19 Colonel Pendlebury to Earl Rivers, August 6, 1711, HMC Portland Papers, V, 63
20 By kind permission of Lord Cadogan
21 WSC IV, 860
22 Kane, *op cit*, 89
23 The 1711 campaign on the French border and subsequent events are covered in Coxe, III, 190–242; GMT III, 129–34; WSC IV, 842–72
24 Huntington, *op cit*, 31
25 *Ibid*
26 Veenendaal, *op cit*, 48, quoting N. Japikse, *Correspondentie van William III* in Portland II, S Gravenhage (1928), 521

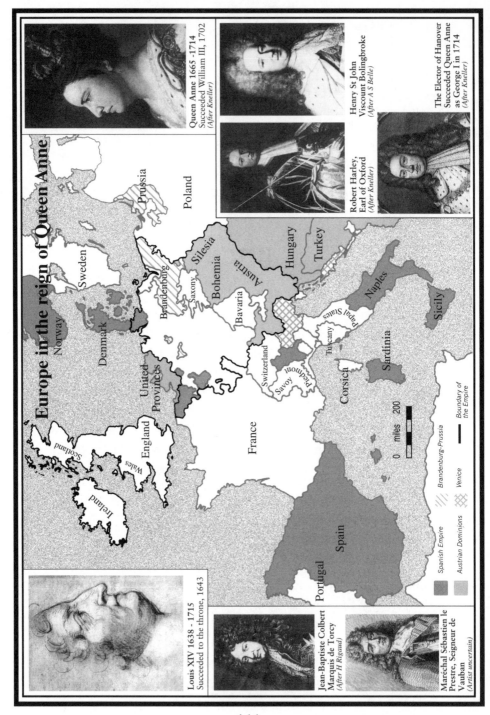

Europe in the reign of Queen Anne

Queen Anne 1665 -1714
Succeeded William III, 1702
(After Kneller)

Henry St John
Viscount Bolingbroke
(After A S Belle)

Robert Harley,
Earl of Oxford
(After Kneller)

The Elector of Hanover
Succeeded Queen Anne
as George I in 1714
(After Kneller)

Louis XIV 1638 - 1715
Succeeded to the throne, 1643
(After H Rigaud)

Jean-Baptiste Colbert
Marquis de Torcy
(After H Rigaud)

Maréchal Sébastien le
Prestre, Seigneur de
Vauban
(Artist uncertain)

Norway

Sweden

Prussia

Poland

Brandenburg

Saxony

Silesia

Bohemia

Austria

Hungary

Turkey

Bavaria

Denmark

United
Provinces

Scotland

Wales

England

Ireland

Switzerland

Savoy

Piedmont

Tuscany

Papal States

Naples

Sardinia

Sicily

Corsica

France

Spain

Portugal

0   miles   200

Spanish Empire

Austrian Dominions

Brandenburg-Prussia

Venice

Boundary of
the Empire

16

The Redcoats' Shame

(1712)

To Cadogan's intense dismay the Captain General was found guilty of the trumped-up charges levelled by the Tory government. On 31 December 1711 the Queen dismissed Marlborough from all his appointments and, next day, sent him a most ungracioius and ungrateful letter informing him of the decision. Adam de Cardonnel, formerly Secretary-at-War, and Robert Walpole, who was to become prime minister under George I, were also indicted. Cadogan wrote to his 'dear Judge' again on 24 January 1712 expressing his sorrow at this turn of events:

Wee have Dear Judge in the course of our long acquaintance generally agreed in our opinions of men and things, this makes it easy for me to guess at the indisposition of mind you complain of, and the cause of it. I am deeply affected in the same Part, and by the same Distemper, and am so far gone in it, as not only to be tired of business and Employments, but even weary of Life itself. You know the bottome of my Heart, therefore can better imagine then I describe the afliction and weight of Grief I am under. I am uncertain and I assure you unconcerned as to what becomes of my self. I shall act according to the strictest rules of Gratitude Duty and Honour, in Relation to our Great unfortunate Benefactor, and my Zeal Inclination and desire to serve and suffer for him are equal to the vast obligations and Favours I have received from him. As to the rest, I shall doe as People att Sea when the violence of the storm obliges them to abandon the Helm and cut down the masts, I commit myself to the mercy of the wind and waves. Whether they force me to split on Rocks or whether my good Fortune may throw a Plank in my way to carry me ashore, I am grown so insensible or so resigned as to be no longer in Pain about. [1]

And Cadogan wrote to Marlborough from Brussels on 12 January 1712, saying:

My Concern and astonishment att the fatal news of your Graces being removed is as hard to be expressed as the terror and consternation all people will here ... By the same hand Your Grace receives this letter I send to Mr Cardonnel certificates and attestations concerning the business of the bread. For these five and thirty years past, it was an established custom to present the General commanding in Chief with a considerable annual gratification in proportion to the number of troops the army was composed of ... I persuade myself 'tis unnecessary to repeat the assurances of my intention to follow your Grace in all fortunes. [2]

Cadogan's sentiments were roundly echoed throughout the army. A Lieutenant Halswell wrote to a brother-officer in the Royal Scots exclaiming that the Duke's dismissal gave 'moral reflection to the unsteddiness of human affairs'. [3] Corporal Bishop asked, 'Must we part from such a Man whose Fame has spread throughout all the World? On hearing that it was confirmed that he was no longer to command it terrified my

Soul to such a degree, that I could not rest Night or Day.'[4] Captain Parker showed the disgust felt by the Grand Alliance when he recorded that 'it must affect every man of virtue or spirit, to see him [Marlborough] oppressed by a set of men, who at the same time were selling their country, and his great actions to the declared enemies of the nation'.[5] Kane was even more blunt declaring that the dismissal was 'done by a set of vile profligate men who had insinuated themselves into the Favour of the ... Queen, and were at this time carrying on a scandalous underhand Treaty with the Grand Enemy of Europe'.[6]

The French, of course, were cock-a-hoop. 'Who could have foreseen,' the Marquis de Torcy wondered, 'that the prosperity of an Alliance so formidable for France and Spain was at an end; that the Supreme Being who fixes the boundaries of oceans and calms the impetuosity of the waves ... should stem the torrents of so many victories?' King Louis exclaimed that 'the affair of displacing the Duke of Marlborough will do all for us we desire'.[7] On 11 February 1712 de Torcy and his team of envoys, having settled in at Utrecht, submitted their own peace proposals. Philip would keep Spain and the Indies, the Elector of Bavaria would have the southern Netherlands, the French must have Lille and Tournai in exchange for Dunkirk, and the Franco-Austrian and Franco-Italian borders would remain the same as they had been at the start of the war. Moderate Tories were, naturally, as appalled by these arrogant French demands as the Whigs.

The new commander of the British army of the Netherlands was to be the inadequate Duke of Ormonde, whom Kane described as 'a good-natured, but a weak and ambitious Man fit to be made a fool of by a set of crafty knaves'.[8] Cadogan offered Ormonde his services in the same capacities that he held under Marlborough and was duly accepted. Ormonde arrived at the Hague on 9 April to take command, but was, obviously in no hurry to join the army, for Cadogan wrote from Tournai to his 'Dear Judge' on the 26th, asking him to deliver the enclosed as soon as your receive them for the wind having been fair and the weather very good these several dayes past, I conclude the Duke of Ormonde is landed, I suppose he will lose no time att the Hague, his Presence being so absolutely necessary here, I wish for his coming on all accounts, but particularly since it will procure me the satisfaction of seeing my dear Judge.[9]

In Cadogan's message to Ormonde he hoped 'this letter will have the Honour to find your Grace safely arrived in Holland.'

I hope to receive your Graces commands very soon in relation to the Place you would have me wait on you in your way to the Army. There are Escorts left at Gant [Ghent] antwerp and oudenard . . . and I will take care of Horses for the Relais, as soon as your Grace will please to let me know the number wanting and the time of your leaving the Hague. The Prince of Savoy [Eugène] arrived here the day before yesterday the army is not yet entirely formed tho all the troops except the Imperialists are come and encamped near this Place [Tournai] Lille and Douay. Monsr de Villars is at Cambray and his Chief attention is to secure all the Passages on the Sensette.[10]

Writing to Ormonde on 3 May from Bouchain, Cadogan displays his tactical instinct again:

I came to this place yesterday by order of the Prince of Savoy to chuse a proper place to encamp and entrench forty Battalions and eight Squadrons which are detached here under command of Monsr Fagel the reason of sending this Corps before the rest of the Army moves, is to prevent the Enemy's possessing themselves of the Heights between the villages of Hordain and Lieu St Arman for if they were [not] posted there it would render very difficult if not impracticable our Passage over the Scheld at Bouchain. I have therefore placed this detachment on the

Height between the . . . two villages, the right at Hordain and the left at Lieu St Amand the entrenchment necessary to secure them was begun yesterday and will be finished this evening. I intend to set out immediately in order to have the Honour of waiting on your Grace at Gant [Ghent] but being obliged to goe with Escortes I cannot make such haste as I wish.[11]

Ormonde (who received precisely the same perks as those which led to Marlborough's indictment of peculation) was not yet aware that his masters in London had no intention of allowing him to engage the enemy. The Dutch, now well acquainted with British treachery, had appointed Prince Eugène as Allied generalissimo. Eugène advanced to besiege Le Quesnoy and Landrècies. A couple of weeks later Ormonde received instructions, in accordance with St John's notorious 'Restraining Orders', not, on any account, to cooperate with Eugène. In fact Ormonde was already in communication with Villars, and had informed him that British military activity would be confined to foraging.

The downright treachery of Harley (Earl of Oxford) and St John (Viscount Bolingbroke) beame increasingly apparent. By now Ormonde – as directed by those two – did not communicate with Eugène at all, and was virtually in cahoots with Villars. Would British troops cooperate in the siege of Le Quesnoy?' Villars demanded of him. Ormonde assured him they would not. Would he promise Villars that the British would refrain from attempting to prevent the French from relieving Le Quesnoy? Ormonde gave that undertaking. Bolingbroke next ordered Ormonde to withdraw his forces altogether. But Cadogan and the other British senior officers refused to desert Eugène who duly captured Le Quesnoy on 4 July. The Savoyard Prince then undertook to besiege Landrècies, but Villars outmanoeuvred him and went on to defeat Eugène, on 24 July, at the Battle of Denain. During the autumn the *Maréchal* retook Douai, Le Quesnoy and Bouchain, thereby nullifying the successes scored by Marlborough, Eugène and Cadogan.[12]

To Eugène's utter amazement he was informed by Ormonde that an armistice had been concluded between the British and French governments without the participation of the Dutch or the Imperialists. Ormonde had by then withdrawn the British expeditionary force to Ghent and Bruges. The scenes of anger and frustration among the officers and men of what had once been Marlborough's proud and gallant army are well documented. Here is Sergeant Millner:

> As they marched off that day both sides [Eugène's and Ormonde's] looked very dejectedly on each other, neither being permitted to speak to the other, to prevent Reflections that might thereby arise, on the strange Revolution between us and our Allies, either by our cessation of Arms, or entrance on an odd Peace with France . . . Ormonde relied on the grateful Fidelity of his own Countrymen for delivering them from the Hardships of War, but great was his Disappointment when, at the close of his first March a suspension of Arms was proclaimed at the head of each Regiment. A burst of Indignation and Abhorrence accompanied this proof of dishonour.[13]

Captain Parker was less restrained:

> Our first day's march was to Avoinlesecq near Bouchain, where the Duke ordered a cessation of arms, between Great Britain and France, to be declared at the head of every regiment: upon which occasion it was expected they would have made a geat huzza: but instead of that nothing was heard but a continued hiss throughout the whole army. This gave the Duke great offence.[14]

Corporal Bishop recalled that 'there was great Disturbance at Ghent amongst the soldiers, which occasioned some to suffer

172

death'.[15] Cadogan's comment must be left to the imagination.

Marlborough and his Duchess received these shaming bulletins at their Hertfordshire home where their greatest friend and the father-in-law of their eldest daughter, Sidney Godolphin, spent much of the summer as their guest, and where the former Lord Treasurer died on 12 September. That was one reason why Marlborough decided to 'exile' himself to the Continent. There was no more sick Godolphin to be cared for. Another reason was that, following the Tories' indictment, he feared that 'Robin the Trickster's' next step would be to impeach him, which would carry the threat of a major financial loss. (His fear was exacerbated by the fact that, at the coroner's inquest into the death, in a duel, of the Tory diplomat Duke of Hamilton and Brandon, it was insinuated that Marlborough had been involved in the challenge.)

Thirdly, he was weary of the continuing campaign of slander and abuse and the Grub Street libels, largely prompted by Oxford and Bolingbroke and penned by Swift and other hacks. Marlborough was also keen to visit the principality of Mindelheim which Emperor Leopold had bestowed on him seven years before. And lastly, knowing that Oxford and Bolingbrooke and the other leading Tories were determined to bring in the Jacobite Pretender if and when the Queen died, he harboured several drastic ideas, including armed invasion, for ensuring the Hanoverian succession.

And that is where General William Cadogan (who had been with his own family in Holland) features again. On 28 November 1712 the Duke, having secured from Oxford the permits necessary for a peer wishing to travel abroad, embarked, as a private passenger on the *North Briton* packet and landed next morning at Ostend, where he was greeted by the trusty Cadogan, who had volunteered to be his eyes and ears and young-man-of-action again, and who would remain his principal agent for the next 21 months.

To quote Winston Churchill again:

The brave, generous Irish soldier, who was never found wanting in fidelity or chivalry, gladly cast away any prospects he might have had under the Tories in order to accompany his old chief. 'The Duke of Marlborough's ill-health,' Cadogan wrote to Oxford, 'the inconvenience of a winter's journey exposes him to, and his being without any one friend to accompany him, make the requesting leave to wait on him an indispensable duty on me, who for so many years have been honoured with his confidence and friendship and [owe] all I have in the world to his favour'. The ministers were not unwilling to oblige him. The Queen's permission was granted; but Cadogan was shortly afterwards dismissed from all his appointments.[16]

Notes

1 By kind permission of Lord Cadogan
2 Pearman, *op cit*, (Quoting 'Blenheim Collection B2–24')
3 *Ibid*, 918
4 Bishop, *op cit*, 235–36
5 Chandler, *op cit*, 114–16
6 Kane, *op cit*, 101–02
7 WSC IV, 913
8 Kane, *op cit*, 90–91
9 By kind permission of Lord Cadogan
10 *Ibid*
11 *Ibid*
12 Burnet VI, 134; WSC IV, 957; GMT III, 222
13 Journal, *op cit*, 356
14 Chandler, *op cit*, 122
15 Bishop, *op cit*, 264–65
16 cf HMC, Portland Papers, V, 257; WSC IV, 977

17

Master Spy

(1712–1714)

The French were duly alarmed to learn that Marlborough was more or less at large on the Continent, the only restriction placed on him by his arch-enemy, Oxford, being that he must not visit Ghent or Bruges where the British expeditionary force was garrisoned. There were a variety of concerns on the Duke's mind during his self-imposed exile. He feared that Oxford might still arrange for him to be impeached, which could involve a heavy fine or even the confiscation of his beloved Blenheim property. Having paved the way, with his hard-won military successes, for a peace that would leave the French little to be proud of, he feared, not without very good cause, that Secretary of State Bolingbroke and the other pro-French elements in the Tory Ministry were permitting the defeated enemy far too many concessions at the peace talks. (The Treaty of Utrecht was to be signed in the spring of 1713.) Marlborough was anxious, as ever, for his wife's safety and he longed to have her with him. He was also, as I say, planning to spend a couple of weeks in his principality of Mindelheim.

Perhaps above all, the Duke was preoccupied with the belief and fear that Bolingbroke and his Jacobite cronies would pave the way for the Pretender to succeed Queen Anne (who was a sick woman, near to death), notwithstanding her contrary wish and the Act of Succession of 1701. Indeed the Duke and Cadogan were convinced that the Tories had already decided to bring in the Pretender and were planning accordingly. They were equally resolved to prevent it. They decided that this could only be effected for sure by armed invasion. So the two old comrades-in-arms were constantly plotting during those 21 Continental months. It was necessary to maintain contact with Antoine Heinsius, Holland's first minister, with Count Sinzendorf, the Emperor's man at the Hague, and with three Hanoverians, Count Bernstorf, that country's prime minister, Jean de Robethon, a French Huguenot member of the Hanoverian government (and *secretaire de les ambassades*) and Count Johann von Bothmar, Hanover's envoy at the Hague.[1]

But those statesmen dared not to be seen in Marlborough's presence, he being in disgrace according to Oxford, and they being unwilling to put a foot wrong with the British government. So it fell to Cadogan to be negotiator and master spy, roles which, both from skill, experience and inclination, suited him very well. He needed, too, to be familiar with the pulse and mood of English politics and to have the latest intelligence at his fingertips. He was in regular touch with the Duke's son-in-law, Sunderland, secretary of the Whig junta, and was kept well informed by James Craggs, formerly secretary of the Ordnance Board and a lifelong Whig intriguer, who transmitted confidential correspondence to a reliable Dutch contact, the Rotterdam banker, Heer Senserf.

James Craggs Jr, who had been General Stanhope's secretary and was formerly English Resident at Barcelona, was also useful. Young Craggs's mistress was the wife of Arthur Moore, the Board of Trade secretary, whose confidential letters from Bolingbroke were copied for him by Mrs Moore, and duly forwarded to Cadogan, who would pass them on to Hanover via von Bothmar. (Incidentally James Craggs Jr was a notorious womanizer. Sarah Marlborough, having turned him out of her Hertfordshire home for attempting to rape one of her servants, held him responsible for two abusive anonymous letters which she received soon afterwards.)

From Ostend Marlborough and Cadogan travelled on to Aix-la-Chapelle where they hatched their invasion plan, and where Marlborough was advised to stay put for fear of an assassination attempt. (Eugène wrote advising that 'your highness will do well to remain as long as possible at Aix-la-Chapelle without causing suspicion, for I know you are watched'.[2]) Cadogan then proceeded to the Hague to arrange meetings with Heinsius, Sinzendorf and von Bothmar, attempting to persuade them, in the first instance, that a coup would soon be attempted in favour of the Pretender, and that, since such action implied a close Anglo-French alliance, it would imperil Holland, Austria and the whole German empire as well as England. Cadogan went on to propose that the Emperor should lease a fleet of Dutch warships upon which a Hanoverian army would embark. The reception of this invasion force would be the responsibility of Sunderland and General Stanhope.

However, Cadogan was obliged to return to Aix with the unhappy news that the project had been dismissed out of hand by all three statesmen. Furious, particularly at the Dutch rebuff and partly because Austrian investments offered more favourable returns, the two soldiers extracted the large amounts of money invested in Holland for Marlborough, transferring them to Imperial stock.[3] It was at about this juncture, too, that Cadogan learned that, because he had aligned himself with the disgraced Duke, he must consider himself deprived of his rank, along with all his appointments and sincecures, and must arrange to sell his regiment, which went to Major General Kellum, who had been the commanding officer during the early years of the war.

Cadogan appears to have taken a philosophical view of these setbacks; he gives the impression of being much more resolute and assertive than Marlborough at this time. He enjoyed, of course, the advantages of a Dutch wife and a Dutch home and freedom to travel to England whenever he liked (although Oxford became increasingly suspicious of his comings and goings).

Sarah Marlborough, that ardent Whig and arch-hater of Oxford and Bolingbroke, who revelled in conspiracy and intrigue at least as strongly as either Cadogan or her husband and whose letters home give some indication of the travellers' situation, was now on her way to join the Duke. She endured a foul Channel crossing. 'I wanted many conveniences that are usual,' the feisty Duchess wrote to Lady Cowper, '& was forc'd to have the door of the place where I lay open in the night when violent sickness put me into a great sweat for a little air to keep me alive, tho' the sea was perpetually dashing in upon me.'[4] Marlborough met her at Maastricht and escorted her coach to Aix from where she penned another letter to Lady Cowper, saying cryptically:

> I have had no hopes a great while but in one thing . . . & I much doubt whether it will happen in time. I can see no human means that will defend us from an Arbitrary Government in a little while . . . If our Enemies do prevail to our utter Ruin I think I had best go into a Monastery. There are several in this Town, and 'tis all the Entertainment I have to visit the Nuns and the Churches. I supp'd with about twenty of them 'tother night, but 'twas a very slight one, nothing but brown bread and butter . . . They were as fond of me as if I had not been a Heretick . . . I don't see what can happen to trouble such as think of nothing but of Heaven'.[5]

That spring found Marlborough and Cadogan in league with Count Bernstorf for a plan whereby the moment Queen Anne died (which everyone saw as being sooner rather than later) the Elector of Hanover (the future George I) would hasten to

London as lieutenant general to his mother (the new 'Queen Sophia') while his son, the Electoral Prince (the future George II) repaired to the Netherlands to take command of the British expeditionary force. At the same time Cadogan was also to proceed to London, seize the Tower and other key places and administer the oath (to the new Queen) to all the home forces. Marlborough would be reappointed Captain General.

While Cadogan sifted through such intelligence that there was to be had in Holland the Marlboroughs journeyed to Frankfurt where, in the bitter cold, Sarah, left alone while the duke pushed on to his principality, Mindelheim, suffered from toothache and complained of her German stove 'which makes my head so uneasy I can't bear it'. As she told the Cowpers she was 'alone in this place where I have no pleasure but the fresh air, & yet I do protest I would not change my condition for any of my enemies that have done so much mischief to their country'.[6]

Marlborough returned, after two weeks' absence, informing Sarah that Mindelheim had been restored to the Elector of Bavaria, but that he, the Duke, might call himself an Imperial prince. The Emperor Charles VI, who had given that verdict, was in a bitter frame of mind. Having refused to have the shameful 'peace preliminaries' at Utrecht signed, he was still at war with France (as he would continue to be until the Treaty of Rastadt in March, 1714). But, although Eugène was his supreme field commander, the Austro-Hanoverian army suffered nothing but defeat in the Netherlands. For, since the close of the Grand Alliance war, Louis kept Villars on that front with a much superior army. When the Treaty of Utrecht was signed Coxe observed that 'all the articles of the grand alliance which related to the security of Europe, or the welfare of England, the great objects of this just and successful war, were either violated or abandoned . . . The Dutch, irritated by the shameful desertion of their cause . . . conceived an aversion to England . . . the house of Austria, the only power then capable of balancing France, and the natural ally of England was treated with still more neglect and indignity.'[7]

Doubtless Marlborough and Cadogan who had worked so hard and risked so much to achieve a just and honourable peace, were considerably more indignant than Coxe was in retrospect.

The Tories were swept back to power with an increased majority in the 1713 general election. However Cadogan contested and won Woodstock for the Whigs again. Many despaired of the sorry state of British politics. ('Good God how this poor nation has been governed in my time,' exclaimed the recently dismissed Lord Steward, the Duke of Buckingham. 'During the reign of King Charles the Second we were governed by a parcel of French whores: in King James the Second's time by a parcel of Popish priests: In King William's time by a parcel of Dutch footmen: and now we are governed by a dirty chambermaid, a Welsh attorney and a profligate wretch that has neither honour nor honesty'.[8]) Sarah Marlborough, in typically plain-spoken mood, wrote to James Craggs Sr, referring to 'the Sorcerer' [Oxford] being a far more dangerous man than that 'cowardly wretch' [Bolingbroke], 'although the latter was far more bear-faced (sic) for the Pretender . . . 'tis very odd to have the Sorcerer pretend to give so much satisfaction to honest men . . . & at the same time to have his brother [Edward Harley, Auditor of the Imprest] goe about with teares in his eyes (as I hear he had lately Don) complaining of Ld B: and his designs to bring in the P of W."[9]

Returning from London to Frankfurt to escort the Marlboroughs to Holland, Cadogan rented a house for them at Antwerp. Sarah, arriving there, wrote to her friend, Mrs Boscawen: 'We came allmost 250 miles in Elleven days . . . I believe I shall like this place much better than Frankford, for here is not so much Company and very good Provissions: 'tis the finest old Town I beleive in the World, but grown poor and ruined for want of Trade which will bee soon the Decay of England.'[10]

Sarah's pessimism was doubtless exacerbated by Cadogan's latest bulletin from London, from which city the best news seemed to be that Oxford and Bolingbroke were now bitter enemies. (The antagonism began, it was said, in the autumn of 1712 when Bolingbroke, without authority, and sidelining the prospect of Utrecht, went to Paris to negotiate the peace treaty single-handed. Oxford promptly deprived Bolingbroke of responsibility for foreign affairs, transferring it to the other Secretary of State, Lord Dartmouth.) But the Tories, said Cadogan, were more determined than ever on forging the closest partnership possible with France and on bringing in the Pretender. As part of their guile they wrote openly to princes in countries which would never receive the Pretender urging them not to so so, while secretly encouraging his retention in Lorraine, but informing Parliament that they had urged the French to exile him. They gave as many key appointments as possible to Jacobites. They put the government of Scotland into the hands of the Earl of Mar, a personal friend of the Pretender(and soon to be deputy leader of the '15 rebellion), and entrusted that of Ireland to Sir Constantine Phipps, another notorious Jacobite.

Cadogan, who clearly had no time whatsoever for the Pretender, must have often despaired at the Jacobite antics of Marlborough 'the trimmer'; the Marlborough who had never got over the guilt he suffered at having 'betrayed' James II in 1688, at having deserted the King who had launched him on his career and seen him half-way up the ladder; the Marlborough who, during the past quarter of a century, had so often felt the pricks of a goad telling him to atone for that guilt. And now, since there was this real danger that the Tories might bring in the Pretender, the Duke did not wish to be caught on the wrong foot. But Victoria Glendinning is wrong to state, in her recent and entertaining biography of Swift, that 'Marlborough went to France to court the Pretender'. She is also at fault in asserting, on the same page,[11] that 'the Queen now hated

Marlborough'. On the contrary Anne, surrounded by so many untrustworthy advisers, yearned for the impossible – a return for the good old days of the Marlborough- Godolphin partnership.

During the autumn of 1713 James II's widow, Mary of Modena, plotting at St Germains on behalf of her son, the Pretender, and remembering how readily her old friend and servant, John Churchill, had been so often prepared to run with the hare at the same time as hunting with the hounds – dispatched her special agent, Tunstal, to Antwerp, to sound Marlborough out. Might he be persuaded to change sides? Indeed he might.[12]

The Duke's initial reaction was to send Tunstal back with a request for Franco-Jacobite intercession with Oxford to plead against impeaching him. De Torcy, the French foreign minister and erstwhile leader of the French delegaton at Utrecht, was highly sceptical, remarking that sincerity was 'une virtu qu'il [Marlborough] n'a jamais connue. However, de Torcy agreed with the equally doubtful Duke of Berwick, who had plenty of experience of his uncle's duplicity and who now took over the role of negotiator with him, that 'one might reap some wood of this gentleman's fears'.[13] But Cadogan must have felt exasperated, however earnestly he meant his intention of 'following the fortunes, good or bad, of the great man to whom I am under such infinite obligations . . . I would be a monster if I did otherwise', he had added.[14]

Tunstal soon returned to Antwerp with Berwick's three conditions for bringing his uncle into the Jacobite plot. They were that Marlborough should support the Pretender publicly, that he should in no way oppose Louis XIV and that he must concur with Queen Anne for a Jacobite succession if that was her wish, to none of which the wily Duke was ready to comply.[15] Bolingbroke commenting on Marlborough's double-dealing said that 'it is hard for so old a gamester to leave off playing'[16], which was rich coming from him! Even so it was a truthful remark. The Duke, a past master at double bluff, was regularly transmitting Jacobite intelligence to the Whigs in London. All the same Marlborough secured a pardon from the Pretender for his duplicitous treatment of the Stuarts, which Berwick had persuaded his half-brother to grant, adding 'I see no harm in it, and one may give to those sort of people as good as they bring, for I see nothing else in all Marlborough says, and indeed he has never behaved himself otherways'.[17] On 16 December 1713 von Bothmar was writing to Bernstorf that 'both the Duke of Marlborough and Cadogan have provisional orders from the Electress to take command of the troops and garrison in case of the Queen's death. Cadogan told me it would be proper to have a particular one for Mr Armstrong, Quartermaster-General at Dunkirk, to seize upon that place, and execute the orders of Mr Cadogan.'[18]

When Anne suffered a serious illness around the period of Christmas and New Year 1713–14, so much so that death seemed imminent, Marlborough and Cadogan were told of the hectic consternation among the Tory ministers, especially Bolingbroke. They concluded that the English government's plans for a Jacobite coup were not sufficiently far ahead, which prompted Sarah to comment that they were 'sure to quicken their measures now'.[19]

As Cadogan well knew, Queen Anne had no intention of revoking the Act of Settlement. When it was suggested she might do so she exclaimed to her doctor and friend, Sir David Hamilton, 'Oh fye, there is no such thing. What, do they think I'm a child, and to be imposed upon?'[20] Quite apart from that the Pretender had affirmed that he had no intention of renouncing his Catholic faith if he was nominated heir to the throne. He was therefore unacceptable. Yet he continued to call himself 'Prince of Wales' and, often, 'James III', for he regarded his half-sister as a usurper, and he still counted on a French invasion force to impose himself on Anglican Britain, the reality of which Cadogan was soon to witness. As late as 22 July

1713 Cadogan was writing (from Frankfurt) to Bernstorf saying, 'it appears that the return of the Pretender is the design of our ministry so it cannot be doubted they will attempt it during the Queen's lifetime . . . If I may therefore give our opinion I beleive *(sic)* it will be for his Electoral Highness service to enter into a strict confidence with him [Marlborough] and impart from time to time the measures that shall be taken which may be done by Mons Bothnar or my self.'[21]

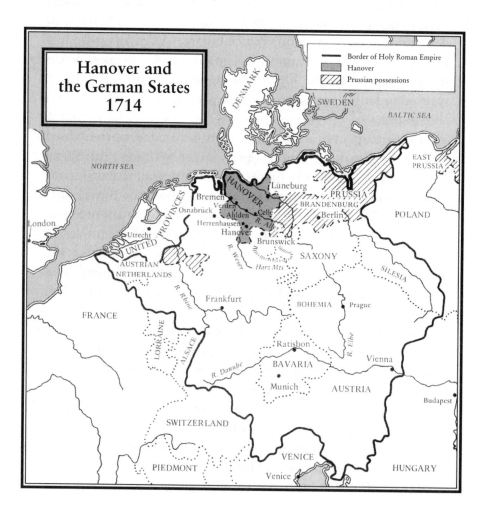

With the spring and early summer of 1714 seeing a confusion of intrigues centred on the court of Hanover Cadogan found himself having to shadow Oxford's double agent (the Treasurer's cousin, Auditor Edward Harley) as well as keeping abreast of the Jacobite intrigues. This necessitated maintaining close contact with a young Irishman called Samuel Molyneux, the MP for Dublin University, whom the Marlboroughs had appointed to keep an eye on things in Hanover. The Electress Sophia, whose life's ambition was the English throne, hoping to push her foot a few inches further into the door leading there, instructed her envoy in London, Baron von Schutz, to demand that her grandson, Prince George Augustus, who had been created Duke of Cambridge, be summoned to take his seat in the Lords. But the Elector, more astute than his mother, refused to let his son go to London without an invitation from the Queen.

As the prospect of a Stuart restoration receded, both Oxford and Bolingbroke – 'never two falser villains', in Sarah Marlborough's opinion – increased their attempt to gain favour with Hanover. The Treasurer and Secretary of State, now loathing one another more than ever, and knowing that Marlborough would be a favourite in the event of a Hanoverian succession, each opened secret negotiations with the Duke, the Treasurer through Cadogan and Auditor Harley, Bolingbroke through Craggs Sr.[21] The Electress Sophia died on 8 June 1714, aged 84.

When, towards the end of June, Berwick (a *sine qua non* of the Jacobite movement) left Paris to lead a siege of Barcelona it was clear to Marlborough and Cadogan that there could be no Franco-Jacobite invasion in the near future. So they made known their decision to return to London in July, which greatly alarmed the Tory government, fearing as they did that their presence in England might cause a civil war. (Matthew Prior wrote from Paris that 'M. de Torcy has very severe, and I fear, very exact accounts of us; we are all frightened out of our wits upon the Duke of Marlborough going into England.')[23] Meanwhile Cadogan and the Duke and Duchess found ample distractions at Antwerp, 'a folly for almost every day of the year',[24] Sarah told her friend Mrs Clayton. 'The D of Marl and I go constantly every Day in the Afternoon, and stop the Coach and go out wherever we see a place that looks hard and clean,' she wrote to her cousin, Robert Jennings, 'which does me a great deal of good'.[25]

Cadogan sailed ahead of the Marlboroughs, with the mission of taking command at the Tower and ensuring that all was calm in London for a Hanoverian sucession. The Marlboroughs set out from Antwerp for Ostend on 27 July (the very day that the Queen dismissed Oxford from office and Bolingbroke went into hiding and later to France. Ormonde and Oxford were to be impeached for high treason.) The Duchess wrote to Mrs Clayton saying that she would be happy to be several days at the port waiting for a calm day rather than risk a repeat of her stormy night crossing in February 1713, 'because it is intolerable to go to bed in those boats'.[26]

As the Marlborough's packet approached Dover a small boat came alongside. A messenger went aboard with the news that Queen Anne was dead (she died on 1 August). Thus Britain missed having a 'Queen Sophia' by a mere eight weeks, the cry being now 'God save King George' and the Whigs in power again with Walpole as Chancellor. During the Queen's last hours the Whig General Stanhope wrote to the Emperor Charles VI saying, 'This accident, sudden and unforeseen, came like a thunderbolt to the Jacobites . . . I venture to assure your Imperial Majesty that, if the doctors prophesy truly, Monsr l'Electeur of Hanvr will be proclaimed King . . . I hope I shall be saying nothing new in assuring you that all who are honest people are disgusted at the *treachery* of the late Ministry to your Imperial Majesty . . . and that they will, when the occasion offers, do their best to repair this dishonour of the nation.'[27]

The first German monarch to set foot on English soil, being

in no hurry to leave his beloved Hanover, did not disembark at Greenwich until 18 September. He was accompanied by his mistress, the ugly Baronin von Kilmansegge, and by his son, Prince George Augustus, Prince of Wales, he and his princess being the only members of the party who could speak English well. However, the King mastered a set-piece question to ask Marlborough, 'My Lord duke I hope your troubles are now all over?' (The dialogue between statesmen, diplomats and politicians was French, which was the language used between George I and his English ministers.)

Certainly Cadogan's troubles appeared to be over. He was reinstated as a lieutenant general and as Lieutenant of the Tower. On 11 August he was appointed Colonel of the Second Foot Guards (the Coldstream). He was a rich man and one of extensive property and one greatly respected by the King (whose language he spoke), not only for his efficiency both as a soldier and as a civil administrator, but also as a companion. Cadogan was a very happy family man, too, and was soon reunited with his wife and daughters. For that autumn he returned to Holland as Envoy Extraordinary and Minister Plenipotentiary. In that capacity he represented Great Britain at the Third Barrier Treaty conferences which then opened at Antwerp, where 'international espionage intensified. Cadogan took steps to ensure that his agents were vigilant'.[28] He had by no means yet finished with the Jacobites.[29]

Notes

1　The authority for much of this chapter is taken from the finely researched article *Marlborough in Exile, 1712–1714*, by Professor Edward Gregg (of the University of South Carolina) in the *Historical Journal*, XV, 4 (1972) pp 593–618

2　Gregg, *op cit*, 599

3　Coxe III, 327

4　Sarah to Lady Cowper, Feb 17, 1713

5　*Ibid*, April 9, 1713; cf Harris, 192–93

6　*Ibid*, June 6, 1713; cf Harris 194

7　Coxe III, 334–35

8   WSC, IV, 1008
9   Stowe MS 751, f 106; Grigg, *op cit*, 612–13
10 Sarah to Mrs Boscawen, September 26, 1713; cf Harris, 196–97
11 *Jonathan Swift* (Random House, 1998), p 114
12 Gregg, *op cit*, As he points out: 'Sir Winston Churchill . . . contended that [Marlborough] "never swerved from his fidelity to the Protestant Succession". But . . . a search of Hanoverian, French and British archives has yielded new material which illuminates Marlborough's political activities during his exile'.
13 HMC, Stuart papers, Vol 51, p 278; Berwick to 'James III', October 13, 1713
14 PRO, FO Records, Flanders, nos 132–35
15 Gregg, *op cit*, 605
16 Gregg, *op cit*, 606
17 *Ibid*
18 HMC Stuart Papers *op cit*, p 308
19 Sarah to Mrs Boscawen, Jan 28, 1714; cf Harris, 198
20 P. Roberts, Hamilton's Diary, 44
21 Huntington, *op cit*, 371
22 Gregg, *op cit*, 611–14
23 Coxe, III, 370
24 BL Add MS 61463, f123 Sarah to Robert Jennings, May 5, 1714
25 *Ibid*, f137
26 *Ibid*
27 HM Imbert-Terry *A Constitutional King: George I*, p 121 (Quoting Leibnitz, III, p 504)
28 Patricia Dickson, *op cit* Pt 1, p 161
29 The events of this chapter are largely related in Coxe III, 325–73; GMT III, 271–307; WSC IV, 977–1018

18

Scourge of the Jacobites

(1715–1716)

Honoured and wholly reinstated by King George, Lieutenant General William Cadogan must have been a happy man in 1715. As Envoy and Plenipotentiary to Holland he represented Britain at the negotiations for the Third Barrier Treaty whereby he was working to obtain for his wife's people the maximum number of fortresses (far more than that allowed by the Tories) beyond their border, including several along the French frontier. This work involved exhausting journeys between Vienna, London, Antwerp, Brussels and the Hague. On 31 July he succeeded General Webb (a Jacobite sympathiser) as Captain of the Isle of Wight and Governor of Carisbrooke Castle.[1] On 11 August he was appointed Colonel of the Second Guards (Coldstream).

However, viewing the state of British politics during the first year and more of the new reign, he took a somewhat jaundiced view. Given a Whig ministry headed by Robert Walpole (Chancellor of the Exchequer), with the strong personalities (though lesser abilities) of Stanhope and Townshend as Secretaries of State – the former for the south, the latter for the northern department and mainly responsible for foreign affairs

– it seemed as though the nation was set for a long and peaceful term of Hanoverian government. But there were two principal factors blurring that outlook. One was the unpopularity of King George and the other was the seemingly romantic image of Prince James Edward Stuart, the Pretender, whom many people, besides dyed-in-the-wool Jacobites, saw as the rightful inheritor of the throne, notwithstanding his Catholicism.

Not only could George of Hanover speak virtually no English, but he was dour and made little effort to be liked by his new subjects, who were made to feel as though they were foreigners, and that this German King who was thrust upon them much preferred Hanover (which indeed he did). A great majority of the Scots – who had always been opposed to both the Act of Succession and the Act of Union – were Jacobite, while the movement also enjoyed wide support, particularly in the north of England and in the West Country. Noisy demonstrations were rife in the major English towns, as much against the impeachment of Oxford, Ormonde and Strafford (Cadogan's old friend, formerly Lord Raby) as against the King.

In September 1715, while Louis XIV lay dying at Versailles,[2] his nephew, the Duke of Orleans was virtually master of France and poised to be Regent for the delicate five-year-old prince who would be Louis XV. Bolingbroke had been appointed Secretary of State to the Pretender (who was to grow increasingly mistrustful of him). In July Ormonde had also joined the court of the Pretender, whose half-brother, the Duke of Berwick, had been once again immersed in Jacobite politics from the moment he returned from soldiering in Spain in November, 1714. Those three now persuaded Prince James Edward that Britain was ripe for a Jacobite uprising. But the Prince did not move before the end of October. (The Prussian Resident in London, Bonet, writing home that summer, stated that 'the Jacobite cause has made more progress in eight months of King George's reign than in the whole four years of the Tory ministry'. But if the Pretender had struck a year or more earlier, when George of Hanover was proclaimed and Louis XIV still sat on the French throne, things might have gone better for his cause. Whereas, by the autumn of 1715 the Jacobite ardour had cooled somewhat while the French Regent was lukewarm about Jacobitism, and the Whig government was more readily geared to deal with a rebellion.)

Industrious Cadogan, aside from his day-to-day work as British envoy to Holland and his deep involvement in the Barrier Treaty negotiations, was active in his old pursuit of espionage and counter-espionage. An example of this activity occurred in the summer of 1715 when one of his agents informed him that some 500,000 Louis d'ors had been dispatched from Paris to a Monsieur Pels, a well known French banker. As Cadogan informed both Heinsius and Townshend, the money was clearly intended to support a Jacobite invasion. Cadogan then had Bolingbroke and Ormonde watched more closely than ever. Using his ambassadorial powers he also urged the Dutch government to order their provincial governors to examine strangers in transit and to stop all British subjects coming from, and going to, Germany and France; to send him their details and to detain them pending his reply. Captains of ships were not to receive British subjects on board unless they held passports bearing Cadogan's signature. His memoir to the States General concluded as follows:

As the undersigned Ambassador cannot doubt the sincere friendship of your High Powers for the King his Master, and of their anxiety to foil the Pretender's designs, he is strongly persuaded that your High Powers will carry out as soon as possible the orders according to this Memoir, and that they take other measures such as they think fit, to prevent the passage of the 'Pretender' and his adherents.[3]

Meanwhile the rebellion was already underway. In July the Jacobite John Erskine, Earl of Mar, Secretary of State for Scotland, being cold-shouldered by the King and dismissed, sailed for the Fife coast, rode to Braemar, issued an invitation to the Highland chiefs to attend a 'deer hunt' on his Aberdeenshire estate and informed them on arrival that he had received a commission from 'King James' appointing him commander-in-chief, Scotland. Mar then set up the Jacobite standard in the nearby village of Kirkmichael to which some 9,000 volunteers rallied. But Mar proved to be a most inept leader.

Although Marlborough was no longer fit to take the field he was still Captain General of the British army, and as such ordered the Duke of Argyll to take the offensive with some 3,000 horse and foot. On 14 September the expeditionary force reached Edinburgh where Argyll was informed that Mar's rebels, having secured Perth, were now at Dunblane. Although Argyll had served as a capable formation commander under Marlborough he was now hampered by conflicting loyalties and affections, half the lairds of his clan, the Campbells, having joined the rebels and he himself harbouring much sympathy for the Jacobite cause. Indeed Argyll had protested that he did not want the Scottish command (only accepting because Marlborough had ordered it). However, he met Mar's 9,000 clansmen on 24 November at Sheriffmuir, near Dunblane, where, not withstanding the fact that the rebels outnumbered the Hanoverians by three to one, a drawn battle was fought. Argyll then concentrated his little army on Stirling.

There were other revolutionary attempts. A number of the Scottish chieftains, imposing little faith in Mar, marched their men south, crossing the Esk into England on 1 November, to link up with the considerable dissident elements in Cumberland, Northumberland and Lancashire. By the time this Anglo-Scottish Jacobite army reached Preston it had swollen to over 20,000. But its commander, Thomas Forster,

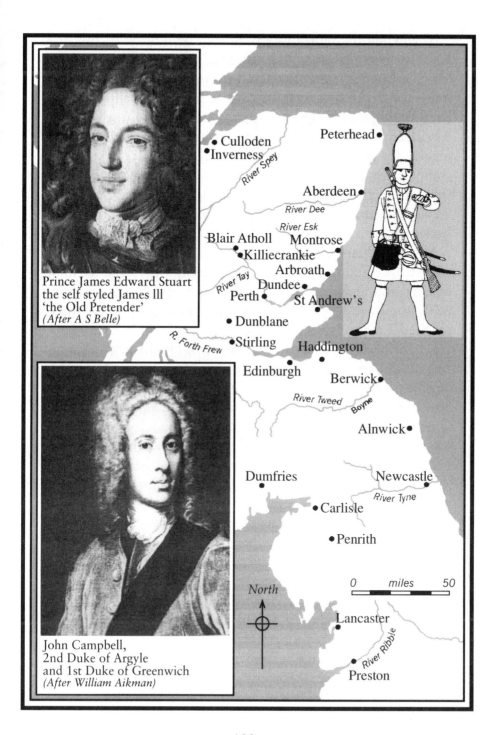

Prince James Edward Stuart
the self styled James lll
'the Old Pretender'
(After A S Belle)

John Campbell,
2nd Duke of Argyle
and 1st Duke of Greenwich
(After William Aikman)

Culloden
Inverness
River Spey
Peterhead
Aberdeen
River Dee
River Esk
Blair Atholl   Montrose
Killiecrankie
Arbroath
River Tay   Dundee
Perth   St Andrew's
Dunblane
R. Forth Frew   Stirling   Haddington
Edinburgh
Berwick
River Tweed   Boyne
Alnwick
Dumfries   Newcastle
River Tyne
Carlisle
Penrith
North
0   miles   50
Lancaster
River Ribble
Preston

MP for Northumberland, proving even more incompetent than Mar, allowed his army to be surrounded in Preston where he surrendered on 13 November. During October the Duke of Ormonde had made two sorties from France to the Devon coast, expecting thousands of West Country sympathizers to throng to his Standard. But in the face of well-prepared Georgian defences he withdrew to France without even landing. On 15 September the Lords Justice issued a proclamation ordering 'payment of 100,000 to any one who should seize and secure the Pretender in case he shall land in Great Britain or Ireland'.

It was indeed now the Pretender's turn. Better late than never, perhaps. Disguised as an Abbé, he arrived (from Lorraine) in Paris on 30 October. And next day, hotly pursued by an agent employed by the British ambassador, the Earl of Stair, as well as by one of Cadogan's, the young Prince made for the Normandy coast, arriving at St Malo on 8 November.[4] He wrote to Berwick instructing him to join his 'invasion', but Berwick declined, replying that, being a Marshal of France, he was precluded from leaving the country without the Regent's sanction (which Berwick, forseeing the uprising as being potentially abortive, took no trouble to obtain. The frustrated Pretender was to write to Bolingbroke, three weeks later, saying, 'I must suffer the humiliation of courting a disobedient subject and a bastard too.')

However, Berwick's son, Lord Teignmouth, sailed ahead of the hopeful Prince. Then, on 6 December and, not withstanding Admiral Byng's vigilance, the Pretender, with a few adherents, left from Dunkirk, disembarking at Peterhead, near Aberdeen, on 2 January 1716.[5] Having been proclaimed King James VIII at Fetteresso two days later, he proceeded to Perth where he reviewed Mar's motley army (or what was left of them, many having deserted). The Pretender was brave and handsome but he lacked resolution and charisma and looked glum. The Highlanders were not impressed. His mood was not helped by the fact that Teignmouth's ship was wrecked off St Andrew's carrying 100,000 ducats of gold bars, sent by the King of Spain. (The Hanoverians recovered them.)

From Stirling, 30 miles south of Perth, the unfortunate Argyll had sent a number of dispatches to Townshend requesting reinforcements. Eventually the British government, invoking the Anglo-Dutch pact of 1715, whereby Holland was obliged to provide 6,000 troops in the event of any threat to the Hanoverian succession, ordered Cadogan to take command of such a force (which would include Swiss, as well as Dutch, troops) and sail them from Antwerp to Scotland in support of Argyll. Robert Walpole's brother, Horatio, stood in for Cadogan at the Hague.

This diversion dovetailed nicely in Cadogan's career, his work for the Third Barrier Treaty having been concluded, in November, to the complete satisfaction of the Whig government.[6] He arrived with his 6,000 men at Stirling during the third week of December. There had never been much love lost between Cadogan and Argyll, the latter being a somewhat jealous and touchy man. To further deteriorate the situation Cadogan was sent more in the capacity of a government agent than a joint (or subordinate) commander. Cadogan kept nagging his Scottish colleague to advance, with his superior force, on Perth and attack. Argyll's army now amounted to over 10,000 soldiers. Argyll excused himself on the grounds that the road was snowbound. Cadogan countered by saying there were plenty of labourers to clear the way.

As for the enemy Mar submitted an order for the Pretender's signature, a warrant which was one of the factors proving fatal to the Jacobite cause. It was for five villages on the Perth-Stirling road to be burned in order to deny provisions to Argyll's army. The burning took place between 25–29 January. Thus the destitute villagers were obliged to stand in the snow watching their homes go up in flames and with nowhere then to lay their heads. Notwithstanding that brutality, the Jacobites made the decision, on 28 January, to withdraw from Perth and, next day, started their long march towards Dundee. On 3 February the Pretender wrote to the Regent of France begging help, men, money, and supplies. On the 4th, however, he and Mar came to the conclusion that their position was untenable.

Meanwhile Argyll, with Cadogan at his elbow constantly pressing him to advance, had been in a quandary. He wrote to Marlborough asking to be relieved of his command, adding that 'while I have the name of Commander-in-Chief the testimony of others is more listened to'.[7] And, once the march to Perth was completed, Cadogan posted a letter to the Captain General on 1 February telling him that 'the Duke of Argyle grows so intolerable uneasy that 'tis almost impossible to live with him any longer; he is enraged at the success of this expedition tho' he and his creatures attribute to themselves the honour of it'.[8] Argyll, for his part, may have found Cadogan's demeanour somewhat overbearing. Following a brief rest in Perth the Hanoverian army set off on the road to Dundee and Montrose.

On 4 February Mar and the Pretender admitted defeat. Mar handed over command of what was left of the rebel army to General Alexander Gordon of Auchintoul, while the Pretender wrote his 'letter of adieu to the Scotch'. And, to the everlasting fury of the loyal Highlanders, the two Jacobite 'leaders' sailed from Montrose to France where they were horrified to discover that Bolingbroke had murmured indiscreet confidences about the uprising to his mistress, Claudine de Tencin, who also happened to be the lover of the French foreign minister, Abbé Dubois, who, for mercenary reasons, supported England's Hanoverian government. So the Jacobite plans had been given away during the previous autumn. The Pretender's cause was effectively over. The Regent, after a good deal of prevarication, exiled him to Italy in February 1717. The Pretender died in Rome in 1766.

There remained, in the Highlands, the remnants of a rebel force to be dealt with. By now Alexander Gordon had ordered an evacuation of Aberdeen. Marlborough, on receipt of Cadogan's latest complaint, transferred the Scottish command to him and ordered Argyll to return to London. Cadogan, in his forthright and decisive way, sent his troops into the hills and glens to 'exterminate all the clans that will not give up their arms'. Early in April he was writing to Marlborough from the Blair of Athol telling him that 'all the Rebels in these Parts have bought in their arms and surrendered att discretion as they have likewise done in several places where I have sent detachments.'

The campaign against the rebels continued far into the Highlands and into the Hebrides. The correspondence of Frances, the widowed Countess of Seaforth, whose son, the Earl, had raised 800 Horse and 3,000 Foot for Mar, presents a sidelight. In April, when Cadogan was marching from Perth to Inverness, he received from her a request for a pass, which he sent to her. He added this: 'I am very sorry your coach and horses were taken away . . . Mine are at your Ladyship's service'. He goes on to inform her that the Seaforth estate will be garrisoned ' 'til my Lord Seaforth comes in and his People give up their Arms as their Neighbours have don, and indeed it appears unaccountable that his Lordship who was one of the first that offered to submit, should be one of the last to do it'. Cadogan goes on to offer protection for Lady Seaforth's 'House and Goods' and assures her that 'the garrison will pay for everything furnished them'.[9]

By 10 April he was at Inverness reporting to his chief that 'all the Clans have submitted except Lord Seaforth's and Macdonald's of the Isles who [would] come in as the others had done and would deliver their arms by Saturday next'. On 11 May he was writing from Edinburgh to say that 'as there is not a single Rebel now in arms, and that as the public peace and tranquility is restored in all parts of the Kingdom I judge it unnecessary for me to stay any longer.' Thus it was Cadogan who was largely responsible for quelling the uprising. On 25 May Townshend wrote to Horatio Walpole as follows:

His Majesty having no further occasion for the Dutch Troops is desirous to send them home as soon as may be Convenient, and would have you inform your self of the Pensry [Heinsius] whether those that are now about London may not be sent over separately . . . or whether it will be insisted on that they should all come over at one embarcation.[10]

A month later, Argyll having been branded a Jacobite sympathizer, Townshend told Walpole that 'ye Duke of Argyle & Ld Isla [Argyll's brother, the Earl of Islay] are removed from all their posts which will occasion his Majy's continuing here some days longer . . . you will be surprised at Argyle's disgrace but it was absolutely necessary for ye Kg's service'.[11]

Early in May Cadogan, mission accomplished, returned to London to be greeted by King George as the hero of the hour and to be rewarded with a Knighthood of the Thistle and a peerage as Lord Cadogan of Reading and of Oakley at which, having no son, he applied for his brother, Charles, to succeed to the barony of Oakley.[12] It was virtually through Cadogan's triumphant and conclusive campaign in 1716 that the Highlands of Scotland were fully assimilated into the United Kingdom.

Meanwhile the diplomat Charles Whitworth, whose regular posting was Berlin, was ordered to help Horatio Walpole to keep Cadogan's place at the Hague warm as explained in this letter from Stanhope to Whitworth of 11 March 1716:

There being at this time Affairs of ye greatest Importance to be transacted at the Hague with regard to the Publick Tranquillity of Europe as well as the Peace and Safety of his Majestys Dominions and his Majestys Service making it absolutely necessary that [Cadogan] should continue here . . . his Majesty has made choice of you to come to the Hague in the Quality of his Envoy Extraordinary.'[13]

Notes

1 BL Add MS 46501, f25

2 Louis died on 16 September 1715

3 Dickson, *op cit*, pt II (quoting States-General archives), which is also the authority for the previous paragraph

4 Saint-Simon gives a graphic description of the Pretender's journey through France to Scotland; *vide* Vol V of Arkwright's translation of the *Memoires*, pp 388–96

5 Tayler, 145

6 BL Egerton MS 3124, f 209 (Sunderland-Townshend corres)

7 *Ibid, vide* Coxe, III, p 392 '[Cadogan's] activity and zeal were strongly contrasted with the temporising and lukewarm conduct of Argyle'

8 BL Add MS 9128 cxxx.vii.63; cf Coxe III, 392–93; Tayler, 146

9 BL Add MS 28239, 45–46

10 BL Egerton MS 3124, (Townshend Papers, 25.5.16), f 87

11 *Ibid*, f 107

12 Cadogan, having been notified, when he was at Aberdeen, of the impending peerage by Marlborough, replied:

> Your Grace, having been pleased to order me to let you know the name of the Barony I desire to be called by . . . the place I propose is called Cadogan near Wrexham on the borders of Wales, on the Cheshire side, and as I am not so happy as to have a son . . . I have settled a great part of my fortune on my Brother Charles, it would be an infinite satisfaction to me, if the title was limited to him, should I leave no male issue. (*from the Blenheim Papers*) BL Add MS 37364, ff1–3]

13 BL Add MS 37364, ff 1–3

19

Diplomat and Statesman

(1716–1720)

On 14 September 1716, Cadogan was writing to Townshend from Holland to say that 'I have the honour to acquaint your Lordship that my Lord Sunderland and I landed on Thursday at Ostend and I design tomorrow for Brussels from whence his Lordship will goe in a day or two to Aix, and I intend at the same time to set out for the Hague'.[1]

Now aged 44, Lord Cadogan must once again have reflected on his life with great satisfaction. Starting out with a soundly based education but no great social advantage, he had come through a dozen and more violently fought military campaigns with geat distinction, yet without any serious injury, while achieving the rank of general at a remarkably tender age. And he had led the force which finally put paid to the 'Fifteen rebellion. Having proved himself as a master of espionage he was convincing King George and the Whig ministry that he was, too, a diplomat of singular ability and confidentiality. He had married a beautiful landowning woman from a prominent Dutch 'Regency' family and had fathered two pretty daughters. And here he was back in Lady Cadogan's homeland – speaking the language of her people (or French or German to foreign

200

diplomats) – as Ambassador Extraordinary and Plenipotentiary, for which appointment he resided at the Hague, at the stately Mauritshuis (where Charles the Second had stayed before returning to England as King in 1660).

Not that Cadogan carried all the diplomatic responsibility at the Hague. He was the Plenipotentiary, his assistant being Charles Whitworth, who, having been transferred from Berlin for the time being, continued to act in partnership with him (and independently during Cadogan's absences), while both kept close touch with Leathes, the Resident Minister at Brussels.[2] The Hague had become Europe's principal hub of diplomatic activity. It being usual, when a sovereign died, to renew treaties, a fresh Anglo-Dutch pact of friendship had been signed in February 1716.

As a Member of the House of Lords and the holder of several senior posts Cadogan returned to England at least once a year during this tour of duty as a diplomat (1716–20). 1717 was a good year for him except for one setback. Soon after being sworn in as a Privy Councillor in March he was indicted in the House of Commons by a clique of Tory Jacobites furious with him for his crowning success in Scotland. The charge was that he had defrauded the Government in the context of the transport for the Dutch and Swiss troops which he led against the uprising. There were few commanders who did not take a bit on the side for themselves when an opportunity occurred and, as we have seen, Cadogan, ever devious in money matters, was probably one of the last officers to have proved an exception to that. The pro-Jacobite MPs, knowing his reputation, were simply waiting for the dust to settle on the rebellion before making their accusation. However, Stanhope and other Whigs sprang to his defence and the Tory motion was easily defeated.[3] It is surely a strong reflection on Cadogan's wiliness that, considering his record of embezzlement, apparently no charge against him was ever upheld.

Southern Europe enjoyed a long period of comparative peace

following the Treaty of Utrecht. Yet the Continental Europe to which Cadogan returned after quelling the 'Fifteen' was a continent in considerable turmoil and Cadogan was a diplomat who always viewed international problems in a global context. Spain, with the sinister Cardinal Alberoni having chief influence with Bourbon Philip, laid claim to certain Austrian possessions in Italy and the Mediterranean and actually invaded and occupied Austrian Sardinia. Cadogan also took a close interest in the Austrian successes against the Turks. But he was more preoccupied with the 'Northern War', which was largely a quarrel between Russia (in the person of the Czar, Peter the Great) and Sweden's young king, that aggressive knight-errant, Charles XII, who, having on separate occasions defeated armies of Russia, Poland and Denmark, was himself thoroughly trounced by the Czar's army at Poltava in the Ukraine in 1709. The Czar, who in 1703 had founded St Petersburg as a port from which to hold sway in the Baltic and to give himself a marine window to the West, began to build a fine navy. And, following Poltava, he proceeded to snatch a number of Swedish properties along the Baltic's east coast. It seemed, too, as though Peter's predatory eyes looked towards Danzig and further – into west Germany.

In December 1716 the Czar arrived in Holland with the express purposes of examining the Dutch maritime industry and of raising a substantial loan from Amsterdam bankers. Cadogan, appreciating the threat posed by the Russian dictator's growing naval power, hastened to Amsterdam where he spoke to his old friend Antoine Heinsius and the burgomasters, warning them that it would not be in their country's interest to cooperate with the Russian leader. Back at the Hague, he told Hanover's Jean de Robethon exactly what he had done and why. For to curb the Czar was in Hanover's interest, and, to some extent, in England's too.[4] All the same, while the British ministers were happy for Admiral Sir John Norris to proceed to the Baltic with a squadron of gunboats to protect British trading interests, they were also concerned that their German monarch might drag their country into an expensive war that had little else to do with England. In order to provide Hanover with extra safeguards against Russian expansionism, George, who, accompanied by Stanhope, was in Hanover between July 1716 and January 1717, concluded two 'treaties of mutual guarantees', the first with Austria, and the second, more importantly, with France.

The Abbé Dubois, acting for Orleans, was a tricky individual. He found every excuse he could think up for postponing the exile of the Pretender (as did his equally devious successor, Chateauneuf). Dubois also kept finding excuses for delaying the Anglo-French treaty, one of which was to object that Cadogan lacked sufficient diplomatic stature to sign for Britain. On 10 November 1716 Townshend wrote to Cadogan, saying that 'it was with the utmost surprise that his Royal Highness [the Prince of Wales acting for his absent father] observed this fresh obstacle, which the Abbé has thrown in the way to his signing the Treaty, & whch is all together groundless & frivolous cannot but confirm his Royal Highness in the opinion that the Abbé has an undoubted backwardness in signing, not withstanding the professions he affects to make to the contrary.'[5]

However, the Anglo-French treaty was eventually signed by the Abbé Dubois and Stanhope in Hanover on 9 October and by Dubois and Cadogan at the Hague on 28 November. Cadogan was also instrumental in preparing the terms of the Triple Alliance (between France and the Maritime Powers) which George approved and countersigned at the Hague on his way back to London, accompanied by Cadogan and Stanhope, in January 1717. Cadogan then remained in England until May.

The Czar thought next to try his luck with France and her Regent. Charles Whitworth, writing on 20 April 1717 to Stanhope from the Hague (on his way to Berlin), remarked that, 'You will have heard that the Czar went away from hence very much piqu'd against us, and would not sign the orders which had been got ready for the removal of his Troops from Mecklenburg.[6] ... The Czar will go on to Paris ... if any opportunity ... should offer itself of promoting what he thinks his advantage or revenge 'tis probable he will not neglect it.'[7]

The finalization of the Barrier treaty was not achieved without considerable trouble as Cadogan intimated to Craggs Sr in a letter from the Hague dated 28 June 1718:

> More Lies are writt over here than my Lord Oxford's, or even the comptroler ever told. Mr Whitworth's and my Joynt Dispatch by this Post will inform you that our busyness goes on pretty well in this Place and that we shall force the Treaty through the States of Holland before the end of this week ... the negotiating this Affair has been more troublesome if possible than solicitting the House of Commons . . . The Emperor having it now in his Power to make Peace with the Turk, the Depart of our Fleet to the Mediterranean and this Republic's coming into his Majesty's Measures will I hope determine and fix the Regent and frighten the mad Cardinal into a Complyance and have some effect on our mad men at home.[8]

On 12 July Whitworth penned a letter, in his own name and that of Cadogan, to both Stanhope and Stair, complaining of the duplicity of the French minister at the Hague:

> We hope the mistake Monr de Chateauneuf so very maliciously endeavoured to draw his Count into a relation to a *Contre Lettre*, is rectified by the Explanations we gave in our last to your Excellencies on that matter. We cannot however forbear remarking that he designedly deceived the Regent in this affair, since the very day the Resolution of the States of Holland passed for signing the Project of Alliance I Whitworth at the desire of my Ld Cadogan went to inform him that the Resolution was *simple, pur, et sans restriction ou limitation* . . . We are told by some of our best friends that he continues to do Us privately all

204

the mischief he can and indeed it is not natural a Person should do otherwise who, in his Inclinations and Principles is against the Treaty and is entirely under the Influence of the Faction in France which has always opposed it.[9]

Following Charles XII's defeat at Poltava, Sweden's German provinces were parcelled out, Bremen and Verden eventually going to Hanover, acquisitions that gave George command of the mouth of the Elbe. On 2 July 1718 Cadogan and Whitworth wrote to Norris, who was acting in concert with the Dutch admiral to safeguard merchant ships in the Baltic. 'If there should be any appearance of Peace between the Swedes and the Muscovites and of their fleets acting in Conjunction in order to pass the Sound', they informed him, 'this State [Holland] will equip more ships to reinforce you.' The Hanoverians were no sooner installed on the banks of the Elbe than George declared war on Sweden. Meanwhile Charles XII, struggling to regain some of his lost territory on the east Baltic coast, had marshalled a fresh army and a fresh navy, his response to George's aggression being to pretend common cause with the Stuarts. He threatened to sail his new army to Scotland[10] and the young warrior-king might have done so had he not been killed by a sniper's bullet in Norway in December 1718. There would have been a sigh of relief on the lips of many people, not least on those of the Captains of Dutch and Danish merchant ships in the Baltic. With the death of King Charles of Sweden that threat almost disappeared.

Shrewd Cadogan, whose agents were as far afield as Holland and the Balkans, Berlin and Paris, Sweden and Spain, was well aware of that danger and, quite apart from his involvement in international politics, he was as deeply engrossed as ever in the game of espionage with particular reference to the Jacobites, whose own spies, recognizing the Plenipotentiary as the most astute of their opponents, kept a close watch on him.[11] Cadogan's heavy build, insouciance and bluff manner may have been an asset to him in this work. For such characteristics were inclined to give the impression of a blunt intellect, whereas they concealed a mercurial mind and a great craftiness.

All this was a hazardous extra involvement for a busy, dedicated diplomat. At least one letter addressed to Cadogan fell into the hands of the Jacobite leader, Lord Mar (who had been nominated a 'duke' by the Pretender). Mar forwarded this letter to his colleague, Sir Hugh Stirling, with a covering note, dated 17 September 1717: 'It is fit that Lord Cadogan shall be the opener of it himself and he should not have it till after Tuesday next, but as soon after that as possible. You will get the address put on it with all necessary appellations and you had best put it in the common post at Leyden, Rotterdam, or one of those places after the time I mentioned and you are sure he is arrived.'[12]

On 5 November Whitworth, back at the Hague, was telling Sunderland that 'on the 3rd Inst His Majtys Man of War the Dragon arrived at Helvoetsluys to convoy over my Lord Cadogan, but the wind having been since that time directly contrary his Exly is still detained on this side of the water . . . my Lord Cadogan and I have had the honour to inform your Lordship . . . of the vigorous measures which the Province of Holland was disposed to take for the Protection of their Commerce in the Baltick. This has extreamly alarmed the Swedish partisans'.

A little later Cadogan uncovered a plot by the Jacobite 'Privy Council' to have King George assassinated. On another occasion an agent of his in Spain reported that the defecting Duke of Ormonde had gone to Madrid to raise troops, supplies and money for another Jacobite invasion of Britain. It was Cadogan who tipped off the British government. (As it was, Ormonde's flotilla, conveying a force of 5,000 men, sailed from Cadiz in March 1718, but, being caught in a hurricane, was quickly scattered. However, two frigates, carrying three Scottish lords and 300 Spanish troops managed to avoid the hurricane. 1500 clansmen joined them, but the rebellion was crushed at the Pass of Glenshiel in June, 1719.[13]

One of Cadogan's Netherlands agents was Edward Burke, an Irish officer garrisoned in Flanders, who addressed the spymaster as 'Mr John Williams'. Burke must have been terrified of being found out, for he implored Cadogan never to 'let any body see my letters, but immediately burn them when you read them'.[14] Of course all Cadogan's spies had to be paid handsomely for such risky work. In writing about the assassination plot against King George Burke requested 'a letter of advice of the said summe without which I will doe no thing'.[15] Cadogan reassured him. 'You may depend on having a very considerable pension for your life, and a present great reward in ready mony, provided you can either produce or put me or any other of His Majesty's servants in a way of intercepting letters from England concerning offers to rise in Arms or proposals to serve the Pretender, or doing any thing else for the Pretender's interest'.[16] A few weeks later Burke requested that their correspondence be temporarily suspended as he had become 'an object of suspicion to the commander'.[17]

Cadogan now turned his attention to the Quadruple Alliance, by which Austria was brought into the treaty (already signed by Britain, France and Holland). He refers to the 'negotiating this affair' as being more onerous than 'soliciting the House of Commons'.[18] The pact, hatched by Stanhope, von Bothmar and Bernstorf, included a promise that the British navy would, if desired, cooperate with the Imperial forces against Spain in the Mediterranean. It was signed by Britain, France and Austria in July 1718, but not by Holland, whose leaders were lukewarm about the inclusion of Austria, until the following spring and then only reluctantly (with a good deal of cajoling by Cadogan).[19]

By now Cadogan had been made Earl. Among the papers appertaining to him, which are the property of the present Earl, there is a warrant signed by George the First on 24 November

1719, sending Cadogan on a highly important mission to Vienna, an assignment to follow up the Quadruple Alliance Treaty, and one that would test his skills and powers of persuasion to the full. It is headed *Private Instructions for our Right Trusty & Right Wellbeloved Cousin and Councillor William Earl of Cadogan whom We have appointed to go to our Good Brother the Emperor of Germany* [the Holy Roman Emperor] *upon certain matters of the utmost importance . . . You shall therefore repair forthwith to Vienna and demand an audience of* [the Emperor].[20]

Cadogan's first original task was to dissuade the Emperor from consenting to the marriage of the youngest of his 'Josephine archduchess nieces' to the Prince of Piedmont, the elder son of the King of Sardinia, a militant supporter of the Jacobite Pretender, whose aim was to obstruct the Quadruple Alliance, to disrupt the accord between England, France and the Empire and 'whose practices have given so just grounds of jealousy both to us and to the Regent of France'. However an adjunct to the document tells Cadogan that, since it was drafted, the Emperor had made clear that he declined to agree to the marriage.

The King goes on to warn Cadogan that some of the Emperor's subjects in the Netherlands are 'in mischievous league with the Court of Spain'. The King adds that 'It will be easy for you to demonstrate to the Emperor how much he would suffer by the Loss of our Friendship and that of France, and how little amends would be made him by acquiring that of the Court of Turin [the King of Sardinia's government] or of the Court of Madrid. Whatever wild Projects his new Ministers may have formed, they can never abide the Examination of so judicious a Prince as he is'.[21]

The document is couched in terms of courteous suspicion of the motives of the Emperor, who 'may have heard that Rumours among our Subjects were occasioned by the Escape of his Cousin German and Princess Sobiesky & how difficult it must be to destroy the general opinion that it did not happen without his Connivance'.

The warrant next refers Cadogan to the late conflicts in northern Europe and, in particular, to urge the Emperor to allow Prussia permanent possession of 'the town of Stettin and its District' and the Elector of Hanover [ie King George himself] 'the Dutchys of Bremen and Verden . . . You shall . . . support in our Name . . . both by word of mouth and in writing the Demands that shall be made in behalf of the Crown of Prussia and of the Electorate of Hanover of the said Investitures . . . Likewise the Emperor must support the return of Livonia and Esthonia to Prussia . . . and whilst we are obviously satisfying our engagements with the Emperor . . . it would be very hard if he should give any Obstruction to the Performance of what he owes to Us, and of what we owe to a Prince [King of Prussia], without whose Allyance we must have suffered Sweden to have been destroyed by the Czar'.

Cadogan is further enjoined 'to endeavour to induce [the Emperor] to concurr in acting with a good body of Troops against [the Czar] in case he should refuse to come into a Safe and Equitable Peace and you shall . . . support the Representations which shall be made on that head by the ministers of Sweden.' Cadogan must also persuade the Emperor to exert his influence more effectively to prevent the persecution of Protestants throughout the empire, 'particularly in the Palatinate . . . such notorious breaches of [the Treaty of Westphalia] of depriving the Protestants of their Catechism . . . and taking from them their Churches and the Revenues out of which their Ministers were maintained . . . which Persecution We look upon to be an Artifice of the Court of Rome to . . . create such Disturbances in the Empire as may occasion the Emperor losing the Assistance of his Allys.'

Comprising twenty-three lengthy paragraphs that elegant, if ponderous, document ran to twenty-six pages. Nor was that all. Shortly afterwards Cadogan received from the King 'additional

Instructions' in which he is urged 'upon Receipt of these Dispatches to set forward towards that Court [Vienna] without loss of time' and on the way, to call at Berlin on Charles Whitworth (who had recently returned from the Hague) 'and to assure his Prussian Majty of our unalterable purpose,' etc.[22]

Given Cadogan's formidable presence, profound knowledge of European affairs and impeccable diplomatic finesse, he accomplished the commission, apparently without undue difficulty, shortly after attending the marriage of his elder daughter, Sarah, to Lord March, which is to be one of the subjects of the next chapter. He remained in Vienna until October, 1720.[23]

Cadogan's attendance was now called for to be permanently at home where he was needed to fill his role as Master of Robes to the King more fully, for home politics and to display a closer interest in his various sinecures and honorary colonelcies, while Marlborough, having suffered two strokes in 1716,[24] required a military deputy who could act promptly and decisively for him as C-in-C. But Cadogan's diplomatic career was by no means finished.

Clearly his flagrant ambition showed, and was the subject of some ridicule, as reflected in this note from Stanhope to Stair, written on 10 March 1719.

> Good Lord Cadogan, though he has made the utmost profession of friendship and deference to other peoples measures, had certainly blown the coals; he has a notion of being premier ministre, which I believe you will with me think a very Irish idea.[25]

Notes

1   PRO SP 84/254
2   BL Add MS 37368, ff 48-49.(Stanhope to Whitworth March 11, 1717.)
3   Sunderland pointed out that the attack on Cadogan 'was butt leading one to others that were settled by the new faction against the whole

administration & indeed against the King himself'. (BL Add MS 61443, ff 65-67)

4   Dickson, *op cit*, Pt II
5   Egerton MS 3124 (Townshend Papers) ff 229-30
6   In April 1716 the Czar married his niece to the Duke of Mecklenburg and put Russian troops at the Duke's disposal. George I feared a Russian invasion of Hanover.
7   BM Add MS 37, 364, f 34; see *Saint-Simon Memoirs, op cit*, pp 506-15, for details of the Czar in Paris
8   Stowe, 246, Craggs corres.
9   BL Add MS 37368, Whitworth Papers, Vol XXI, f 387
10 BM Add MS 37, 364, ff 36-37. '. . . assurances have been given by the said Baron [Gortz of Sweden] that the King of Sweden would be very soon ready to invade Scotland with 12,000 men.' (Stanhope to Leathes, April 20, 1717). In that context the evidence against the Swedish ambassador to Britain, Count Gyllenborg, was so strong that, notwithstanding diplomatic immunity, he was placed in house arrest and his papers seized. Gortz, Sweden's envoy to the United Provinces, was also arrested.
11 'His movements were closely watched and reported on under the code-names "The Cobbler" and "Mc Cheyn"'. Dickson, *op cit*, pt II
12 *Ibid*
13 HMC Stuart MSS, f 189; cf Hatton, *George I*, 239, and Imbert-Terry, 261
14 Dickson, *op cit*, Pt II
15 *Ibid*
16 *Ibid*
17 *Ibid*
18 BL Add Ms Stowe 246 (Cadogan to Craggs, June 28, 1718)
19 The Dutch feared that the treaty might involve them in committing resources in a war with Spain
20 By kind permission of Lord Cadogan
21 BL Add MS 37365, f 498
22 By kind permission of Lord Cadogan
23 PRO SP80/41, f325
24 Cadogan had been virtually commander-in-chief from the time of Marlborough's first stroke. Argyll, the more senior lieutenant general (but who had 'blotted his copybook' in Scotland) was furious at being passed over.
25 HMC 2nd Report, f 189, 10.3.1719

20

Commander-in-Chief

(1720–1726)

Whereas we thought fit, about two years since, to give the rank and dignity of a Peer of this realm to William Lord Cadogan, by the title of Baron of Reading, in consideration of his great and eminent services; and particularly those performed by him during the war in Flanders, and after that, in the late rebellion in Scotland, as is more fully set forth in the preamble of our patent for creating him Baron of Reading; and we having great reason to be extremely satisfied with the services he has since done in several important negotiations transacted by him, as our Ambassador extraordinary in Holland; and with his conduct and behaviour in his station as General of our Foot and Commander of our Forces next under the Duke of Marlborough; and he having continued to give us upon all occasions, and in the most difficult times, singular and undoubted proofs of his zeal for our service, and of his steady, firm and inviolable, and unalterable affection to our person and government; and we having further an intention to send him speedily into Holland, to negotiate with the States General their entering into the alliance between ourselves, the Emperor, and the French King; which is an affair of the utmost importance to the good of these our Kingdoms in particular, and of Europe in general; and we in likewise having given him orders to make a public entry, in quality of our Ambassador extraordinary at the Hague, to assure the States, in the most solemn manner, of our constant friendship and affection to their Commonwealth. For these reasons, and to give a greater lustre and dignity to the commission we now employ him in, we have thought fit to create him Earl of Cadogan, in Denbighshire; Viscount of Caversham in Oxfordshire; and Baron Oakley, in Buckinghamshire.

George I's preamble to the patent for Cadogan's earldom, 1718.

During the years following the 'Fifteen' rebellion Cadogan's head was not only packed with problems and projects regarding his career as a diplomat, his involvement in espionage, his royal duties and the obligations of his various sinecures, it was also filled with concerns and hopes for his family and his properties, which must be in due proportion to his new status, that of his earldom (although, owing to the fact that 'Cadogan', as a place, proved to be no more than a tiny hamlet on the borders of Wales and Cheshire, the 'of' must, in due course, be dropped.) In April of the same year – having sold the various properties in Dublin, Co. Meath and Co. Limerick, which he inherited from his father – he bought the freehold of his Caversham (Causham) estate for a mere £6,000 and set about having a magnificent three- storey manor house built on the property, while London found him installed in his Hanover Square mansion. Colen Campbell describes the Caversham landscape, in his *Vitruvius Britannicus*, as . . . this magnificent place:

The situation is very high, but the ascent so easy and gradual that you rise insensibly to it; where the Eye is entertained with most beautiful Prospects; particularly that from the grand Terras, 1200 Feet long towards Reading and the Thames. The Descent from this Terras, to the bottom of the Parterre, is 50 feet perpendicular, by Two double Flights of Steps, all Portland stone. The

213

Parterre is nobly adorned with Fountains, Vases and Statues, particularly Four Originals in Statuary Marble of King William, King George, Duke of Marlborough and Prince Eugène.[1]

Owing to Cadogan's influence his brother, Charles, had been elected MP for Reading in 1716. But neither brother was popular locally (where Jacobitism prevailed); they gained the reputation of being mean and arrogant. There was little local sympathy for Lord Cadogan when the deer at Caversham were poached. According to Edward Thompson, in his *Whigs and Hunters*:

Earl Cadogan's deer-park and fishing-canals and obelisks cannot have been loved by the local inhabitants, upon whom he had suddenly descended somewhat like Gulliver's flying island of Laputa. Nor had Cadogan succeeded in endearing himself to the citizens of Reading, just across the Thames. The borough was an open constituency, with some 600 electors, which he tried but failed to bring into his pocket. The citizens clearly identified him with the Hanoverian interest: in the election of 1714–15 he failed to secure the seat in the face of crowds demonstrating under slogans of 'No Hanover, no Cadogan', and 'no Foreign Government'. His brother Colonel Charles Cadogan . . . lost his seat after a bitter conflict, in 1722. The Tory Dr Stratford wrote to Harley [Oxford] 'Reading has dealt the most honourably of any borough I have yet heard of. They shut their doors against Cadogan's brother . . . and declared that though they starved, they would not be bribed this election.' In the aftermath of his family's defeat the town teemed with Cadogan's soldiers. The navigations in his park had done nothing to improve the condition of Watry Lane, the only road between Caversham and Reading, an important market route flooded and impassable for many weeks in the year. Cadogan had promised that, if the borough chose his brother, he would drain and mend the road. The electors were left to do the work by public subscription (to which the Earl contributed not one penny) and by donations of their own gravel, labour and carts.[2]

It seems extraordinary that someone who suceeded, in youth, in carrying with him the hearts and minds of countless sub-ordinates on campaign, should, in middle age, allow himself to become unpopular at home. The reason was local Jacobitism.

Although Cadogan was now virtually retired from diplomacy he was sent, in 1721, on another most significant mission. Since the death of William III the Dutch had had no Stadtholder and it was in the interests of both Britain and Hanover 'to root out the false and pernicious maxims' of the republican Amsterdam regents *de ne prendre point de part aux Affaires Etrangères, de tacher de subsister sans Alliances Engagemens*. In other words Britain and Hanover wished to negotiate inter-state affairs through a Royal head of state with an Anglo-Hanoverian connection. They saw in Prince Willem of Orange-Nassau, the son of the soldier Prince Jan Willem Friso (William III's nephew) and his widow, Princess Maria Louise, the obvious choice. Willem, now 10 years old, had been elected at birth to his father's position as Stadtholder and captain-general of Friesland.[3]

Cadogan, who had already made a name for himself with the prince and his mother, sailed for Holland again that September, being empowered to offer the boy in marriage to one of George I's grand-daughters as soon as he should come of age. Cadogan reported on his journey and delivered his *Relation de l'Etat des Affaires en Hollande*, spelling out the various steps by which the pro-Stadtholder party might achieve its goal. This planning put another feather, if only a posthumous one, in Cadogan's cap. The marriage between Willem and Anne, the eldest daughter of George II, took place in 1734, and was followed three years later by the election of Willem IV as Stadtholder of the United Provinces.[4]

215

When Cadogan was made a baron in 1716 he had asked (having no sons as mentioned in Chapter 17) that his brother, Charles, might inherit the secondary Oakley title. In 1717 Charles (who would in due course become the second Baron Cadogan of Oakley) married well. His bride was Elizabeth, daughter of the immensely rich Irish physician Sir Hans Sloane (1660–1753), who had treated the late Queen during her last illness and who was, more significantly, Lord of the Manor of Chelsea[5] Through Elizabeth the Cadogan family became owners of the famous London estate which still bears their name.

Two years later came another very important family coup. William and Margaretta Cadogan's elder daughter, Sarah was 12 years old in 1719 and it was time to find her a suitable match. Socially-aspiring Cadogan had his eye on the 18-year-old Earl of March, son and heir of the Duke of Richmond, whose parents were the late Charles II and Louise de Kerouaille, Duchess of Portsmouth (then living in Paris). A substantial dowry was called for and it was typical of 'lucky' Cadogan to be owed a gambling debt by the Duke, with which to offset a considerable portion of the sum requested. The marriage took place at the Hague in 1719 (shortly before Cadogan began a special diplomatic mission to Berlin and Vienna). Lord March then proceeded, as most young aristocrats did, on a grand tour of the Continental towns, accompanied by his tutor, Mr Hill.

Cadogan, keeping track of his privileged son-in-law, wrote to him from the Hague in October, 1721:

> I assure your Lordship there are few things in the world that I desire more than to have the Pleasure of seeing you, but att the same time I am of opinion your Lordship should not return home till Spring, that is till the Sessions of Parliament is over . . . I think your Lordship cannot chuse a better Place to pass three months att than Luneville in Lorrain, tis near England and att a distance from those Parts of France which are infected. The

academy there is the best in Europe, The Court very polite and the Duke of Lorrain infinitely civil to the English, I approve therefore extremely of your Lordship going thither especially since you seem seriously resolved to be on your guard against Play . . . you will find Lord Albermarle [March's brother-in-law] at Munich, the Prince Electoral having invited him to pass the Winter there, as that Court is very agreeable. You will do right to stay there some little time. Lady Margaret [the Cadogans' second daughter] who was dangerously ill of the small Pox is God be thanked now out of danger, her Recovery is a kind of Miracle as she will not be able to goe abroad in three months she desires extremely that Lady March should keep her Company in her Confinement and Lady March begs it so very earnestly her self that I can hardly refuse their request I consent to it the less unwillingly because your Lordship must pass through this Country in your way to England from Lorrain in order to avoid the quarantain.[6]

Anticipating March's return in the spring of 1722, Cadogan, obviously a little apprehensive as to whether the couple would 'hit it off', wrote to him, from London, as follows:

My dear Lord, I was extremely glad to find by your Lordship's letter of the 21st of this month ns [new style] that you were safely arrived at Luneville and I hope to have very soon the Pleasure of seeing you in Holland. I design to embark the latter end of this week, and as soon as I get to the Hague, I shall give your Lordship immediate notice and expect you there with Impatience. The King goes the 16th of May os [old style] so that your Lordship will have an opportunity to wait on Him as he passes through Holland, and you may come for England with Lady March afterwards in the Yatch that has carried his Majesty over. My Lady Dutchess intends to be in Town about that time to meet your Lordship and Lady March, and her Grace and I have agreed that you shall pass part of the Summer att

217

Goodwood and part at Causham. I doubt not that her Grace has given your Lordship a particular account of this Plan we have formed for you . . . [There was a ps]: My most humble service to Mr Hill I beleive he is not a little pleased to have got so near Home.[7]

According to a later Lord March, his ancestor's sister, Lady Anne Lennox, was, like Cadogan,

contemplating his home coming with somewhat mixed feelings . . . For when they found themselves, much to Tom Hill's relief, once more at the Hague, en route for London, naturally enough Lord March was in no great hurry to resume relations with the poor little bride of whom he had nought but the distasteful recollections occasioned by the sordid circumstances of their union. And so, instead, [Lady Anne related] he repaired to the theatre intending to spend what he bitterly imagined to be his remaining hours of happiness in the enjoyment of the drama . . . And then he would honourably surrender to the inevitable. And now mark you what befell the unwilling bridegroom of three years ago. Dame Fortune had come there as well in haste to make amends. Facing him, and admiringly ogled, by not a few pretty fellows there sat a beauteous lady with whom he promptly fell over head and ears in love at first sight . . . And yet had he known it, that hackneyed expression was in no wise applicable. For, in response to his eager enquiry of those around him their eyebrows raised in astonishment that so proper a young man could display such surprising ignorance that the damsel was none other than the reigning toast, the beautiful Lady March.[8]

Cadogan was duly comforted:

My dear Lord, I most heartily congratulate your Lordship and my Daughter on your safe arrival in Holland, and hope to have very soon the pleasure of seeing you both here [London]. I conclude that before this can get to you, your Lordship will have returned all the Civilities and Visits you received on the occasion which brought you to Raphorst [Lady Cadogan's country seat].[9] I therefore desire your Lordship would lose no time in coming for England, for besides the infinite Impatience of your Friends here to see you, the King designs to review the Horse Guards towards the latter end of this month, and it will be extremely right for your Lordship to be then present. In case my wife should think it necessary for your Lordship to make a short visit to her Relations att Amsterdam four or five dayes will be sufficient for it and my Lady Dutchess[10] is of opinion with me this ceremony should not be omitted.[11]

That was written on 5 June 1722. A fortnight later Cadogan's old comrade-in-arms and benefactor, the Duke of Marlborough, died at Windsor Lodge, aged 72. Foremost in the procession for the burial at Westminster Abbey walked Cadogan at the head of a group of generals who had fought under Marlborough in the Spanish Succession War. Spitefully, Cadogan's Jacobite enemies accused their *béte noir* of appearing at the funeral 'indecorously dressed and betraying his want of sympathy by his looks and gestures'.[12] (See Prologue). The Bishop of Rochester, who had spent some time in the Tower for his Jacobite rantings, hated Cadogan and may have been behind that insulting description. The following Rochester diatribe, a clearly libellous one, written following Marlborough's funeral, doubtless reflects much of the venom felt by the Jacobites. For clearly it was Cadogan's swaggering, self confident, and probably rather loud-voiced, mien, as much as anything, that irritated them:

Unaw'd by Mercy and by Shame
Th'undoubted spawn of Hangman and of Bawd:
Ungrateful to th'ungrateful man he grew by,
A bawling blustering boystrous bloody booby.[13]

219

One reason for those jibes was that the Jacobite-leaning Duke of Argyll, albeit the senior lieutenant general, having incurred the displeasure of King George and the Ministry for his Jacobitism and faltering conduct in Scotland, was passed over in favour of Cadogan, who was, besides, the more capable of the two, for the posts of commander-in-chief (acting as such under the King) and master general of the ordnance. Cadogan was by all accounts the King's favourite Englishman (not only, perhaps, because he was a faithful Hanoverian and spoke German, but also because there was something rather Germanic in his bluff, extrovert, hail-fellow-well-met demeanour). Reflecting his prestige he personally commanded the troops encamped in Hyde Park in 1722 and was a member of the Regency Council during the King's absence in Hanover in 1723.

Sarah Marlborough comments cryptically on Rochester's hostile verse: 'it is some part of my Lord Cadogan's character: it would be too long to make it compleat, & would swell to as large a bulk as his person'.[13] Later in 1722 a friend of Sarah's informed her that Cadogan's 'great passion for Mrs Pulteney [the wife of William Pulteney MP] is . . . the Joke of the Town. He is the most ridiculous sight imaginable in all public places.'[14]

One wonders what thoughts went through Cadogan's mind while he walked with the Marlborough cortege on that solemn July day of 1722. Were they of the march to the Danube for which, at the age of 32, he had been administratively responsible? Of the shrapnel that hit him as he rode up the heights of the Schellenberg? Of that French cannon-ball that plunged into the clay at the feet of his and the Duke's chargers, while he, Cadogan, sent the aides-de-camp about their business at Blenheim? Of the cavalry charge he led after the Lines of Brabant were turned? Of that foggy reconnaissance-in-force before Ramillies? Of the Wynendael day? Of those flat-bottomed boats he had built to resupply the troops besieging Lille? Of his good fortune, having exposed himself 50 times over, in emerging from Oudenarde and Malplaquet alive? Of

220

his and the Duke's intrigues during the exile months? And now he wore Marlborough's mantle. He had reached the pinnacle of his military career. He also inherited from Marlborough the Colonelcy of the 1st Guards, (Grenadiers).

There was another pressing family issue. It was time to find a suitable husband for Sarah Cadogan's younger sister, Margaret. In a chatty letter of 23 October 1723 Cadogan wrote to the Duke of Richmond, with whom he appears to have struck up a close friendship, saying:

> I thank your Grace for the particular detail you sent of the Dutchess of Portsmouth's affairs . . . Before your Grace leaves the Hague, Lord Carnarvon will very probably be there the Duke of Chandos [James Brydges][15] has proposed him for Lady Margaret, and offers such conditions as I doe not dislike. I shall not however resolve positively on any thing till I see your Grace. I must beg of you to be particularly civil to him, and to find out his inclinations as to Whig and Tory, for should he have any tendency towards being the latter I shall think no more of the match . . .[16]

That particular proposal for Margaret Cadogan fell through. She eventually married an Anglo-Dutch aristocrat like herself, Count Bentinck, a son of William III's favourite, the 1st Earl of Portland. (Bentinck was a Count of the Holy Roman Empire.)

Although Cadogan was not much over fifty the campaigning years of toil and danger and privation had taken their toll. There was little time left to him. A month after Marlborough's funeral he was writing to one of his generals of ' such a violent Fluxion on my eyes.'[17] On 1 August 1724 he told the Duke of Richmond that he 'got safe to Town before it was dark on Thursday and was God be thanked very well that day, but yesterday I had a violent Feaverish fit which lasted a great while. Sir Hans Sloane [father-in-law of his brother, Charles] ordered the Bark [quinine] of which I have taken already no small quantity . . . I have still a pain in my head which makes the writing uneasy to me.'[18]

Yet he was as busy as ever, telling Richmond on the 20th of that month that 'I goe three times a week to Windsor [in his capacity as Master of the King's Robes], so that I almost live upon the road. The King is most extremely delighted with the Place, and talks of making a Garden below the Terasse.'[19]

Cadogan's unfortunate financial speculation after Marlborough had entrusted him with £50,000 for investment in Holland in 1712, now caught up with him. For Cadogan had, as we have seen, reinvested the money in Austrian securities, which at that time were paying a much higher dividend. Subsequently, however, those fell heavily on the market, to such an extent that Marlborough lost a lot of money. His widowed duchess, now a rather bitter, as well as avaricious, old woman, who had always been jealous of her husband's fondness for his closest comrade-in-arms, claimed recompense. She sued Cadogan and won. That came at a difficult time for him, considering there was still a large sum to be paid on Caversham and more outstanding on the Richmond dowry. ('Marlborough's brave and faithful comrade, always lax in money matters,' comments Winston Churchill, 'had great difficulty in making the necessary restitution.'[20])

In the spring of 1725 Cadogan's health had become such a liability that he was asked to resign the taxing appointment of Master General of the Ordnance. In a letter to Richmond of 1 May, a letter reflecting once again George I's prejudice (and his own, too), he wrote:

> I cannot better explain to your Grace my present situation than by transmitting here enclosed the letter I received from Lord Townshend [by then Lord President of the Council] to signify my dismission from the ordnance, to which I may add, that it was with the utmost reluctancy that the King consented to my

removal. The Duke of Argyle [created also Duke of Greenwich 1719] is to have nothing to do with the command of the army and the Duke of Bolton is made the Constable of the Tower, he however keeps his Regt.[21] His Majesty having declared that the Duke of Argyle shall neither have that Regiment nor any other.[22] I send back your Grace's commissions . . . I am not so rebuted by the present stroke but that I still hope and beleive, I shall have it one day in my Power to shew my gratitude by some thing more solid than thanks . . . I design to go to Causham the day after the King embarks. I desire your Grace to assure Lady Dutchess of my most tender affections.[23]

Writing to Richmond from Caversham in mid-July Cadogan saw prospects of a complete recovery:

Tho my being still obliged to keep my bed makes writing a little uneasy, yet I could not refuse my self the Pleasure of thanking you by the very first opportunity for your kind and obliging letter of the 15th. I continue God be thanked to grow better and better, and the Surgeons say I recover as fast as any body did after so severe an operation . . . When I write next to Prince Eugène I shall not fail to recommend Faustina [a celebrated singer] . . . I rejoice to hear that she is engaged by our Royal Academy of Musique after she leaves Vienna . . . I am afraid your Grace will be hardly able to read this Scrawl I am forced to write it in twenty different Postures.'[24]

By the end of that summer Cadogan was still optimistic about his health (but the modern reader's mind boggles at the thought of the primitive method of surgical operations then practised, not to mention the scarcely effective anaesthetics). He wrote to the Duke on 14 September, to say that:

I received yesterday in the afternoon your Graces letter by your running Footman and am infinitely obliged to you for your kind

223

Enquiry and concern about my health I have been extremely ill since the last operation, of the Stone Cholick, but am now God be praised very easy, and my wound begins to mend tho slowly I rest well; and have a good stomach; and am allowed to eat a Chicken every day. What retards the cure is a sharp Humour That falls upon the Wound, and to dry up this Humour the Surgeons use [illegible word] and Inward means, which begin to have in some measure their effect, for it lessens every day . . . Little Carolina [his eldest granddaughter, and also Richmond's, aged two][25] is mighty well and amuses me extremely.[26]

Five days later he added that:

Since writing last to your grace I have God be thanked mended a good deal, and as Sir Hans Sloan and Mr Busiere are of opinion I should hasten to London, to have their advice and assistance in case of new accidents, I design to goe there as soon as I can bear the jolting of a Coach, which if the wound continues to heal as it has done of late, will I hope be in a very few dayes. When I can fix the time, I shall let your Grace know it. Little Carolina is in perfect Health she will goe in the coach with my nieces [daughters of his sister, Penelope Lady Prendergast]. My brother and sister came here on Thursday last.[27]

Cadogan was a born optimist. But, notwithstanding the courage and persistent cheerfulness reflected in those letters, he did not recover from his operation. He died on 17 July, 1726, aged only 54. 'The Earl Cadogan dyed in top dress', said an observer, 'and kept on him to the last his great wig, imbroydered coat, brocade vest, red top shoes, diamond buckles . . .'[28] He was buried in Westminster Abbey four days later.

To his enemies he was brash and unhealthily conceited, much too full of himself, arrogant and overbearing, mean, grossly acquisitive and dishonest, greatly overrated by Marlborough (another villain) and was as undeservedly lucky in his career, as he was as a gambler. And, as we have seen, Cadogan's negative side all too often showed. He was a bit of a rogue – as well as a military, diplomatic and secret service genius. To his admirers he was frank and open, amiable and brave as a lion, an outstanding military administrator and leader of men, a diplomatic negotiator with a sharp intellect and a global sense of politics. In short, to those supporters, he was a paragon and something of a genius.

The Duke of Marlborough was Britain's greatest soldier-diplomat, arguably a general of even higher accomplishment than the Black Prince, Henry V or Wellington and certainly of higher stature than any of those soldiers who followed in the 19th and 20th centuries. An intuition that was to prove one of Marlborough's principal triumphs was that of recognizing the very young William Cadogan as a budding military genius. Marlborough's decision to appoint the youthful Cadogan to be his chief of staff, quartermaster general and director of intelligence over the heads of many senior officers was itself a mark of the Captain General's shrewd judgement.

Marlborough was, more or less, a sick man throughout the Spanish Succession War and was frequently dependent upon the ultra-fit and energetic Cadogan to lead crucial missions, missions that required not only outstanding courage, considerable resourcefulness and tactical initiative but also geat ingenuity, qualities not entirely possessed by any of the other generals. As another soldier-diplomat, the Earl of Strafford [Raby], wrote to Lord Chancellor Harley in 1713 'I do believe the greatest part of Lord Marlborough's victories are owing to him [Cadogan], and even the Pensionary [Antoine Heinsius, Holland's Chancellor] said to me *si vous voulez avoir un duc de Marlborough, un Cadogan est Necessaire*'. But Cadogan was much more than Marlborough's 'other military half'. Nor was he simply a brilliant commander and military administrator. That bluff and haughty presence concealed the incisive mind that rendered him such a first-class diplomat and master of espionage. Notwithstanding his weaknesses, his stubbornness and haughtiness, his financial avarice and addictive gambling, surely we can now accord him the high place in Britain's history that he has so far been denied? Whatever else is in question his place as Britain's first star military administrator must be difficult to challenge.

Notes

1 Vol III (1725) pp 11–12
2 Page 101. Thompson quotes *Particulars of the Manor of Caversham; a list of the Subscribers for mending the road from Reading to Caversham; An Account of the Riots Tumults and other Treasonable Practices since his Majesty's Accession to the Throne.* Romney Sedgwick, *History of Parliament: The House of Commons, 1715–54,* 1970.
3 Hatton, *George I,* pp 267–68; Hatton, *Diplomatic Relations between Great Britain and the Dutch Republic, 1714–1721,* p 221
4 *Ibid*
5 In addition Sir Hans Sloane's library and art collection formed the basis for the foundation, in 1753, of the British Museum
6 Goodwood MS 106, L21
7 *Ibid*, L23
8 March, Earl of. *A Duke and his Friends: the Life and Letters of the 2nd Duke of Richmond,* Vol I, p 64
9 Raaphorst Castle, set in a 520-acre estate, lay 10 miles from the Hague
10 March's mother, Anne, daughter of Francis, Lord Brudenell, had been the widow of Henry, Lord Belasyse of Worlaby
11 Goodwood MS 106, L24
12 DNB
13 Blenheim MSS
14 *Ibid*
15 Brydges became Earl of Carnarvon in 1714. He was created Duke of Chandos in 1719. His son thus assumed the courtesy title of Earl of Carnarvon.
16 Goodwood MS 106, f 8
17 Huntington, Stowe MS, f 104
18 Goodwood MS 106, f 10
19 *Ibid*, f 11
20 WSC, IV, 1031
21 Bolton was Colonel of the Royal Horse Guards (Blues), 1717–33

22 Argyll was Colonel of the 4th (Scottish) Troop of the Life Guards, 1703–15; Colonel of the Royal Horse Guards, 1715–17, 1733–40 and 1742; and Colonel of the 2nd Dragoon Guards (Scots Greys),1726–33

23 Goodwood MS 106, f 10

24 *Ibid*, f 30

25 The Marchs' eldest child, Lady Georgiana Carolina Lennox, born London, 1723

26 Goodwood MS 106, f 38

27 Goodwood MS 106, f 40

28 DNB

Epilogue

The Succeeding Dynasty

1726–2001

Second Baron Cadogan of Oakley (1685–1776)
Charles Cadogan, the 2nd Baron of Oakley, appears to have
lacked entirely the hubris and deviousness of his illustrious
elder brother as well as the genius and brilliant practical ability.
It is also apparent that Charles would have left little mark on
the world, would have been a man of minor account, but for
William. Charles had the Earl to thank for his barony of Oakley
besides his appointments as MP for Reading (1716–22) and for
Newport, Isle of Wight (1722–26). It is doubtful, too, that
Charles would have looked an eligible candidate for the hand
of Sir Hans Sloane's daughter, whom he married in 1717, had
he not been declared his brother's heir. It is therefore reasonable to add that the Cadogan dynasty, still thriving today, owes
its original lustre and estate largely to the great general.

We know little of the second Baron Cadogan of Oakley
except that he, too, spent his youth as a regular soldier. Being
originally commissioned in the Second Foot Guards (the
Coldstream) he bought his regimental promotion in Colonel
Rooke's Foot, fought at Oudenarde and Malplaquet and
became a general in 1761, by which time he was 76 years old.

The deceased Earl's debts gave him quite a lot of trouble, particularly that still owing on the dowry due to the Lennox family. (His niece, Sarah, became the second Duchess of Richmond in 1723.[1]) Charles Cadogan raised a substantial sum by selling the Manor of Oakley to Sarah, Duchess of Marlborough (who was, then, incidentally, reputed to be the richest woman in Europe). There was still a deficit when William's Countess, Margaretta Cecilia, died in 1749. She spent her widowhood in Holland, at Raaphorst, and the proceeds of the sale of that estate also went mostly to the 2nd Duke of Richmond.

Charles Cadogan lived at a succession of three London houses and at Caversham until his death, aged 91, in 1776. During the latter part of his life he also spent time at Cadogan House, also known as Chelsea House, which stood on the site of what is now the Duke of York's headquarters, off King's Road, and which he used as an administrative headquarters for the estate.

Sir Hans Sloane bought the Manor of Chelsea in 1712. It was at that time an essentially rural parish, much of it planted out with market orchards and vegetable gardens. The adjacent Thames was fished for salmon, while the river was thick with traffic, Chelsea's Cheyne Walk berth being one of the most convenient mooring-places.

The Cadogan estate was created on the death of Sir Hans. There were two heiresses to his will, Lady Cadogan and her elder sister, Mrs Stanley. But a large proportion of the Stanley land reverted through bequest to the Cadogans, so that only a quarter of the Stanley estate passed to Sir Hans Sloane's great-nephew, Hans Sloane Stanley. In 1771 Henry Holland, the architect son-in-law of 'Capability' Brown, leased 90 acres, stretching from Knightsbrige to a little way south of what is now Sloane Square. Building began six years later. Hence that part of the Cadogan estate, originally known as 'Hans Town'.

The First Earl of the New Creation (1728–1807)

The heir to the barony, Charles Sloane Cadogan, was a successful politician, beginning his career as MP for Cambridge at the age of 21, and holding the seat for the next 27 years.

His marital life was ill-starred. He married, first, into a somewhat emotionally unstable family, she being Frances Bromley the daughter of the first Lord Montfort, who committed suicide. Thirteen years later Frances herself 'dyed raving mad'.[2] Meanwhile she had borne Cadogan eight sons, but only one of whom was to outlive his father. Shortly after the death of his own father the new Baron Cadogan married again (1777), this time to Mary Churchill, a cousin of the then Duke of Marlborough and granddaughter of Sir Robert Walpole, (subsequently Earl of Orford), Britain's first prime minister. She produced another three sons and two daughters for him, but then ran off with a vicar, several years her junior, called Cooper, with a living near Caversham. Hoping to retrieve the situation Lord Cadogan promptly sold Caversham, removing his erring wife and their children to East Anglia and setting up a new family home, Downham Hall, Suffolk. But, as the move failed to abate Mary's extra-marital passion, he divorced her in 1796, citing the clergyman, who had been forced to relinquish his living.

This third Baron Cadogan of Oakley, a man of many political and administrative parts – he held among other appointments, the Mastership of the Mint (1769–84) – was created Earl Cadogan and Viscount Chelsea in 1800.

The present holder of the title, the 8th Earl and owner of the Cadogan estate, was born in 1937. He married in 1963, Lady Philippa Wallop (died, 1984) a daughter of the 9th Earl of Portsmouth, his heir being Viscount Chelsea, to whom he has delegated the running of the London estate.

Notes

1 Four of Sarah's daughters were the subject of Stella Tillyard's widely-acclaimed *Aristocrats*: Caroline, who married the 1st Lord Holland;

Emily, who became Countess of Kildare, and then Mrs William Ogilvie; Louisa, who married Thomas Conolly; and Sarah, who was first Lady Bunbury and, secondly, Mrs George Napier

2 Pearman, *The Cadogan Estate*, p67, quoting L-W Mackzenzie, *Twelve Lordships since the Conquest; Caversham Park: a Retrospect;* and *The Letters and Journals of Lady Mary Coke,* Vol II

Sources and
Select Bibliography

Contemporary Unpublished Sources

British Library
Add MSS 9114 (Archdeacon Hare's Journal): 22196 (Strafford Papers/Raby-Cadogan corres): 37209 (Earl of Orrery, diplomatic corres, 1711–14); 31, 134 (Raby's political corres); 37364, 37365, 37368, 37371 and 37373 (Whitworth Papers); 37209 (Complaints against Cadogan by the Netherlands Council, 31.3.10); 4456 (Verses addressed to Cadogan in 1718); 38500 (Townshend Papers); 46501 (Warrant for Cadogan's Appointment as Captain of the Isle of Wight and Governor of Carisbrooke Castle); 3516 (Sloane MS); 28, 239 (corres of Frances Countess of Seaforth); 46936 (Warrant for Cadogan's grandfather as Governor of Trim); 5136; 21494; 37200; 37209 (Lord Orrery's diplomatic corres) and 61351

Public Record Office
SP 77 (Flanders) 57, 58, 59, 60 and 64
SP 80 (Holy Roman Empire) 40, 41 and 42
SP 84 (Holland) 254, 254, 257, 258, 262, 267, 268, 273 and 274

Huntington Library (California, USA)
Cadogan, letters of 5.11.01; 25.6.06; 29.10.06; 31.3.07; 10, 25, 28 and 30.4.07; 25.4.17 and 10.7.22

Royal Commission on Historical Manuscripts
Bath, Checquers Court, Cowper, Egmont, Lansdowne, Northumberland, Stopford Sackville, Stowe and Stuart MSS

West Sussex Record Office
Correspondence between Cadogan and the 1st Duke of Richmond and the Earl of March. Goodwood MS 106 – L21 (28.10.21); L22 (16.2.22); L23

232

(24.4.22); L24 (5.6.22); L8 (22.10.23); L10 (1.8.24); L12 (1.5.25); L30 (15.7.25); L38 (14.9.25) and L40 (19.9.25)

The Cadogan Estate
A substantial collection of documents appertaining to the 1st Earl and dated between 1705 and 1719. (These were discovered recently in a loft by Viscount Chelsea, the present Earl's son).

Contemporary Published Sources

Ailesbury, Thomas Bruce, Earl of, *Memoirs*, Vol II (Roxburghe Club, 1890)
Berwick, Maréchal James FitzJames, Duke of. *Memoires*, 2 Vols. (Ed London, 1779)
Bishop, Corporal Matthew, *Life and Adventures* (1744)
Blackadder, Colonel John, *Diary, 1700–1728* (Ed A. Crichton, 1824)
Burnet, Bishop Gilbert, *History of His Own Time*, Vols V and VI (Ed 1823)
Campbell, Colen, *Vitruvius Britannicus*, Vol III (1717)
Carleton, Capt George, *Military Memoirs*, 1672
Chandler, David, *Two Soldiers of Marlborough's Wars*: Memoirs of Capt Robert Parker and Comte Eugène-JeanPhilippe de Mérode-Westerloo, including Parker's *Memoirs of the Most Remarkable Military Transactions, 1693–1718* (1746) and Merode-Westerloo's full *Memoires* (Paris, 1840; republished by Longmans, 1968))
Colonie, J. M. de la, *The Chronicles of an Old Campaigner*, 1692–1717. (Translated by W.C.Horsley, John Murray, 1909)
Coxe, Archdeacon William. *Memoirs of the Duke of Marlborough* (with his original – contemporary – correspondence), 3 Vols, ed John Wade (Henry Bohn, 1847-8)
Deane, Private J. M. (Foot Guards), *Journal of the Campaign in Flanders, 1708* (ed. 1846)
Defoe, Daniel, *The Life and Adventures of Mother Ross*
Drake, Capt Peter, *Amiable Renegade* (ed Stanford University Press, 1960). Foreword by Paul Jordan-Smith; introduction by S.A.Burrell
Farquhar, George, *The Recruiting Officer*, 1706 (Rupert Hart-Davis edition, 1965)
Hamilton, Sir David, *Diary, 1709–1714* Memoirs of Queen Anne's doctor, ed Philip Roberts, (Clarendon Press, Oxford, 1975)
Hare, Rev Dr Francis, *The Conduct of the Duke of Marlborough during the Present War* (1712)
Hoff, Van'T, (ed the Hague 1891) *The Correspondence of John Churchill Duke of Marlborough and Antoine Heinsius, 1701–1711.*

Hooke, Nathaniel, *The Conduct of the Duchess of Marlborough* ('Written under the Duchess's inspection, 1742')

Kane, Brig Gen Richard, *A System of Camp Discipline and other Regulations for the Land Forces and the Campaigns of King William and Queen Anne (1747)*. The first part of the book (pp1–83) contains the *System of Discipline*. The second part (146pp) covers the campaigns of William III and Marlborough (National Army Museum no 355 541)

Lediard, Thomas, *The Life of John, Duke of Marlborough*, 3 vols (London 1736)

Luttrell, *Brief Historical Relation of State Affairs*, Vols V and VI (ed. 1857)

Mérode-Westerloo, Comte Eugène-Jean-Philippe, *Memoires* (ed 1840). His journal and that of Capt Robert Parker were republished in David Chandler's *Two Soldiers of Marlborough's Wars*, from which my references are taken.

Millner, Sergeant John, *A Compendious Journal, 1701–1712* (London, 1733)

Murray, George. (Ed). *The Letters and Dispatches of John Churchill, 1st Duke of Marlborough*, 5 Vols (London, 1845)

Orkney, George Hamilton, Earl of, *Four Letters of the First Lord Orkney during Marlborough's Campaigns*. (Ed H.H.E. Cra'ster in the English Historical Review, April, 1904)

Parker, Capt. Robert, *Memoirs of the Most Remarkable Military Transactions from 1683 to 1718*. (1746). See Chandler

Saint-Simon, Louis de Rouvroy, Duc de, (1675–1755). *Memoires*. 6 Vols. Translated by Francis Arkwright (Stanley Paul, 1918) Vols II, III, IV and V are relevant

Secondary Printed Sources

Atkinson, C. T., *Marlborough and the Rise of the British Army* (G P Putnam, 1921)

—— *Marlborough's Sieges*, (In the Journal of the Society for Army Historical Research (1934) pp195–205

Bevan, Bryan. *Marlborough the Man* (Robert Hale, 1975)

—— *King James the Third of England: A Study of Kingship in Exile*. (Robert Hale 1967)

Black, Jeremy, *European Warfare, 1660–1815* (UCL Press, 1994)

Carleton, J. D., *Westminster (Blackie, 1938)*

Carman, W. Y., *The Dress of Erle's Regiment in 1704 and 1709* (in the Journal of the Society for Army Historical Research, Vol 46, 1968)

Chandler, David, *Marlborough as Military Commander* (Batsford, 1973)

— *The Art of Warfare in the Age of Marlborough* (Batsford, 1976)

— See also under 'contemporary published sources'.

Churchill, Winston S., *Marlborough His Life and Times*, (Harrap, 1947). The first edition of this monumental work was published in 4 vols in 1933, these being reduced to two books, from which my references are taken, in 1947

Clark, Sir George, *War and Society in the 17th Century* (CUP 1958).

Clode, Charles M., *Military Forces of the Crown*, Vol I (John Murray, 1869)

Dalton, Charles, *George the First's Army*. 2 vols. (Eyre and Spottiswoode, 1910 and 1912)

Davies, Godfrey, *The Seamy Side of Marlborough's War*. In the *Huntington Library Quarterly*, Vol 15, 1951–52, pp21–44

Dickson, Patricia, *Red John of the Battles. John, 2nd Duke of Argyll and 1st Duke of Greenwich*, 1680–1743. (Sidgwick and Jackson, 1973)

— *Lieutenant General William Cadogan's Intelligence Service*, in Vol 109 of the *Army Quarterly*, in two parts (Jan and April, 1979)

Dictionary of National Biography, Vol VIII. (Smith Elder edition, edited by Leslie Stephen, 1886)

Ferguson, James (ed): *Papers illustrating the History of the Scots Brigade in the Service of the United Netherlands, 1572–1782* (Vol VIII. Edinburgh University Press, 1901)

Fortescue, J., *Marlborough*. (Peter Davies, 1934)

—— *History of the British Army*, Vol I (London 1889)

Fosten, D S V., *Blenheim*. Artwork by B. Fosten (Almark, 1974)

Francis, David, *Marlborough's March to the Danube*, 1704, in the *Journal of the Society for Army Historical Research*, Vol 50, 1972, pp 78–100

Gregg, Edward, *Queen Anne* (Ark Paperbacks, 1984)

—— *Marlborough in Exile*, 1712–1714, in the *Historical Journal*, XV, 4 (1972), pp 593–618

Grimblot, J. (Ed), *Letters of William III and Louis XIV and their Ministers, 1697–1700*. 2 Vols (Longmans, Brown and Green, 1848)

Gutman, Myron P., *War and Rural Life in the Early Modern Low Countries* (Princeton University Press, 1980)

Harris, Francis, *A Passion for Government. The Life of Sarah, Duchess of Marlborough* (Clarendon Press, 1991)

Hatton, Ragnhild, *George I: Elector and King*. (Thames and Hudson, 1978)

—— *Diplomatic Relations between Great Britain and the Dutch Republic, 1714–21*. (London, 1950)

Imbert-Terry, H. M., *A Constitutional King: George I*. (John Murray, 1927)

Jackson, Major E. S., *The Inniskilling Dragoons* (Humphries, 1909)

Kemp, Anthony, *Weapons and Equipment of the Marlborough Wars* (Blandford Press, 1980)

Kipling, Arthur, *Uniforms of Marlborough's Wars*, with illustrations by Frank Wilson (Charles Knight, 1970)

Legge-Pomeroy, Major Hon Ralph, *The Story of a Regiment of Horse*. The

History of Princess Charlotte of Wales's (the 5th) Dragoon Guards. 2 Vols (Blackwood, Edinburgh, 1924)

McDowell, R. B. and Webb, D. A., *Trinity College, Dublin* (Cambridge University Press, 1982)

Maclysaght, Edward, *Irish Life in the 17th Century* (Cork University Press 1950)

March, Earl of, *A Duke and his Friends* (Hutchinson, 1911)

O'Brien, R. Barry. *Studies in Irish History 1649–1775* (Browne and Nolan, 1903)

Ogg, D., *Europe in the 17th Century*, Clarendon Press, 1948)

—— *England in the Reigns of James II and William III* (Clarendon Press, 1963)

Pearman, Robert, *The Cadogan Estate* (Haggerston Press, 1986).

—— *The First Earl Cadogan* (Haggerston Press, 1988)

Pelet, J. J. G. and De Vault, F. E., *Memoires Militaires relatifs a la Succession d'Espagne sous Louis XIV* (Paris, 1850)

Petrie, Charles, *The Marshal Duke of Berwick* (Eyre and Spottiswoode, 1953)

Plumb, J. H., *Sir Robert Walpole: The Making of a Statesman* (Cresset Press, 1956)

Robb, Nesca, *William of Orange* (Heinemann, 1966)

Scouller, R.E., *The Armies of Queen Anne* (OUP, 1966)

Simms, J. G., *The Williamite Confiscation in Ireland – Vol VII of Studies in Irish History* (Faber, 1956)

Tayler, A. and H., *1715: The Story of the Uprising* (Thomas Nelson, 1936)

Taylor, F, *The Wars of Marlborough* (London, 1921)

Thomson, A. D., *Memoirs of the Jacobites*, Vol I (London, 1845)

Thompson, E. P., *Whigs and Hunters.* (Penguin, 1975). This includes several references to Cadogan at Caversham

Tillyard, Stella, *Aristocrats: Caroline, Emily and Sarah Lennox 1740–1832*, (Chatto & Windus 1994)

Trevelyan, G. M., *England in the Reign of Queen Anne.* 3 Vols. (Longmans Green, 1930)

Veenendaal, A. J., *The Opening Phase of Marlborough's Campaign of 1708 in the Netherlands.* (In the February and June, 1950, issues of *History*, pp34–48

Verney, Peter., *The Battle of Blenheim* (Batsford 1976)

Walton, Clifford., *History of the British Standing Army, 1660–1700* (Harrison, 1894)

Wyon, G.W., *The History of Great Britain during the Reign of Queen Anne* (London, 1876)

236

Index

239

Brussels, 100, 101, 105, 112, 127, 189, 200
Buckingham, Duke of (*quoted*), 180
Burgundy, Duc de, Grandson of Louis XIV, 112–123, 125–126, 127
Burke, Edward, ("John Williams"), 207
Burnet, Gilbert, Bishop of Salisbury, *quoted*, 65
Busby, Dr Richard, 2, 3
Bülow, Lt Gen Count, 56–57
Byng, Admiral Sir George, 99, 194

Cadogan,
  Ambrose, brother of General William, 2
  Charles, 3rd Baron and 1st Earl (of the new creation), 230
  Charles, 2nd Baron of Oakley, brother of General William, 2, 198, 214, 216, 221, 228–229
  Charles, 2nd Earl (of the new creation), 230
  Charles, 8th Earl, xiv, 230
  Henry, father of General William, 2
  Henry, brother of General William, 2
  William ('Old William'), grandfather of General William, 1
  General William, Earl, ancestry, 2–3; boyhood and schooling, 15; at Trinity College, Dublin, 4–5; at the Battle of the Boyne, 7; regimental service, 8–17; appointed Quartermaster General to the Grand Alliance, 17; marriage, 27; on the march to the Danube, 28–43; at the Schellenberg, 47–51; at Blenheim, 52–62; on the Moselle, 64–66; on the Lines of Brabant, 67–68; MP for Woodstock, 71; at Ramillies, 74–84; captured, 88–89; Lieutenant of the Tower of London, 89- 90; receives Prussian Order of Generosity, 90–91; buys Manor of Oakley, 92; in London (1707), 92–93; returns to Flanders base, 93–94; Envoy Extraordinary to South Netherlands, 99–100; his avarice, 91–102, 108–110; his march to Oudenarde, 113–114; at Oudenarde, 114–123; with siege train for Lille, 126–127; at Wynendael, 127–130; and the Lille convoys, 130–131; at Malplaquet, 137–148; wounded at the siege of Mons, 147; in the 1711 campaign, 155–161; buys Caversham, 163; with Marlborough in exile 1712–14, 173–176; deprived of appointments, 174; espionage, 1712–14, 175–185; sells regiment, 177; reinstated on accession of George I, 187–189; appointed Colonel of the 2nd Guards, 187; returns to Holland as Envoy Extraordinary and Minister Plenipotentiary, 189–191; Captain of Isle of Wight and Governor of Carisbrooke Castle, 189; commands army against 1715–16 Jacobite rebellion, 194–198; Knight of the Thistle, 198; granted peerage, 198; Privy Councillor, 1717, 201; as diplomat, 1715–20, 200-210; created Earl, 207–213; his next mission to Vienna, 1719, 208–210; Master of the Robes, 210; his Caversham property and London house, 213–214; Commander in Chief and Colonel of the 1st Guards, 221; last illness and death, 224; assessment of character, 225–226
Bridget, mother of General William, 2
Elizabeth (née Roberts) grandmother of General William, 1
Penelope (Lady Prendergast), sister of General William, 2, 146–147, 224
Countess (née Churchill), 2nd wife of 1st Earl of new Creation, 230
Countess (née Munter), General William's wife, 20, 25, 73, 90, 200, death of, 229

95, 136–146, 152, 155–161, 170, 179

Villeroi, Maréchal François de Neufville, Duc de, 23, 41, 66, 67, 70, 74

Villingen, fortress of, 30, 40

Walch, Helen, xv
Wales, George, Prince of, 203
Waller, Sir Hardress, 2
Wallop, Lady Philippa (married 8th Earl Cadogan), 230
Walpole, Sir Robert, 186, 189, 230
Horatio, 197, 198
Wangé, fortress of, 67
Warneton, fortress of, 125
Waterloo (1705), 70
Watkins, Henry, Deputy Judge Advocate, 71, 102, 155, 160, 167–168, 169–170
Watson, Sheila, xiv
Watson, Lavinia, xiv
Webb, Gen John, 127–130, 184
Week, Brig Gen, 121
Wentworth, Lady (mother of Lord Raby), (*quoted*), 93
Wernitz, rivulet of (1704), 47
Werwick, fortress of,

Westbrook, Ellen, xiii
Westminster Abbey, 224
Westphalia,Treaty of, 209
West Sussex Record Office, xiii
Whigs, 134, 150, 152, 153, 161, 176, 180, 183, 186, 191, 195, 200, 201
Whitworth, Charles, diplomat, 198, 201, 203, 204, 206, 210
Wight, Isle of, 189
'Wild Geese', 7, 144
William III, King of England, 4, 5, 7, 15, 17, 20, 180
Wilson, Sergeant, (*quoted*), 35–36
Withers, General Henry, 145
Wizard, Susan, xiv
Woodstock, constituency of, 71, 92, 180
Wratislaw, Count, Austrian envoy, 22, 41
Wren, Sir Christopher, 2
Würtemburg, Duke of, 58, 109
Wynendael, Battle of, 127–130, 220

York's, Duke of, HQ, 229
Ypres, 88, 125

Zeeland, 98, 127
Zweibrücken, 40

248